CISCO

Course Booklet

Introduction to Networks

Version 6

ciscopress.com

Cisco | Networking Academy
Mind Wide Open

Introduction to Networks v6 Course Booklet

Published by:
Cisco Press
800 East 96th Street
Indianapolis, IN 46240 USA

Printed in the United States of America

2   17

Library of Congress Control Number: 2016953365

ISBN-13: 978-1-58713-359-6

ISBN-10: 1-58713-359-8

Warning and Disclaimer

This book is designed to provide information about Introduction to Networks. Every effort has been made to make this book as complete and as accurate as possible, but no warranty or fitness is implied.

The information is provided on an "as is" basis. The authors, Cisco Press, and Cisco Systems, Inc. shall have neither liability nor responsibility to any person or entity with respect to any loss or damages arising from the information contained in this book or from the use of the discs or programs that may accompany it.

The opinions expressed in this book belong to the author and are not necessarily those of Cisco Systems, Inc.

Editor-in-Chief
Mark Taub

Alliances Manager, Cisco Press
Ron Fligge

Executive Editor
Mary Beth Ray

Managing Editor
Sandra Schroeder

Senior Project Editor
Tonya Simpson

Editorial Assistant
Vanessa Evans

Cover Designer
Chuti Prasertsith

Composition
codeMantra

Trademark Acknowledgments

All terms mentioned in this book that are known to be trademarks or service marks have been appropriately capitalized. Cisco Press or Cisco Systems, Inc., cannot attest to the accuracy of this information. Use of a term in this book should not be regarded as affecting the validity of any trademark or service mark.

Feedback Information

At Cisco Press, our goal is to create in-depth technical books of the highest quality and value. Each book is crafted with care and precision, undergoing rigorous development that involves the unique expertise of members from the professional technical community.

Readers' feedback is a natural continuation of this process. If you have any comments regarding how we could improve the quality of this book, or otherwise alter it to better suit your needs, you can contact us through email at feedback@ciscopress.com. Please make sure to include the book title and ISBN in your message.

We greatly appreciate your assistance.

Americas Headquarters
Cisco Systems, Inc.
San Jose, CA

Asia Pacific Headquarters
Cisco Systems (USA) Pte. Ltd.
Singapore

Europe Headquarters
Cisco Systems International BV
Amsterdam, The Netherlands

Cisco has more than 200 offices worldwide. Addresses, phone numbers, and fax numbers are listed on the Cisco Website at **www.cisco.com/go/offices.**

CCDE, CCENT, Cisco Eos, Cisco HealthPresence, the Cisco logo, Cisco Lumin, Cisco Nexus, Cisco StadiumVision, Cisco TelePresence, Cisco WebEx, DCE, and Welcome to the Human Network are trademarks; Changing the Way We Work, Live, Play, and Learn and Cisco Store are service marks; and Access Registrar, Aironet, AsyncOS, Bringing the Meeting To You, Catalyst, CCDA, CCDP, CCIE, CCIP, CCNA, CCNP, CCSP, CCVP, Cisco, the Cisco Certified Internetwork Expert logo, Cisco IOS, Cisco Press, Cisco Systems, Cisco Systems Capital, the Cisco Systems logo, Cisco Unity, Collaboration Without Limitation, EtherFast, EtherSwitch, Event Center, Fast Step, Follow Me Browsing, FormShare, GigaDrive, HomeLink, Internet Quotient, IOS, iPhone, iQuick Study, IronPort, the IronPort logo, LightStream, Linksys, MediaTone, MeetingPlace, MeetingPlace Chime Sound, MGX, Networkers, Networking Academy, Network Registrar, PCNow, PIX, PowerPanels, ProConnect, ScriptShare, SenderBase, SMARTnet, Spectrum Expert, StackWise, The Fastest Way to Increase Your Internet Quotient, TransPath, WebEx, and the WebEx logo are registered trademarks of Cisco Systems, Inc. and/or its affiliates in the United States and certain other countries.

All other trademarks mentioned in this document or website are the property of their respective owners. The use of the word partner does not imply a partnership relationship between Cisco and any other company. (0812R)

Contents at a Glance

Contents

Command Syntax Conventions

The conventions used to present command syntax in this book are the same conventions used in the IOS Command Reference. The Command Reference describes these conventions as follows:

- **Boldface** indicates commands and keywords that are entered literally as shown. In actual configuration examples and output (not general command syntax), boldface indicates commands that are manually input by the user (such as a **show** command).

- *Italic* indicates arguments for which you supply actual values.

- Vertical bars (|) separate alternative, mutually exclusive elements.

- Square brackets ([ ]) indicate an optional element.

- Braces ({ }) indicate a required choice.

- Braces within brackets ([{ }]) indicate a required choice within an optional element.

About This Course Booklet

Your Cisco Networking Academy Course Booklet is designed as a study resource you can easily read, highlight, and review on the go, wherever the Internet is not available or practical:

- The text is extracted directly, word-for-word, from the online course so you can highlight important points and take notes in the "Your Chapter Notes" section.

- Headings with the exact page correlations provide a quick reference to the online course for your classroom discussions and exam preparation.

- An icon system directs you to the online curriculum to take full advantage of the images embedded within the Networking Academy online course and reminds you to perform the labs, Interactive activities, Packet Tracer activities, watch videos, and take the chapter quizzes and exams.

The *Course Booklet* is a basic, economical paper-based resource to help you succeed with the Cisco Networking Academy online course.

Course Introduction

0.0 Welcome to Introduction to Networks

0.0.1 Message to the Student

0.0.1.1 Welcome

Welcome to the CCNA Introduction to Networks course. The goal of this course is to introduce you to fundamental networking concepts and technologies. These online course materials will assist you in developing the skills necessary to plan and implement small networks across a range of applications. The specific skills covered in each chapter are described at the start of each chapter.

You can use your smart phone, tablet, laptop, or desktop to access your course, participate in discussions with your instructor, view your grades, read or review text, and practice using interactive media. However, some media are complex and must be viewed on a PC, as well as Packet Tracer activities, quizzes, and exams.

Refer to
Online Course
for Illustration

0.0.1.2 A Global Community

When you participate in the Networking Academy, you are joining a global community linked by common goals and technologies. Schools, colleges, universities, and other entities in over 160 countries participate in the program. Click here to view a video about how Cisco Networking Academy is changing the world.

Look for the Cisco Networking Academy official site on Facebook© and LinkedIn©. The Facebook site is where you can meet and engage with other Networking Academy students from around the world. The Cisco Networking Academy LinkedIn site connects you with job postings, and you can see how others are effectively communicating their skills.

Refer to
Online Course
for Illustration

0.0.1.3 More Than Just Information

The NetSpace learning environment is an important part of the overall course experience for students and instructors in the Networking Academy. These online course materials include course text and related interactive media, Packet Tracer simulation activities, real equipment labs, remote access labs, and many different types of quizzes. All of these materials provide important feedback to help you assess your progress throughout the course.

The material in this course encompasses a broad range of technologies that facilitate how people work, live, play, and learn by communicating with voice, video, and other data. Networking and the internet affect people differently in different parts of the world. Although we have worked with instructors from around the world to create these materials, it is important that you work with your instructor and fellow students to make the material in this course applicable to your local situation.

Refer to
Online Course
for Illustration

0.0.1.4 How We Teach

E-doing is a design philosophy that applies the principle that people learn best by doing. The curriculum includes embedded, highly interactive e-doing activities to help stimulate learning, increase knowledge retention, and make the whole learning experience much richer – and that makes understanding the content much easier.

Refer to
Online Course
for Illustration

0.0.1.5 Practice Leads to Mastery

In a typical lesson, after learning about a topic for the first time, you will check your understanding with some interactive media items. If there are new commands to learn, you will practice them with the Syntax Checker before using the commands to configure or troubleshoot a network in Packet Tracer, the Networking Academy network simulation tool. Next, you will do practice activities on real equipment in your classroom or accessed remotely over the internet.

Packet Tracer can also provide additional practice any time by creating your own activities or you may want to competitively test your skills with classmates in multi-user games. Packet Tracer skills assessments and skills integration labs give you rich feedback on the skills you are able to demonstrate and are great practice for chapter, checkpoint, and final exams.

Refer to
Online Course
for Illustration

0.0.1.6 Mind Wide Open

An important goal in education is to enrich you, the student, by expanding what you know and can do. It is important to realize, however, that the instructional materials and the instructor can only facilitate the process. You must make the commitment yourself to learn new skills. The following pages share a few suggestions to help you learn and prepare for transitioning your new skills to the workplace.

Refer to
Online Course
for Illustration

0.0.1.7 Engineering Journals

Professionals in the networking field often keep Engineering Journals in which they write down the things they observe and learn such as how to use protocols and commands. Keeping an Engineering Journal creates a reference you can use at work in your ICT job. Writing is one way to reinforce your learning – along with Reading, Seeing, and Practicing.

A sample entry for implementing a technology could include the necessary software commands, the purpose of the commands, command variables, and a topology diagram indicating the context for using the commands to configure the technology.

Refer to
Online Course
for Illustration

0.0.1.8 Explore the World of Networking

Packet Tracer is a networking learning tool that supports a wide range of physical and logical simulations. It also provides visualization tools to help you understand the internal workings of a network.

The pre-made Packet Tracer activities consist of network simulations, games, activities, and challenges that provide a broad range of learning experiences. These tools will help you develop an understanding of how data flows in a network.

Refer to
Online Course
for Illustration

0.0.1.9   Create Your Own Worlds

You can also use Packet Tracer to create your own experiments and networking scenarios. We hope that, over time, you consider using Packet Tracer - not only for experiencing the pre-built activities, but also to become an author, explorer, and experimenter.

The online course materials have embedded Packet Tracer activities that will launch on computers running Windows® operating systems, if Packet Tracer is installed. This integration may also work on other operating systems using Windows emulation.

Refer to
Online Course
for Illustration

0.0.1.10   How Packet Tracer Helps Master Concepts

Educational Games

Packet Tracer Multi-User games enable you or a team to compete with other students to see who can accurately complete a series of networking tasks the fastest. It is an excellent way to practice the skills you are learning in Packet Tracer activities and hands-on labs.

Cisco Aspire is a single-player, standalone strategic simulation game. Players test their networking skills by completing contracts in a virtual city. The Networking Academy Edition is specifically designed to help you prepare for the CCENT certification exam. It also incorporates business and communication skills ICT employers seek in job candidates. Click here to learn more about Cisco Aspire Networking Academy Edition.

Performance-Based Assessments

The Networking Academy performance-based assessments have you do Packet Tracer activities like you have been doing all along, only now integrated with an online assessment engine that will automatically score your results and provide you with immediate feedback. This feedback helps you to more accurately identify the knowledge and skills you have mastered and where you need more practice. There are also questions on chapter quizzes and exams that use Packet Tracer activities to give you additional feedback on your progress.

Refer to
Online Course
for Illustration

0.0.1.11   Course Overview

As the course title states, the focus of this course is on learning the fundamentals of networking. In this course, you will learn both the practical and conceptual skills that build the foundation for understanding basic networking. You will do the following:

- Examine human versus network communication and see the parallels between them
- Be introduced to the two major models used to plan and implement networks: OSI and TCP/IP
- Gain an understanding of the "layered" approach to networks
- Examine the OSI and TCP/IP layers in detail to understand their functions and services
- Become familiar with the various network devices and network addressing schemes
- Discover the types of media used to carry data across the network

By the end of this course, you will be able to build simple LANs, perform basic configurations for routers and switches, and implement IP addressing schemes.

Explore the Network

1.0 Introduction

1.0.1.1 Exploring the Network

We now stand at a critical turning point in the use of technology to extend and empower our ability to communicate. The globalization of the Internet has succeeded faster than anyone could have imagined. The manner in which social, commercial, political and personal interactions occur is rapidly changing to keep up with the evolution of this global network. In the next stage of our development, innovators will use the Internet as a starting point for their efforts, creating new products and services specifically designed to take advantage of the network capabilities. As developers push the limits of what is possible, the capabilities of the interconnected networks that form the Internet will play an increasing role in the success of these projects.

This chapter introduces the platform of data networks upon which our social and business relationships increasingly depend. The material lays the groundwork for exploring the services, technologies, and issues encountered by network professionals as they design, build, and maintain the modern network.

Refer to
Lab Activity
for this chapter

1.0.1.2 Class Activity - Draw Your Concept of the Internet

Welcome to a new component of our Networking Academy curriculum: Modeling Activities! You will find them at the beginning and end of each chapter.

Some activities can be completed individually (at home or in class), and some will require group or learning-community interaction. Your instructor will be facilitating so that you can obtain the most from these introductory activities.

These activities will help you enhance your understanding by providing an opportunity to visualize some of the abstract concepts that you will be learning in this course. Be creative and enjoy these activities!

Here is your first modeling activity:

Draw Your Concept of the Internet

Draw and label a map of the Internet as you interpret it now. Include your home or school/university location and its respective cabling, equipment, devices, etc. Some items you may wish to include:

- Devices/Equipment
- Media (cabling)
- Link Addresses or Names

■ Sources & Destinations

■ Internet Service Providers

Upon completion, save your work in a hard-copy format, as it will be used for future reference at the end of this chapter. If it is an electronic document, save it to a server location provided by your instructor. Be prepared to share and explain your work in class.

Refer to **Video**
in online course

1.1   Globally Connected

1.1.1   Networking Today

1.1.1.1   Networks in Our Daily Lives

Among all of the essentials for human existence, the need to interact with others ranks just below our need to sustain life. Communication is almost as important to us as our reliance on air, water, food, and shelter.

In today's world, through the use of networks, we are connected like never before. People with ideas can communicate instantly with others to make those ideas a reality. News events and discoveries are known worldwide in seconds. Individuals can even connect and play games with friends separated by oceans and continents.

Click Play in the figure to view how connected we are.

Click here to read the transcript of this video.

Refer to
Online Course
for Illustration

1.1.1.2   Technology Then and Now

Imagine a world without the Internet. No more Google, YouTube, instant messaging, Facebook, Wikipedia, online gaming, Netflix, iTunes, and easy access to current information. No more price comparison websites, avoiding lines by shopping online, or quickly looking up phone numbers and map directions to various locations at the click of a button. How different would our lives be without all of this? That was the world we lived in just 15 to 20 years ago. But over the years, data networks have slowly expanded and been repurposed to improve the quality of life for people everywhere.

Click Play in the figure to watch how the Internet emerged over the last 25 years and see a glimpse into the future! What else do you think we will be able to do using the network as the platform?

Refer to
Online Course
for Illustration

1.1.1.3   No Boundaries

Advancements in networking technologies are perhaps the most significant changes in the world today. They are helping to create a world in which national borders, geographic distances, and physical limitations become less relevant presenting ever-diminishing obstacles.

The Internet has changed the manner in which social, commercial, political, and personal interactions occur. The immediate nature of communications over the Internet encourages the creation of global communities. Global communities allow for social interaction that is independent of location or time zone. The creation of online communities for the exchange of ideas and information has the potential to increase productivity opportunities across the globe.

Cisco refers to this as the human network. The human network centers on the impact of the Internet and networks on people and businesses.

How has the human network affected you?

Refer to
Online Course
for Illustration

1.1.1.4   Networks Support the Way We Learn

Networks have changed the way we learn. Access to high quality instruction is no longer restricted to students living in proximity to where that instruction is being delivered. Click Play in the figure to view a video about the ways that the classroom has expanded.

Online distance learning has removed geographic barriers and improved student opportunity. Robust and reliable networks support and enrich student learning experiences. They deliver learning material in a wide range of formats including interactive activities, assessments, and feedback.

Click here to read the transcript of this video.

Refer to
Online Course
for Illustration

1.1.1.5   Networks Support the Way We Communicate

The globalization of the Internet has ushered in new forms of communication that empower individuals to create information that can be accessed by a global audience.

Some forms of communication include:

- **Texting** – Texting enables instant real-time communication between two or more people.

- **Social Media** – Social media consists of interactive websites where people and communities create and share user-generated content with friends, family, peers, and the world.

- **Collaboration Tools** – Without the constraints of location or time zone, collaboration tools allow individuals to communicate with each other, often across real-time interactive video. The broad distribution of data networks means that people in remote locations can contribute on an equal basis with people in the heart of large population centers.

- **Blogs** – Blogs, which is an abbreviation of the word "weblogs", are web pages that are easy to update and edit. Unlike commercial websites, blogs give anyone a means to communicate their thoughts to a global audience without technical knowledge of web design.

- **Wikis** – Wikis are web pages that groups of people can edit and view together. Whereas a blog is more of an individual, personal journal, a wiki is a group creation. As such, it may be subject to more extensive review and editing. Many businesses use wikis as their internal collaboration tool.

- **Podcasting** – Podcasting allows people to deliver their audio recordings to a wide audience. The audio file is placed on a website (or blog or wiki) where others can download it and play the recording on their computers, laptops, and other mobile devices.

- **Peer-to-Peer (P2P) File Sharing** – Peer-to-Peer file sharing allows people to share files with each other without having to store and download them from a central server. The user joins the P2P network by simply installing the P2P software. P2P file sharing has not been embraced by everyone. Many people are concerned about violating the laws of copyrighted materials.

What other sites or tools do you use to share your thoughts?

1.1.1.6   Networks Support the Way We Work

Refer to **Online Course** *for Illustration*

In the business world, data networks were initially used by businesses to internally record and manage financial information, customer information, and employee payroll systems. These business networks evolved to enable the transmission of many different types of information services, including email, video, messaging, and telephony.

The use of networks to provide efficient and cost-effective employee training is increasing in acceptance. Online learning opportunities can decrease time-consuming and costly travel, yet still ensure that all employees are adequately trained to perform their jobs in a safe and productive manner.

There are many success stories illustrating innovative ways networks are being used to make us more successful in the workplace. Some of these scenarios are available through the Cisco web site at http://www.cisco.com/web/about/success-stories/index.html.

1.1.1.7   Networks Support the Way We Play

Refer to **Online Course** *for Illustration*

The Internet is used for traditional forms of entertainment. We listen to recording artists, preview or view motion pictures, read entire books, and download material for future offline access. Live sporting events and concerts can be experienced as they are happening, or recorded and viewed on demand.

Networks enable the creation of new forms of entertainment, such as online games. Players participate in any kind of online competition that game designers can imagine. We compete with friends and foes around the world as if we were all in the same room.

Even offline activities are enhanced using network collaboration services. Global communities of interest have grown rapidly. We share common experiences and hobbies well beyond our local neighborhood, city, or region. Sports fans share opinions and facts about their favorite teams. Collectors display prized collections and get expert feedback about them.

Whatever form of recreation we enjoy, networks are improving our experience.

How do you play on the Internet?

Refer to **Lab Activity** *for this chapter*

1.1.1.8   Lab - Researching Network Collaboration Tools

In this lab, you will complete the following objectives:

- Part 1: Use Collaboration Tools

- Part 2: Share Documents with Google Drive

- Part 3: Explore Conferencing and Web Meetings

- Part 4: Create Wiki Pages

Refer to
Online Course
for Illustration

1.1.2 Providing Resources in a Network

1.1.2.1 Networks of Many Sizes

Networks come in all sizes. They can range from simple networks consisting of two computers to networks connecting millions of devices. Click the images in the figure to read about networks of different sizes.

Simple networks installed in homes enable sharing of resources, such as printers, documents, pictures and music between a few local computers.

Home office networks and small office networks are often set up by individuals that work from a home or a remote office and need to connect to a corporate network or other centralized resources. Additionally, many self-employed entrepreneurs use home office and small office networks to advertise and sell products, order supplies and communicate with customers.

In businesses and large organizations, networks can be used on an even broader scale to provide consolidation, storage, and access to information on network servers. Networks also allow for rapid communication such as email, instant messaging, and collaboration among employees. In addition to internal benefits, many organizations use their networks to provide products and services to customers through their connection to the Internet.

The Internet is the largest network in existence. In fact, the term Internet means a 'network of networks'. The Internet is literally a collection of interconnected private and public networks, such as those described above.

Refer to
Online Course
for Illustration

1.1.2.2 Clients and Servers

All computers connected to a network that participate directly in network communication are classified as hosts. Hosts are also called end devices.

Servers are computers with software that enable them to provide information, like email or web pages, to other end devices on the network. Each service requires separate server software. For example, a server requires web server software in order to provide web services to the network. A computer with server software can provide services simultaneously to one or many clients. Additionally, a single computer can run multiple types of server software. In a home or small business, it may be necessary for one computer to act as a file server, a web server, and an email server.

Clients are computers with software installed that enable them to request and display the information obtained from the server. An example of client software is a web browser, like Chrome or FireFox. A single computer can also run multiple types of client software. For example, a user can check email and view a web page while instant messaging and listening to Internet radio.

Refer to
Online Course
for Illustration

1.1.2.3 Peer-to-Peer

Client and server software usually runs on separate computers, but it is also possible for one computer to carry out both roles at the same time. In small businesses and homes, many computers function as the servers and clients on the network. This type of network is called a peer-to-peer network.

The advantages and disadvantages of peer-to-peer networking are shown in the figure.

Refer to
Online Course
for Illustration

1.2 LANs, WANs, and the Internet

1.2.1 Network Components

1.2.1.1 Overview of Network Components

The path that a message takes from source to destination can be as simple as a single cable connecting one computer to another, or as complex as a collection of networks that literally spans the globe. This network infrastructure provides the stable and reliable channel over which these communications occur.

The network infrastructure contains three categories of network components:

- Devices

- Media

- Services

Click each button in the figure to highlight the corresponding network components.

Devices and media are the physical elements, or hardware, of the network. Hardware is often the visible components of the network platform such as a laptop, PC, switch, router, wireless access point, or the cabling used to connect the devices.

Services include many of the common network applications people use every day, like email hosting services and web hosting services. Processes provide the functionality that directs and moves the messages through the network. Processes are less obvious to us but are critical to the operation of networks.

Refer to
Online Course
for Illustration

1.2.1.2 End Devices

The network devices that people are most familiar with are called end devices. Some examples of end devices are shown in Figure 1.

An end device is either the source or destination of a message transmitted over the network, as shown in the animation in Figure 2. To distinguish one end device from another, each end device on a network is identified by an address. When an end device initiates communication, it uses the address of the destination end device to specify where the message should be sent.

Refer to
Online Course
for Illustration

1.2.1.3 Intermediary Network Devices

Intermediary devices connect the individual end devices to the network and can connect multiple individual networks to form an internetwork. These intermediary devices provide connectivity and ensure that data flows across the network.

Intermediary devices use the destination end device address, in conjunction with information about the network interconnections, to determine the path that messages should take through the network. Examples of the more common intermediary devices and a list of functions are shown in the figure.

Refer to
Online Course
for Illustration

1.2.1.4   Network Media

Communication across a network is carried on a medium. The medium provides the channel over which the message travels from source to destination.

Modern networks primarily use three types of media to interconnect devices and to provide the pathway over which data can be transmitted. As shown in Figure 1, these media are:

- **Metallic wires within cables** – data is encoded into electrical impulses
- **Glass or plastic fibers (fiber optic cable)** – data is encoded as pulses of light
- **Wireless transmission** – data is encoded using wavelengths from the electromagnetic spectrum

Different types of network media have different features and benefits. Not all network media have the same characteristics, nor are they all appropriate for the same purpose.

Figure 2 displays criteria to consider when choosing network media.

Refer to
Online Course
for Illustration

1.2.1.5   Network Representations

Diagrams of networks often use symbols, like those shown in Figure 1, to represent the different devices and connections that make up a network. A diagram provides an easy way to understand how devices in a large network are connected. This type of "picture" of a network is known as a topology diagram. The ability to recognize the logical representations of the physical networking components is critical to being able to visualize the organization and operation of a network.

In addition to these representations, specialized terminology is used when discussing how each of these devices and media connect to each other. Important terms to remember are:

- **Network Interface Card** – A NIC, or LAN adapter, provides the physical connection to the network at the PC or other end device. The media that are connecting the PC to the networking device, plug directly into the NIC (Figure 2).
- **Physical Port** – A connector or outlet on a networking device where the media is connected to an end device or another networking device.
- **Interface** – Specialized ports on a networking device that connect to individual networks. Because routers are used to interconnect networks, the ports on a router are referred to as network interfaces.

Note   Often, the terms port and interface are used interchangeably.

Refer to
Online Course
for Illustration

1.2.1.6   Topology Diagrams

Topology diagrams are mandatory for anyone working with a network. They provide a visual map of how the network is connected.

There are two types of topology diagrams:

- **Physical topology diagrams** – Identify the physical location of intermediary devices and cable installation. (Figure 1)
- **Logical topology diagrams** – Identify devices, ports, and addressing scheme. (Figure 2)

The topologies shown in the physical and logical diagrams are appropriate for your level of understanding at this point in the course. Search the Internet for "network topology diagrams" to see some more complex examples. If you add the "Cisco" to your search phrase, you will find many topologies using similar icons to what you have seen in this chapter.

Refer to
Interactive Graphic
in online course

1.2.1.7   Activity - Network Component Representations and Functions

Refer to
Online Course
for Illustration

1.2.2   LANs and WANs

1.2.2.1   Types of Networks

Network infrastructures can vary greatly in terms of:

■ Size of the area covered

■ Number of users connected

■ Number and types of services available

■ Area of responsibility

The figure illustrates the two most common types of network infrastructures:

■ **Local Area Network (LAN)** – A network infrastructure that provides access to users and end devices in a small geographical area, which is typically an enterprise, home, or small business network owned and managed by an individual or IT department.

■ **Wide Area Network (WAN)** – A network infrastructure that provides access to other networks over a wide geographical area, which is typically owned and managed by a telecommunications service provider.

Click here to view a video in which Cisco's Jimmy Ray Purser explains the difference between LAN and WAN.

Other types of networks include:

■ **Metropolitan Area Network (MAN)** – A network infrastructure that spans a physical area larger than a LAN but smaller than a WAN (e.g., a city). MANs are typically operated by a single entity such as a large organization.

■ **Wireless LAN (WLAN)** – Similar to a LAN but wirelessly interconnects users and end points in a small geographical area.

■ **Storage Area Network (SAN)** – A network infrastructure designed to support file servers and provide data storage, retrieval, and replication.

Refer to
Online Course
for Illustration

1.2.2.2   Local Area Networks

LANs are a network infrastructure that spans a small geographical area. Specific features of LANs include:

■ LANs interconnect end devices in a limited area such as a home, school, office building, or campus.

- A LAN is usually administered by a single organization or individual. The administrative control that governs the security and access control policies are enforced on the network level.

- LANs provide high speed bandwidth to internal end devices and intermediary devices.

Refer to **Online Course** for Illustration

1.2.2.3   Wide Area Networks

WANs are a network infrastructure that spans a wide geographical area. WANs are typically managed by service providers (SP) or Internet Service Providers (ISP).

Specific features of WANs include:

- WANs interconnect LANs over wide geographical areas such as between cities, states, provinces, countries, or continents.

- WANs are usually administered by multiple service providers.

- WANs typically provide slower speed links between LANs.

Refer to **Online Course** for Illustration

1.2.3   The Internet, Intranets, and Extranets

1.2.3.1   The Internet

The Internet is a worldwide collection of interconnected networks (internetworks or internet for short). The figure shows one way to view the Internet as a collection of interconnected LANs and WANs. Some of the LAN examples are connected to each other through a WAN connection. WANs are then connected to each other. The red WAN connection lines represent all the varieties of ways we connect networks. WANs can connect through copper wires, fiber optic cables, and wireless transmissions (not shown).

The Internet is not owned by any individual or group. Ensuring effective communication across this diverse infrastructure requires the application of consistent and commonly recognized technologies and standards as well as the cooperation of many network administration agencies. There are organizations that have been developed for the purpose of helping to maintain structure and standardization of Internet protocols and processes. These organizations include the Internet Engineering Task Force (IETF), Internet Corporation for Assigned Names and Numbers (ICANN), and the Internet Architecture Board (IAB), plus many others.

Note   The term internet (with a lower case "i") is used to describe multiple networks interconnected. When referring to the global system of interconnected computer networks or the World Wide Web, the term Internet (with a capital "I") is used.

Refer to **Online Course** for Illustration

1.2.3.2   Intranets and Extranets

There are two other terms which are similar to the term Internet:

- Intranet

- Extranet

Intranet is a term often used to refer to a private connection of LANs and WANs that belongs to an organization, and is designed to be accessible only by the organization's members, employees, or others with authorization.

An organization may use an extranet to provide secure and safe access to individuals who work for a different organization, but require access to the organization's data. Examples of extranets include:

- A company that is providing access to outside suppliers and contractors.

- A hospital that is providing a booking system to doctors so they can make appointments for their patients.

- A local office of education that is providing budget and personnel information to the schools in its district.

Refer to
Online Course
for Illustration

1.2.4   Internet Connections

1.2.4.1   Internet Access Technologies

There are many different ways to connect users and organizations to the Internet.

Home users, teleworkers (remote workers), and small offices typically require a connection to an Internet Service Provider (ISP) to access the Internet. Connection options vary greatly between ISP and geographical location. However, popular choices include broadband cable, broadband digital subscriber line (DSL), wireless WANs, and mobile services.

Organizations typically require access to other corporate sites and the Internet. Fast connections are required to support business services including IP phones, video conferencing, and data center storage.

Business-class interconnections are usually provided by service providers (SP). Popular business-class services include business DSL, leased lines, and Metro Ethernet.

Refer to
Online Course
for Illustration

1.2.4.2   Home and Small Office Internet Connections

The figure illustrates common connection options for small office and home office users:

- **Cable** – Typically offered by cable television service providers, the Internet data signal is carried on the same cable that delivers cable television. It provides a high bandwidth, always on, connection to the Internet.

- **DSL** – Digital Subscriber Lines provide a high bandwidth, always on, connection to the Internet. DSL runs over a telephone line. In general, small office and home office users connect using Asymmetrical DSL (ADSL), which means that the download speed is faster than the upload speed.

- **Cellular** – Cellular Internet access uses a cell phone network to connect. Wherever you can get a cellular signal, you can get cellular Internet access. Performance will be limited by the capabilities of the phone and the cell tower to which it is connected.

- **Satellite** – The availability of satellite Internet access is a real benefit in those areas that would otherwise have no Internet connectivity at all. Satellite dishes require a clear line of sight to the satellite.

■ **Dial-up Telephone** – An inexpensive option that uses any phone line and a modem. The low bandwidth provided by a dial-up modem connection is usually not sufficient for large data transfer, although it is useful for mobile access while traveling.

Many homes and small offices are more commonly being connected directly with fiber optic cables. This enables an ISP to provide higher bandwidth speeds and support more services such as Internet, phone, and TV.

The choice of connection varies depending on geographical location and service provider availability.

Refer to
Online Course
for Illustration

1.2.4.3   Businesses Internet Connections

Corporate connection options differ from home user options. Businesses may require higher bandwidth, dedicated bandwidth, and managed services. Connection options available differ depending on the type of service providers located nearby.

The figure illustrates common connection options for businesses:

■ **Dedicated Leased Line** – Leased lines are actually reserved circuits within the service provider's network that connect geographically separated offices for private voice and/ or data networking. The circuits are typically rented at a monthly or yearly rate. They can be expensive.

■ **Ethernet WAN** – Ethernet WANs extend LAN access technology into the WAN. Ethernet is a LAN technology you will learn about in a later chapter. The benefits of Ethernet are now being extended into the WAN.

■ **DSL** – Business DSL is available in various formats. A popular choice is Symmetric Digital Subscriber Lines (SDSL) which is similar to the consumer version of DSL, but provides uploads and downloads at the same speeds.

■ **Satellite** – Similar to small office and home office users, satellite service can provide a connection when a wired solution is not available.

The choice of connection varies depending on geographical location and service provider availability.

Refer to **Packet
Tracer Activity**
for this chapter

1.2.4.4   Packet Tracer - Help and Navigation Tips

Packet Tracer is a fun, take-home, flexible software program which will help you with your Cisco Certified Network Associate (CCNA) studies. Packet Tracer allows you to experiment with network behavior, build network models, and ask "what if" questions. In this activity, you will explore a relatively complex network that highlights a few of Packet Tracer's features. While doing so, you will learn how to access Help and the tutorials. You will also learn how to switch between various modes and workspaces.

Refer to **Packet
Tracer Activity**
for this chapter

1.2.4.5   Packet Tracer - Network Representation

In this activity, you will explore how Packet Tracer serves as a modeling tool for network representations.

Refer to
Online Course
for Illustration

1.3   The Network as a Platform

1.3.1   Converged Networks

1.3.1.1   Traditional Separate Networks

Consider a school built thirty years ago. Back then, some classrooms were cabled for the data network, telephone network, and video network for televisions. These separate networks could not communicate with each other, as shown in the figure. Each network used different technologies to carry the communication signal. Each network had its own set of rules and standards to ensure successful communication.

Refer to
Online Course
for Illustration

1.3.1.2   The Converging Network

Today, the separate data, telephone, and video networks are converging. Unlike dedicated networks, converged networks are capable of delivering data, voice, and video between many different types of devices over the same network infrastructure, as shown in the figure. This network infrastructure uses the same set of rules, agreements, and implementation standards.

Refer to
Lab Activity
for this chapter

1.3.1.3   Lab – Researching Converged Network Services

In this lab, you will complete the following objectives:

- Part 1: Survey Your Understanding of Convergence
- Part 2: Research ISPs Offering Converged Services   •
- Part 3: Research Local ISPs Offering Converged Services
- Part 4: Select Best Local ISP Converged Service
- Part 5: Research Local Company or Public Institution Using Convergence Technologies

Refer to
Online Course
for Illustration

1.3.2   Reliable Network

1.3.2.1   Network Architecture

Networks must support a wide range of applications and services, as well as operate over many different types of cables and devices, which make up the physical infrastructure. The term network architecture, in this context, refers to the technologies that support the infrastructure and the programmed services and rules, or protocols, that move data across the network.

As networks evolve, we are discovering that there are four basic characteristics that the underlying architectures need to address in order to meet user expectations:

- Fault Tolerance
- Scalability

- Quality of Service (QoS)
- Security

Refer to
Online Course
for Illustration

1.3.2.2   Fault Tolerance

The expectation is that the Internet is always available to the millions of users who rely on it. This requires a network architecture that is built to be fault tolerant. A fault tolerant network is one that limits the impact of a failure, so that the fewest number of devices are affected. It is also built in a way that allows quick recovery when such a failure occurs. These networks depend on multiple paths between the source and destination of a message. If one path fails, the messages can be instantly sent over a different link. Having multiple paths to a destination is known as redundancy.

One way reliable networks provide redundancy is by implementing a packet-switched network. Packet switching splits traffic into packets that are routed over a shared network. A single message, such as an email or a video stream, is broken into multiple message blocks, called packets. Each packet has the necessary addressing information of the source and destination of the message. The routers within the network switch the packets based on the condition of the network at that moment. This means that all the packets in a single message could take very different paths to the destination. In the figure, the user is not aware and is unaffected by the router dynamically changing the route when a link fails.

This is not the case in circuit-switched networks traditionally used for voice communications. A circuit-switched network is one that establishes a dedicated circuit between the source and destination before the users may communicate. If the call is unexpectedly terminated, the users must initiate a new connection.

To learn more about packet-switched and circuit-switched networks, refer to the Appendix for this chapter.

Refer to
Online Course
for Illustration

1.3.2.3   Scalability

A scalable network can expand quickly to support new users and applications without impacting the performance of the service being delivered to existing users. The figure shows how a new network can be easily added to an existing network. In addition, networks are scalable because the designers follow accepted standards and protocols. This allows software and hardware vendors to focus on improving products and services without worrying about designing a new set of rules for operating within the network.

To learn more about scalability as a requirement for reliable networks, refer to the Appendix for this chapter.

Refer to
Online Course
for Illustration

1.3.2.4   Quality of Service

Quality of Service (QoS) is also an ever increasing requirement of networks today. New applications available to users over internetworks, such as voice and live video transmissions, create higher expectations for the quality of the delivered services. Have you ever tried to watch a video with constant breaks and pauses? As data, voice, and video content continue to converge onto the same network, QoS becomes a primary mechanism for managing congestion and ensuring reliable delivery of content to all users.

Congestion occurs when the demand for bandwidth exceeds the amount available. Network bandwidth is measured in the number of bits that can be transmitted in a single second, or bits per second (bps). When simultaneous communications are attempted across the network, the demand for network bandwidth can exceed its availability, creating network congestion.

When the volume of traffic is greater than what can be transported across the network, devices queue, or hold, the packets in memory until resources become available to transmit them. In the figure, one user is requesting a web page and another is on a phone call. With a QoS policy in place, the router can manage the flow of data and voice traffic, giving priority to voice communications if the network experiences congestion.

To learn more about QoS as a requirement for reliable networks, refer to the Appendix for this chapter.

Refer to
Online Course
for Illustration

1.3.2.5   Security

The network infrastructure, services, and the data contained on network-attached devices are crucial personal and business assets. There are two types of network security concerns that must be addressed: network infrastructure security and information security.

Securing a network infrastructure includes the physical securing of devices that provide network connectivity, and preventing unauthorized access to the management software that resides on them, as shown in Figure 1.

Information security refers to protecting the information contained within the packets being transmitted over the network and the information stored on network attached devices. In order to achieve the goals of network security, there are three primary requirements, as shown in Figure 2:

- **Confidentiality** – Data confidentiality means that only the intended and authorized recipients can access and read data.

- **Integrity** – Data integrity means having the assurance that the information has not been altered in transmission, from origin to destination.

- **Availability** – Data availability means having the assurance of timely and reliable access to data services for authorized users.

To learn more about security as a requirement for reliable networks, refer to the Appendix for this chapter.

Refer to
Interactive Graphic
in online course

1.3.2.6   Activity - Reliable Networks

Refer to
Online Course
for Illustration

1.4   The Changing Network Environment

1.4.1   Network Trends

1.4.1.1   New Trends

As new technologies and end user devices come to market, businesses and consumers must continue to adjust to this ever-changing environment. The role of the network is transforming to enable the connections between people, devices, and information. There are several new networking trends that will effect organizations and consumers. Some of the top trends include:

- Bring Your Own Device (BYOD)
- Online collaboration
- Video communications
- Cloud computing

Refer to
Online Course
for Illustration

1.4.1.2   Bring Your Own Device

The concept of any device, to any content, in any manner, is a major global trend that requires significant changes to the way devices are used. This trend is known as Bring Your Own Device (BYOD).

BYOD is about end users having the freedom to use personal tools to access information and communicate across a business or campus network. With the growth of consumer devices, and the related drop in cost, employees and students can be expected to have some of the most advanced computing and networking tools for personal use. These personal tools include laptops, netbooks, tablets, smartphones, and e-readers. These can be devices purchased by the company or school, purchased by the individual, or both.

BYOD means any device, with any ownership, used anywhere. For example, in the past, a student who needed to access the campus network or the Internet had to use one of the school's computers. These devices were typically limited and seen as tools only for work done in the classroom or in the library. Extended connectivity through mobile and remote access to the campus network gives students tremendous flexibility and more learning opportunities for the student.

Refer to
Online Course
for Illustration

1.4.1.3   Online Collaboration

Individuals want to connect to the network, not only for access to data applications, but also to collaborate with one another. Collaboration is defined as "the act of working with another or others on a joint project." Collaboration tools, like Cisco WebEx shown in the figure, give employees, students, teachers, customers, and partners a way to instantly connect, interact, and achieve their objectives.

For businesses, collaboration is a critical and strategic priority that organizations are using to remain competitive. Collaboration is also a priority in education. Students need to collaborate to assist each other in learning, to develop team skills used in the work force, and to work together on team-based projects.

Refer to **Video**
in online course

1.4.1.4   Video Communication

Another trend in networking that is critical to the communication and collaboration effort is video. Video is being used for communications, collaboration, and entertainment. Video calls can be made to and from anywhere with an Internet connection.

Video conferencing is a powerful tool for communicating with others at a distance, both locally and globally. Video is becoming a critical requirement for effective collaboration as organizations extend across geographic and cultural boundaries. Click Play in the figure to view how TelePresence can be incorporated into everyday life and business.

Click here to read the transcript of this video.

Refer to
Online Course
for Illustration

1.4.1.5   Cloud Computing

Cloud computing is another global trend changing the way we access and store data. Cloud computing allows us to store personal files, even backup our entire hard disk drive on servers over the Internet. Applications such as word processing and photo editing can be accessed using the Cloud.

For businesses, Cloud computing extends IT's capabilities without requiring investment in new infrastructure, training new personnel, or licensing new software. These services are available on demand and delivered economically to any device anywhere in the world without compromising security or function.

There are four primary types of Clouds, as shown in the figure: Public Clouds, Private Clouds, Hybrid Clouds, and Custom Clouds. Click each Cloud to learn more.

Cloud computing is possible because of data centers. A data center is a facility used to house computer systems and associated components. A data center can occupy one room of a building, one or more floors, or an entire building. Data centers are typically very expensive to build and maintain. For this reason, only large organizations use privately built data centers to house their data and provide services to users. Smaller organizations that cannot afford to maintain their own private data center can reduce the overall cost of ownership by leasing server and storage services from a larger data center organization in the Cloud.

Refer to
Online Course
for Illustration

1.4.2   Networking Technologies for the Home

1.4.2.1   Technology Trends in the Home

Networking trends are not only affecting the way we communicate at work and at school, they are also changing just about every aspect of the home.

The newest home trends include 'smart home technology'. Smart home technology is technology that is integrated into every-day appliances allowing them to interconnect with other devices, making them more 'smart' or automated. For example, imagine being able to prepare a dish and place it in the oven for cooking prior to leaving the house for the day. Imagine if the oven was 'aware' of the dish it was cooking and was connected to your 'calendar of events' so that it could determine what time you should be available to eat, and adjust start times and length of cooking accordingly. It could even adjust cooking times and temperatures based on changes in schedule. Additionally, a smartphone or tablet connection allows the user the ability to connect to the oven directly, to make any desired adjustments. When the dish is "available", the oven sends an alert message to a specified end user device that the dish is done and warming.

This scenario is not long off. In fact, smart home technology is currently being developed for all rooms within a house. Smart home technology will become more of a reality as home networking and high-speed Internet technology becomes more widespread. New home networking technologies are being developed daily to meet these types of growing technology needs.

Refer to
Online Course
for Illustration

1.4.2.2   Powerline Networking

Powerline networking is an emerging trend for home networking that uses existing electrical wiring to connect devices, as shown in the figure. The concept of "no new wires" means the ability to connect a device to the network wherever there is an electrical outlet.

This saves the cost of installing data cables and without any additional cost to the electrical bill. Using the same wiring that delivers electricity, powerline networking sends information by sending data on certain frequencies.

Using a standard powerline adapter, devices can connect to the LAN wherever there is an electrical outlet. Powerline networking is especially useful when wireless access points cannot be used or cannot reach all the devices in the home. Powerline networking is not designed to be a substitute for dedicated cabling in data networks. However, it is an alternative when data network cables or wireless communications are not a viable option.

Refer to
Online Course
for Illustration

1.4.2.3   Wireless Broadband

Connecting to the Internet is vital in smart home technology. DSL and cable are common technologies used to connect homes and small businesses to the Internet. However, wireless may be another option in many areas.

Wireless Internet Service Provider (WISP)

Wireless Internet Service Provider (WISP) is an ISP that connects subscribers to a designated access point or hot spot using similar wireless technologies found in home wireless local area networks (WLANs). WISPs are more commonly found in rural environments where DSL or cable services are not available.

Although a separate transmission tower may be installed for the antenna, it is common that the antenna is attached to an existing elevated structure, such as a water tower or a radio tower. A small dish or antenna is installed on the subscriber's roof in range of the WISP transmitter. The subscriber's access unit is connected to the wired network inside the home. From the perspective of the home user, the setup is not much different than DSL or cable service. The main difference is that the connection from the home to the ISP is wireless instead of a physical cable.

Wireless Broadband Service

Another wireless solution for the home and small businesses is wireless broadband, as shown in the figure. This uses the same cellular technology used to access the Internet with a smart phone or tablet. An antenna is installed outside the house providing either wireless or wired connectivity for devices in the home. In many areas, home wireless broadband is competing directly with DSL and cable services.

Refer to
Online Course
for Illustration

1.4.3   Network Security

1.4.3.1   Security Threats

Network security is an integral part of computer networking, regardless of whether the network is limited to a home environment with a single connection to the Internet or as large as a corporation with thousands of users. The network security that is implemented must take into account the environment, as well as the tools and requirements of the network. It must be able to secure data while still allowing for the quality of service that is expected of the network.

Securing a network involves protocols, technologies, devices, tools, and techniques to secure data and mitigate threats. Threat vectors may be external or internal. Many external network security threats today are spread over the Internet.

The most common external threats to networks include:

- **Viruses, worms, and Trojan horses** – malicious software and arbitrary code running on a user device

- **Spyware and adware** – software installed on a user device that secretly collects information about the user

- **Zero-day attacks, also called zero-hour attacks** – an attack that occurs on the first day that a vulnerability becomes known

- **Hacker attacks** – an attack by a knowledgeable person to user devices or network resources

- **Denial of service attacks** – attacks designed to slow or crash applications and processes on a network device

- **Data interception and theft** – an attack to capture private information from an organization's network

- **Identity theft** – an attack to steal the login credentials of a user in order to access private data

It is equally important to consider internal threats. There have been many studies that show that the most common data breaches happen because of internal users of the network. This can be attributed to lost or stolen devices, accidental misuse by employees, and in the business environment, even malicious employees. With the evolving BYOD strategies, corporate data is much more vulnerable. Therefore, when developing a security policy, it is important to address both external and internal security threats.

Refer to
Online Course
for Illustration

1.4.3.2   Security Solutions

No single solution can protect the network from the variety of threats that exist. For this reason, security should be implemented in multiple layers, using more than one security solution. If one security component fails to identify and protect the network, others still stand.

A home network security implementation is usually rather basic. It is generally implemented on the connecting end devices, as well as at the point of connection to the Internet, and can even rely on contracted services from the ISP.

In contrast, the network security implementation for a corporate network usually consists of many components built into the network to monitor and filter traffic. Ideally, all components work together, which minimizes maintenance and improves security.

Network security components for a home or small office network should include, at a minimum:

- **Antivirus and antispyware** – These are used to protect end devices from becoming infected with malicious software.

- **Firewall filtering** – This is used to block unauthorized access to the network. This may include a host-based firewall system that is implemented to prevent unauthorized access to the end device, or a basic filtering service on the home router to prevent unauthorized access from the outside world into the network.

In addition to the above, larger networks and corporate networks often have other security requirements:

- **Dedicated firewall systems** – These are used to provide more advanced firewall capabilities that can filter large amounts of traffic with more granularity.

- **Access control lists (ACL)** – These are used to further filter access and traffic forwarding.

- **Intrusion prevention systems (IPS)** – These are used to identify fast-spreading threats, such as zero-day or zero-hour attacks.

- **Virtual private networks (VPN)** – These are used to provide secure access to remote workers.

Network security requirements must take into account the network environment, as well as the various applications, and computing requirements. Both home environments and businesses must be able to secure their data while still allowing for the quality of service that is expected of each technology. Additionally, the security solution implemented must be adaptable to the growing and changing trends of the network.

The study of network security threats and mitigation techniques starts with a clear understanding of the underlying switching and routing infrastructure used to organize network services.

Refer to
Interactive Graphic
in online course

1.4.3.3 Activity - Network Security Terminology

Refer to
Online Course
for Illustration

1.4.4 Network Architecture

1.4.4.1 Cisco Network Architecture

The role of the network has changed from a data-only network to a system that enables the connections of people, devices, and information in a media rich, converged network environment. In order for networks to function efficiently and grow in this type of environment, the network must be built upon a standard network architecture.

The network architecture refers to the devices, connections, and products that are integrated to support the necessary technologies and applications. A well-planned network technology architecture helps ensure the connection of any device across any combination of networks. While ensuring connectivity, it also increases cost efficiency by integrating network security and management and improves business processes. At the foundation of all network architectures, and, in fact, at the foundation of the Internet itself, are routers and switches. Routers and switches transport data, voice, and video communications, as well as allow for wireless access, and provide for security.

Building networks that support our needs of today and the needs and trends of the future starts with a clear understanding of the underlying switching and routing infrastructure. After a basic routing and switching network infrastructure is built, individuals, small businesses, and organizations can grow their network over time, adding features and functionality in an integrated solution.

Refer to
Online Course
for Illustration

1.4.4.2   CCNA

As the use of these integrated, expanding networks increase, so does the need for training for individuals who implement and manage network solutions. This training must begin with the routing and switching foundation. Achieving Cisco Certified Network Associate (CCNA) certification is the first step in helping an individual prepare for a career in networking.

CCNA certification validates an individual's ability to install, configure, operate, and troubleshoot medium-size route and switched networks, including implementation and verification of connections to remote sites in a WAN. CCNA curriculum also includes basic mitigation of security threats, introduction to wireless networking concepts and terminology, and performance-based skills. This CCNA curriculum includes the use of various protocols, such as: IP, Open Shortest Path First (OSPF), Serial Line Interface Protocol, Frame Relay, VLANs, Ethernet, access control lists (ACLs) and others.

This course helps set the stage for networking concepts and basic routing and switching configurations and is a start on your path towards CCNA certification.

Refer to
Lab Activity
for this chapter

1.4.4.3   Lab - Researching IT and Networking Job Opportunities

In this lab, you will complete the following objectives:

- Part 1: Research Job Opportunities
- Part 2: Reflect on Research

1.5   Summary

1.5.1   Conclusion

Refer to
Lab Activity
for this chapter

1.5.1.1   Class Activity – Draw Your Concept of the Internet Now

In this activity, you will use the knowledge you have acquired throughout Chapter 1, and the modeling activity document that you prepared at the beginning of this chapter. You may also refer to the other activities completed in this chapter, including Packet Tracer activities.

Draw a map of the Internet as you see it now. Use the icons presented in the chapter for media, end devices, and intermediary devices.

In your revised drawing, you may wish to include some of the following:

- WANs
- LANs
- Cloud computing
- Internet Service Providers (tiers)

Save your drawing in hard-copy format. If it is an electronic document, save it to a server location provided by your instructor. Be prepared to share and explain your revised work in class.

Refer to
Online Course
for Illustration

1.5.1.2   Warriors of the Net

An entertaining resource to help you visualize networking concepts is the animated movie "Warriors of the Net" by TNG Media Lab. Before viewing the video, there are a few things to consider. In terms of concepts you have learned in this chapter, think about when, in the video, you are on the LAN, on the WAN, on the intranet, on the Internet; and what are end devices versus intermediate devices.

Though all animations often have simplifications in them, there is one outright error in the video. About 5 minutes in, the statement is made "What happens when Mr. IP doesn't receive an acknowledgment, he simply sends a replacement packet." This is not a function of the Layer 3 Internet Protocol, which is an "unreliable", best effort delivery protocol, but rather a function of the transport layer TCP protocol. IP is explained in Chapter 6 and TCP is explained in Chapter 9.

Download the movie from http://www.warriorsofthe.net

Refer to
Online Course
for Illustration

1.5.1.3   Exploring the Network

Networks and the Internet have changed the way we communicate, learn, work, and even play.

Networks come in all sizes. They can range from simple networks consisting of two computers to networks connecting millions of devices.

The Internet is the largest network in existence. In fact, the term Internet means a 'network of networks'. The Internet provides the services that enable us to connect and communicate with our families, friends, work, and interests.

The network infrastructure is the platform that supports the network. It provides the stable and reliable channel over which communication can occur. It is made up of network components including end devices, intermediate devices, and network media.

Networks must be reliable. This means the network must be fault tolerant, scalable, provide quality of service, and ensure security of the information and resources on the network. Network security is an integral part of computer networking, regardless of whether the network is limited to a home environment with a single connection to the Internet or as large as a corporation with thousands of users. No single solution can protect the network from the variety of threats that exist. For this reason, security should be implemented in multiple layers, using more than one security solution.

The network infrastructure can vary greatly in terms of size, number of users, and number and types of services that are supported. The network infrastructure must grow and adjust to support the way the network is used. The routing and switching platform is the foundation of any network infrastructure.

This chapter focused on networking as a primary platform for supporting communication. The next chapter will introduce you to the Cisco Internetwork Operating System (IOS) used to enable routing and switching in a Cisco network environment.

Go to the online course to take the quiz and exam.

Chapter 1 Quiz

This quiz is designed to provide an additional opportunity to practice the skills and knowledge presented in the chapter and to prepare for the chapter exam. You will be allowed multiple attempts and the grade does not appear in the gradebook.

Chapter 1 Exam

The chapter exam assesses your knowledge of the chapter content.

Your Chapter Notes

Configure a Network Operating System

2.0 Introduction

2.0.1.1 Configure a Network Operating System

Every computer requires an operating system to function, including computer-based network devices such as switches, routers, access points, and firewalls. These network devices use an operating system called a network operating system.

A network operating system enables device hardware to function and provides an interface for users to interact. In the CCNA course of study, students learn to configure both devices that connect to the network (end devices such as PCs) and devices that connect networks together (intermediary devices like routers and switches). Learning to configure the Cisco Internetwork Operating System (Cisco IOS) on Cisco routers and switches is a large part of the Cisco CCNA program of study.

The Cisco Internetwork Operating System (IOS) is a generic term for the collection of network operating systems used by Cisco networking devices. Cisco IOS is used for most Cisco devices, regardless of the type or size.

Refer to
Lab Activity
for this chapter

2.0.1.2 Class Activity - It Is Just an Operating System

In this activity, imagine that you are employed as an engineer for a car manufacturing company. The company is currently working on a new car model. This model will have selected functions that can be controlled by the driver giving specific voice commands.

Design a set of commands used by this voice-activated control system, and identify how they are going to be executed. The functions of the car that can be controlled by voice commands are:

- Lights
- Wipers
- Radio
- Telephone set
- Air conditioning
- Ignition

Refer to
Online Course
for Illustration

2.1　IOS Bootcamp

2.1.1　Cisco IOS

2.1.1.1　Operating Systems

All end devices and network devices require an operating system (OS). As shown in Figure 1, the portion of the OS that interacts directly with computer hardware is known as the *kernel*. The portion that interfaces with applications and the user is known as the *shell*. The user can interact with the shell using a command-line interface (CLI) or a graphical user interface (GUI).

When using a CLI as shown in Figure 2, the user interacts directly with the system in a text-based environment by entering commands on the keyboard at a command prompt. The system executes the command, often providing textual output. The CLI requires very little overhead to operate. However, it does require that the user have knowledge of the underlying structure that controls the system.

A GUI interface such as Windows, OS X, Apple iOS, or Android allows the user to interact with the system using an environment of graphical icons, menus, and windows. The GUI example in Figure 3 is more user-friendly and requires less knowledge of the underlying command structure that controls the system. For this reason, many individuals rely on GUI environments.

However, GUIs may not always be able to provide all of the features available at the CLI. GUIs can also fail, crash, or simply not operate as specified. For these reasons, network devices are typically accessed through a CLI. The CLI is less resource intensive and very stable when compared to a GUI.

The network operating system used on Cisco devices is called the Cisco Internetwork Operating System (IOS). Cisco IOS is used for most Cisco devices regardless of the type or size of the device.

Note: The operating system on home routers is usually called firmware. The most common method for configuring a home router is by using a web browser-based GUI.

Refer to
Online Course
for Illustration

2.1.1.2　Purpose of OS

Network operating systems are similar to a PC operating system. Through a GUI, a PC operating system enables a user to:

- Use a mouse to make selections and run programs
- Enter text and text-based commands
- View output on a monitor

A CLI-based network operating system like the Cisco IOS on a switch or router enables a network technician to:

- Use a keyboard to run CLI-based network programs
- Use a keyboard to enter text and text-based commands
- View output on a monitor

Cisco networking devices run particular versions of the Cisco IOS. The IOS version is dependent on the type of device being used and the required features. While all devices come with a default IOS and feature set, it is possible to upgrade the IOS version or feature set to obtain additional capabilities.

In this course, you will focus primarily on Cisco IOS Release 15.x. The figure displays a list of IOS software releases for a Cisco Catalyst 2960 Switch. The chapter appendix includes a video that introduces you to Cisco Connection Online. Here you can discover a wealth of information about Cisco products and services.

Refer to **Online Course** for Illustration

2.1.2   Cisco IOS Access

2.1.2.1   Access Methods

A Cisco IOS switch can be implemented with no configuration and still switch data between connected devices. By connecting two PCs to a switch, those PCs will instantly have connectivity with one another.

Even though a Cisco switch will function immediately, configuring initial settings are a recommended best practice. There are several ways to access the CLI environment and configure the device. The most common methods are:

- **Console** – This is a physical management port that provides out-of-band access to a Cisco device. Out-of-band access refers to access via a dedicated management channel that is used for device maintenance purposes only.

- **Secure Shell (SSH)** – SSH is a method for remotely establishing a secure CLI connection through a virtual interface, over a network. Unlike a console connection, SSH connections require active networking services on the device including an active interface configured with an address.

- **Telnet** – Telnet is an insecure method of remotely establishing a CLI session through a virtual interface, over a network. Unlike SSH, Telnet does not provide a securely encrypted connection. User authentication, passwords, and commands are sent over the network in plaintext.

Click the options in the figure to view additional information.

Note   Some devices, such as routers, may also support a legacy auxiliary port that was used to establish a CLI session remotely using a modem. Similar to a console connection, the AUX port is out-of-band and does not require networking services to be configured or available.

Refer to **Online Course** for Illustration

2.1.2.2   Terminal Emulation Programs

There are a number of excellent terminal emulation programs available for connecting to a networking device either by a serial connection over a console port or by a SSH/Telnet connection. Some of these include:

- PuTTY (Figure 1)

- Tera Term (Figure 2)

■ SecureCRT (Figure 3)

■ OS X Terminal

These programs allow you to enhance your productivity by adjusting window sizes, changing font sizes, and changing color schemes.

Refer to
Interactive Graphic
in online course

2.1.2.3   Activity - Accessing Devices

Refer to
Online Course
for Illustration

2.1.3   Navigate the IOS

2.1.3.1   Cisco IOS Modes of Operation

To initially configure a Cisco device, a console connection must be established. Once consoled in, the network technician will have to navigate through various command modes of the IOS CLI. The Cisco IOS modes use a hierarchical structure and are quite similar for both switches and routers.

Click Play in the figure to view a video demonstration of how to establish a console connection with a switch.

Click here to read the transcript of this video.

Refer to
Online Course
for Illustration

2.1.3.2   Primary Command Modes

As a security feature, the Cisco IOS software separates management access into the following two command modes:

■ **User EXEC Mode** – This mode has limited capabilities but is useful for basic operations. It allows only a limited number of basic monitoring commands but does not allow the execution of any commands that might change the configuration of the device. The user EXEC mode is identified by the CLI prompt that ends with the > symbol.

■ **Privileged EXEC Mode** – To execute configuration commands, a network administrator must access privileged EXEC mode. Higher configuration modes, like global configuration mode, can only be reached from privileged EXEC mode. The privileged EXEC mode can be identified by the prompt ending with the # symbol.

The table in the figure summarizes the two modes and displays the default CLI prompts of a Cisco switch and router.

Refer to **Video**
in online course

2.1.3.3   Configuration Command Modes

To configure the device, the user must enter **Global Configuration Mode,** which is commonly called global config mode.

From global config mode, CLI configuration changes are made that affect the operation of the device as a whole. Global configuration mode is identified by a prompt that ends with (config)# after the device name, such as **Switch(config)#.**

Global configuration mode is accessed before other specific configuration modes. From global config mode, the user can enter different sub-configuration modes. Each of these modes allows the configuration of a particular part or function of the IOS device. Two common sub-configuration modes include:

- **Line Configuration Mode** – Used to configure console, SSH, Telnet, or AUX access.
- **Interface Configuration Mode** – Used to configure a switch port or router network interface.

When using the CLI, the mode is identified by the command-line prompt that is unique to that mode. By default, every prompt begins with the device name. Following the name, the remainder of the prompt indicates the mode. For example, the default prompt for line configuration mode is **Switch(config-line)#** and the default prompt for interface configuration mode is **Switch(config-if)#**.

Click Play in the figure to view a video demonstration of navigating between IOS modes.

Click here to read the transcript of this video.

2.1.3.4   Navigate Between IOS Modes

Refer to **Video** in online course

Various commands are used to move in and out of command prompts. To move from user EXEC mode to privileged EXEC mode, use the **enable** command. Use the **disable** privileged EXEC mode command to return to user EXEC mode.

Note   Privileged EXEC mode is sometimes called *enable mode.*

To move in and out of global configuration mode, use the **configure terminal** privileged EXEC mode command. To return to the privileged EXEC mode, enter the **exit** global config mode command.

There are many different sub-configuration modes. For example, to enter line sub-configuration mode, you use the **line** command followed by the management line type and number you wish to access. To exit a sub-configuration mode and return to global configuration mode, use the **exit** command. Notice the changes in the command prompt.

```
Switch(config)# line console 0
Switch(config-line)#
```

To move from any sub-configuration mode of the global configuration mode to the mode one step above it in the hierarchy of modes, enter the exit command.

```
Switch(config-line)# exit
Switch(config)#
```

To move from any sub-configuration mode to the privileged EXEC mode, enter the **end** command or enter the key combination **Ctrl+Z.**

```
Switch(config-line)# end
Switch#
```

You can also move directly from one sub-configuration mode to another. Notice how after the network device name, the command prompt changes from (config-line)# to (config-if)#.

```
Switch(config-line)# interface FastEthernet 0/1
Switch(config-if)#
```

Click Play in the figure to view a video demonstration of how to move between various IOS CLI modes.

Click here to read the transcript of this video.

Refer to
Online Course
for Illustration

2.1.4   The Command Structure

2.1.4.1   Basic IOS Command Structure

A Cisco IOS device supports many commands. Each IOS command has a specific format or syntax and can only be executed in the appropriate mode. The general syntax for a command is the command followed by any appropriate keywords and arguments.

- **Keyword** – a specific parameter defined in the operating system (in the figure, **ip protocols**)

- **Argument** – not predefined; a value or variable defined by the user (in the figure, **192.168.10.5**)

After entering each complete command, including any keywords and arguments, press the Enter key to submit the command to the command interpreter.

Refer to
Online Course
for Illustration

2.1.4.2   IOS Command Syntax

A command might require one or more arguments. To determine the keywords and arguments required for a command, refer to the command syntax. The syntax provides the pattern or format that must be used when entering a command.

As identified in the table in the figure, boldface text indicates commands and keywords that are entered as shown. Italic text indicates an argument for which the user provides the value.

For instance, the syntax for using the **description** command is **description** *string*. The argument is a *string* value provided by the user. The description command is typically used to identify the purpose of an interface. For example, entering the command, **description Connects to the main headquarter office switch**, describes where the other device is at the end of the connection.

The following examples demonstrate conventions used to document and use IOS commands.

- ping ip-address - The command is **ping** and the user-defined argument is the *ip-address* of the destination device. For example, **ping 10.10.10.5**.

- traceroute ip-address - The command is traceroute and the user-defined argument is the *ip-address* of the destination device. For example, **traceroute 192.168.254.254**.

The Cisco IOS Command Reference is the ultimate source of information for a particular IOS command. Refer to the Chapter Appendix to learn more about the Cisco IOS Command Reference.

Refer to **Video**
in online course

2.1.4.3   IOS Help Features

The IOS has two forms of help available:

- Context-Sensitive Help

- Command Syntax Check

Context-sensitive help enables you to quickly find which commands are available in each command mode, which commands start with specific characters or group of characters, and which arguments and keywords are available to particular commands. To access context-sensitive help, simply enter a question mark, **?**, at the CLI.

Command syntax check verifies that a valid command was entered by the user. When a command is entered, the command line interpreter evaluates the command from left to right. If the interpreter understands the command, the requested action is executed, and the CLI returns to the appropriate prompt. However, if the interpreter cannot understand the command being entered, it will provide feedback describing what is wrong with the command.

Click Play in the figure to view a video demonstration of context-sensitive help and command syntax check.

Click here to read the transcript of this video.

Refer to
Online Course
for Illustration

2.1.4.4   Hotkeys and Shortcuts

The IOS CLI provides hot keys and shortcuts that make configuring, monitoring, and troubleshooting easier, as shown in the figure.

Commands and keywords can be abbreviated to the minimum number of characters that identify a unique selection. For example, the **configure** command can be abbreviated to **conf** because **configure** is the only command that begins with **conf**. An abbreviation of **con** will not work because more than one command begins with **con**. Keywords can also be abbreviated.

Refer to **Video**
in online course

2.1.4.5   Video Demonstration – Hotkeys and Shortcuts

Click Play in the figure to view a video demonstration of the various hotkeys and shortcuts.

Refer to the Chapter Appendix to learn more about Cisco IOS commands used to verify and troubleshoot network operations.

Click here to read the transcript of this video.

Refer to **Packet**
Tracer Activity
for this chapter

2.1.4.6   Packet Tracer - Navigating the IOS

In this activity, you will practice skills necessary for navigating the Cisco IOS, including different user access modes, various configuration modes, and common commands used on a regular basis. You also practice accessing the context-sensitive help by configuring the clock command.

Refer to
Lab Activity
for this chapter

2.1.4.7   Lab - Establishing a Console Session with Tera Term

In this lab, you will complete the following objectives:

■ Part 1: Access a Cisco Switch through the Serial Console Port

■ Part 2: Display and Configure Basic Device Settings

■ Part 3: (Optional) Access a Cisco Router Using a Mini-USB Console Cable

Refer to
Online Course
for Illustration

2.2   Basic Device Configuration

2.2.1   Hostnames

2.2.1.1   Device Names

When configuring a networking device, one of the first steps is configuring a unique device name or hostname. Hostnames that appear in CLI prompts can be used in various authentication processes between devices, and should be used on topology diagrams.

If the device name is not explicitly configured, a factory assigned default name is used by the Cisco IOS. The default name for a Cisco IOS switch is "Switch." If all network devices were left with their default names, it would be difficult to identify a specific device. For instance, when accessing a remote device using SSH, it is important to have confirmation that you are connected to the proper device.

By choosing names wisely, it is easier to remember, document, and identify network devices. Guidelines for hostname configuration are listed in Figure 1.

The hostnames used in the device IOS preserve capitalization and lowercase characters. Therefore, it allows you to capitalize a name as you ordinarily would. This contrasts with most Internet naming schemes, where uppercase and lowercase characters are treated identically.

For example, in Figure 2, three switches, spanning three different floors, are interconnected together in a network. The naming convention used took into consideration the location and the purpose of each device. Network documentation should explain how these names were chosen so additional devices can be named accordingly.

Refer to
Online Course
for Illustration

2.2.1.2   Configure Hostnames

Once the naming convention has been identified, the next step is to apply the names to the devices using the CLI.

As shown in Figure 1, from the privileged EXEC mode, access the global configuration mode by entering the **configure terminal** command. Notice the change in the command prompt.

From global configuration mode, enter the command **hostname** followed by the name of the switch and press Enter. Notice the change in the command prompt name.

Note   To remove the configured hostname and return the switch to the default prompt, use the **no hostname** global config command.

Always make sure the documentation is updated each time a device is added or modified. Identify devices in the documentation by their location, purpose, and address.

Use the Syntax Checker in Figure 2 to practice entering a hostname on a switch.

Refer to
Online Course
for Illustration

2.2.2   Limit Access to Device Configurations

2.2.2.1   Secure Device Access

The use of weak or easily guessed passwords continues to be a security issue in many facets of the business world. Network devices, including home wireless routers, should always have passwords configured to limit administrative access.

Cisco IOS can be configured to use hierarchical mode passwords to allow different access privileges to a network device.

All networking devices should limit access as listed in Figure 1.

Use strong passwords that are not easily guessed. Consider the key points listed in Figure 2.

Note   Most of the labs in this course use simple passwords such as **cisco** or **class**. These passwords are considered weak and easily guessable and should be avoided in production environments. We only use these passwords for convenience in a classroom setting or to illustrate configuration examples.

Refer to
Online Course
for Illustration

2.2.2.2   Configure Passwords

The most important password to configure is access to the privileged EXEC mode, as shown in Figure 1. To secure privileged EXEC access, use the **enable secret** *password* global config command.

To secure the user EXEC access, the console port must be configured, as shown in Figure 2. Enter line console configuration mode using the **line console 0** global configuration command. The zero is used to represent the first (and in most cases the only) console interface. Next, specify the user EXEC mode password using the **password** *password* command. Finally, enable user EXEC access using the **login** command. Console access will now require a password before gaining access to the user EXEC mode.

VTY lines enable remote access to the device. To secure VTY lines used for SSH and Telnet, enter line VTY mode using the **line vty 0 15** global config command, as shown in Figure 3. Many Cisco switches support up to 16 VTY lines that are numbered 0 to 15. Next, specify the VTY password using the **password** *password* command. Lastly, enable VTY access using the **login** command.

Refer to
Online Course
for Illustration

2.2.2.3   Encrypt Passwords

The startup-config and running-config files display most passwords in plaintext. This is a security threat since anyone can see the passwords used if they have access to these files.

To encrypt passwords, use the **service password-encryption** global config command. The command applies weak encryption to all unencrypted passwords. This encryption applies only to passwords in the configuration file, not to passwords as they are sent over the network. The purpose of this command is to keep unauthorized individuals from viewing passwords in the configuration file.

Use the Syntax Checker in the figure to practice encrypting passwords.

Refer to **Video**
in online course

2.2.2.4   Banner Messages

Although requiring passwords is one way to keep unauthorized personnel out of a network, it is vital to provide a method for declaring that only authorized personnel should attempt to gain entry into the device. To do this, add a banner to the device output. Banners can be an important part of the legal process in the event that someone is prosecuted for breaking into a device. Some legal systems do not allow prosecution, or even the monitoring of users, unless a notification is visible.

To create a banner message of the day on a network device, use the **banner motd #** *the message of the day* **#** global config command. The "#" in the command syntax is called the delimiting character. It is entered before and after the message. The delimiting character can be any character as long as it does not occur in the message. For this reason, symbols such as the "#" are often used. After the command is executed, the banner will be displayed on all subsequent attempts to access the device until the banner is removed.

Because banners can be seen by anyone who attempts to log in, the message must be worded very carefully. The exact content or wording of a banner depends on the local laws and corporate policies. The banner should state that only authorized personnel are allowed to access the device. Any wording that implies a login is "welcome" or "invited" is inappropriate. Further, the banner can include scheduled system shutdowns and other information that affects all network users.

Click Play in the figure to view a video demonstration of how to secure administrative access to a switch.

Click here to read the transcript of this video.

Refer to
Interactive Graphic
in online course

2.2.2.5   Syntax Checker - Limiting Access to a Switch

Use the Syntax Checker in the figure to practice the commands that limit access to a switch.

Refer to
Online Course
for Illustration

2.2.3   Save Configurations

2.2.3.1   Save the Running Configuration File

There are two system files that store the device configuration:

- **startup-config** – The file stored in Non-volatile Random Access Memory (NVRAM) that contains all of the commands that will be used by the device upon startup or reboot. NVRAM does not lose its contents when the device is powered off.

- **running-config** – The file stored in Random Access Memory (RAM) that reflects the current configuration. Modifying a running configuration affects the operation of a Cisco device immediately. RAM is volatile memory. It loses all of its content when the device is powered off or restarted.

As shown in the figure, use the **show running-config** privileged EXEC mode command to view the running configuration file. To view the startup configuration file, use the **show startup-config** privileged EXEC command.

If power to the device is lost or if the device is restarted, all configuration changes will be lost unless they have been saved. To save changes made to the running configuration to the startup configuration file use the **copy running-config startup-config** privileged EXEC mode command.

Refer to **Video** in online course

2.2.3.2   Alter the Running Configuration

If changes made to the running configuration do not have the desired effect and the running-config file has not yet been saved, you can:

- Restore the device to its previous configuration by removing the changed commands individually.

- Copy the startup configuration file to the running configuration with the **copy startup-config running-config** privileged EXEC mode command.

- Reload the device using the **reload** privileged EXEC mode command.

The downside to using the **reload** command to remove an unsaved running configuration is the brief amount of time the device will be offline, causing network downtime.

When initiating a reload, the IOS will detect that the running config has changes that were not saved to the startup configuration. A prompt will appear to ask whether to save the changes. To discard the changes, enter **n** or **no**.

Alternatively, if undesired changes were saved to the startup configuration, it may be necessary to clear all the configurations. This requires erasing the startup configuration and restarting the device. The startup configuration is removed by using the **erase startup-config** privileged EXEC mode command. After the command is issued, the switch will prompt you for confirmation. Press **Enter** to accept.

After removing the startup configuration from NVRAM, reload the device to remove the current running configuration file from RAM. On reload, a switch will load the default startup configuration that originally shipped with the device.

Click Play in the figure to view a video demonstration on how to save switch configuration files.

Click here to read the transcript of this video.

Refer to **Online Course** for Illustration

2.2.3.3   Capture Configuration to a Text File

Configuration files can also be saved and archived to a text document. This sequence of steps ensures that a working copy of the configuration file is available for editing or reuse later.

For example, assume that a switch has been configured, and the running configuration has been saved on the device.

- Open a terminal emulation software such as PuTTY or Tera Term (Figure 1) connected to a switch.

- Enable logging in the terminal software, such as PuTTY or Tera Term, and assign a name and file location to save the log file. Figure 2 displays that **All session output** will be captured to the file specified (i.e., MySwitchLogs).

- Execute the **show running-config** or **show startup-config** command at the privileged EXEC prompt. Text displayed in the terminal window will be placed into the chosen file.

■ Disable logging in the terminal software. Figure 3 shows how to disable logging by choosing the **None** session logging option.

The text file created can be used as a record of how the device is currently implemented. The file could require editing before being used to restore a saved configuration to a device.

To restore a configuration file to a device:

■ Enter global configuration mode on the device.

■ Copy and paste the text file into the terminal window connected to the switch.

The text in the file will be applied as commands in the CLI and become the running configuration on the device. This is a convenient method of manually configuring a device.

Refer to **Packet Tracer Activity** for this chapter

2.2.3.4   Packet Tracer - Configuring Initial Switch Settings

In this activity, you will perform basic switch configurations. You will secure access to the command-line interface (CLI) and console ports using encrypted and plain text passwords. You will learn how to configure messages for users logging into the switch. These banners are also used to warn unauthorized users that access is prohibited.

Refer to **Online Course** for Illustration

2.3   Address Schemes

2.3.1   Ports and Addresses

2.3.1.1   IP Addresses

The use of IP addresses is the primary means of enabling devices to locate one another and establish end-to-end communication on the Internet. Each end device on a network must be configured with an IP address. Examples of end devices are listed in Figure 1.

The structure of an IPv4 address is called dotted decimal notation and is represented by four decimal numbers between 0 and 255. IPv4 addresses are assigned to individual devices connected to a network.

With the IPv4 address, a subnet mask is also necessary. A subnet mask is a special type of IPv4 address. Coupled with the IPv4 address, the subnet mask determines which particular subnet the device is a member.

The example in Figure 2 displays the IPv4 address (192.168.1.10), subnet mask (255.255.255.0), and default gateway (192.168.1.1) assigned to a host. The default gateway address is the IP address of the router that the host will use to access remote networks, including the Internet.

IP addresses can be assigned to both physical ports and virtual interfaces on devices. A virtual interface means that there is no physical hardware on the device associated with it.

Refer to
Online Course
for Illustration

2.3.1.2   Interfaces and Ports

Network communications depend on end user device interfaces, networking device interfaces, and the cables that connect them. Each physical interface has specifications, or standards, that define it. A cable connecting to the interface must be designed to match the physical standards of the interface. Types of network media include twisted-pair copper cables, fiber-optic cables, coaxial cables, or wireless as shown in the figure.

Different types of network media have different features and benefits. Not all network media has the same characteristics and is appropriate for the same purpose. Some of the differences between various types of media include:

- Distance the media can successfully carry a signal

- Environment in which the media is to be installed

- Amount of data and the speed at which it must be transmitted

- Cost of the media and installation

Not only does each link on the Internet require a specific network media type, but each link also requires a particular network technology. For example, Ethernet is the most common local area network (LAN) technology used today. Ethernet ports are found on end-user devices, switch devices, and other networking devices that can physically connect to the network using a cable.

Cisco IOS Layer 2 switches have physical ports for devices to connect. These ports do not support Layer 3 IP addresses. Therefore, switches have one or more switch virtual interfaces (SVIs). These are virtual interfaces because there is no physical hardware on the device associated with it. An SVI is created in software.

The virtual interface provides a means to remotely manage a switch over a network using IPv4. Each switch comes with one SVI appearing in the default configuration "out-of-the-box." The default SVI is interface VLAN1.

Note   A Layer 2 switch does not need an IP address. The IP address assigned to the SVI is used to remotely access the switch. An IP address is not necessary for the switch to perform its operations.

Refer to
Online Course
for Illustration

2.3.2   Configure IP Addressing

2.3.2.1   Manual IP Address Configuration for End Devices

In order for an end device to communicate over the network, it must be configured with a unique IP address and subnet mask. IP address information can be entered into end devices manually, or automatically using Dynamic Host Configuration Protocol (DHCP).

To manually configure an IP address on a Windows host, open the **Control Panel > Network Sharing Center > Change adapter settings** and choose the adapter. Next right-click and select **Properties** to display the **Local Area Connection Properties** shown in Figure 1.

Highlight Internet Protocol Version 4 (TCP/IPv4) and click **Properties** to open the **Internet Protocol Version 4 (TCP/IPv4) Properties** window shown in Figure 2. Configure the IPv4 address and subnet mask information, and default gateway.

Note   The DNS server addresses are the IP addresses of the Domain Name System (DNS) servers, which are used to translate IP addresses to domain names, such as www.cisco.com.

Refer to
Online Course
for Illustration

2.3.2.2   Automatic IP Address Configuration for End Devices

PCs typically default to using DHCP for automatic IP address configuration. DHCP is a technology that is used in almost every network. The best way to understand why DHCP is so popular is by considering all the extra work that would have to take place without it.

In a network, DHCP enables automatic IPv4 address configuration for every end device that has DHCP enabled. Imagine the amount of time it would consume if every time you connected to the network, you had to manually enter the IP address, the subnet mask, the default gateway, and the DNS server. Multiply that by every user and every device in an organization and you see the problem. Manual configuration also increases the chance of misconfiguration by duplicating another device's IP address.

As shown in Figure 1, to configure DHCP on a Windows PC, you only need to select "Obtain an IP address automatically" and "Obtain DNS server address automatically". Your PC will search out a DHCP server and be assigned the address settings necessary to communicate on the network.

It is possible to display the IP configuration settings on a Windows PC by using the **ipconfig** command at the command prompt. The output will show the IP address, subnet mask, and gateway information received from the DHCP server.

Use the Syntax Checker in Figure 2 to practice displaying the IP address on a Windows PC.

Refer to **Video**
in online course

2.3.2.3   Switch Virtual Interface Configuration

To access the switch remotely, an IP address and a subnet mask must be configured on the SVI. To configure an SVI on a switch, use the **interface vlan 1** global configuration command. Vlan 1 is not an actual physical interface but a virtual one. Next assign an IPv4 address using the **ip address** *ip-address subnet-mask* interface configuration command. Finally, enable the virtual interface using the **no shutdown** interface configuration command.

After these commands are configured, the switch has all the IPv4 elements ready for communication over the network.

Click Play in the figure to view a video demonstration of how to configure a switch virtual interface.

Click here to read the transcript of this video.

Refer to
Interactive Graphic
in online course

2.3.2.4   Syntax Checker - Configuring a Switch Virtual Interface

Use the Syntax Checker in the figure to practice configuring a switch virtual interface.

Refer to **Packet Tracer Activity** for this chapter

2.3.2.5   Packet Tracer - Implementing Basic Connectivity

In this activity, you will first perform basic switch configurations. Then you will implement basic connectivity by configuring IP addressing on switches and PCs. When the IP addressing configuration is complete, you will use various show commands to verify configurations and use the ping command to verify basic connectivity between devices.

Refer to **Video** in online course

2.3.3   Verifying Connectivity

2.3.3.1   Interface Addressing Verification

In the same way that you use commands and utilities like **ipconfig** to verify a PC host's network configuration, you also use commands to verify the interfaces and address settings of intermediary devices like switches and routers.

Click Play in the figure to view a video demonstration of the **show ip interface brief** command. This command is useful for verifying the condition of the switch interfaces.

Click here to read the transcript of this video.

Refer to **Video** in online course

2.3.3.2   End-to-End Connectivity Test

The **ping** command can be used to test connectivity to another device on the network or a website on the Internet.

Click Play in the figure to view a video demonstration using the **ping** command to test connectivity to a switch and to another PC.

Click here to read the transcript of this video.

Refer to **Lab Activity** for this chapter

2.3.3.3   Lab - Building a Simple Network

In this lab, you will complete the following objectives:

- Part 1: Set Up the Network Topology (Ethernet only)
- Part 2: Configure PC Hosts
- Part 3: Configure and Verify Basic Switch Settings

Refer to **Lab Activity** for this chapter

2.3.3.4   Lab - Configuring a Switch Management Address

In this lab, you will complete the following objectives:

- Part 1: Configure a Basic Network Device
- Part 2: Verify and Test Network Connectivity

2.4 Summary

2.4.1 Conclusion

Refer to
Lab Activity
for this chapter

2.4.1.1 Class Activity - Tutor Me

Students will work in pairs. Packet Tracer is required for this activity.

Assume that a new colleague has asked you for an orientation to the Cisco IOS CLI. This colleague has never worked with Cisco devices before.

You explain the basic CLI commands and structure because you want your colleague to understand that the CLI is a simple, yet powerful, command language that can be easily understood and navigated.

Use Packet Tracer and one of the activities available in this chapter as a simple network model (for example, Lab - Configuring a Switch Management Address).

Focus on these areas:

■ While the commands are technical, do they resemble any statements from plain English?

■ How is the set of commands organized into subgroups or modes? How does an administrator know which mode he or she is currently using?

■ What are the individual commands to configure the basic settings of a Cisco device? How would you explain this command in simple terms? Use parallels to real life whenever appropriate.

Suggest how to group different commands together according to their modes so that a minimum number of moves between modes will be needed.

Refer to **Packet Tracer Activity**
for this chapter

2.4.1.2 Packet Tracer - Skills Integration Challenge

As a recently hired LAN technician, your network manager has asked you to demonstrate your ability to configure a small LAN. Your tasks include configuring initial settings on two switches using the Cisco IOS and configuring IP address parameters on host devices to provide end-to-end connectivity. You are to use two switches and two hosts/PCs on a cabled and powered network.

Refer to
Online Course
for Illustration

2.4.1.3 Configure a Network Operating System

Cisco IOS is a term that encompasses a number of different operating systems, which runs on various networking devices. The technician can enter commands to configure, or program, the device to perform various networking functions. Cisco IOS routers and switches perform functions that network professionals depend upon to make their networks operate as expected.

The services provided by the Cisco IOS are accessed using a command-line interface (CLI), which is accessed by either the console port, the AUX port, or through SSH or Telnet. After connected to the CLI, network technicians can make configuration changes to Cisco IOS devices. The Cisco IOS is designed as a modal operating system, which means a network technician must navigate through various hierarchical modes of the IOS. Each mode supports different IOS commands.

Cisco IOS routers and switches support a similar modal operating system, support similar command structures, and support many of the same commands. In addition, both devices have identical initial configuration steps when implementing them in a network.

This chapter introduced the Cisco IOS. It detailed the various modes of the Cisco IOS and examined the basic command structure that is used to configure it. It also walked through the initial settings of a Cisco IOS switch device, including setting a name, limiting access to the device configuration, configuring banner messages, and saving the configuration.

The next chapter explores how packets are moved across the network infrastructure and introduce you to the rules of packet communication.

Go to the online course to take the quiz and exam.

Chapter 2 Quiz

This quiz is designed to provide an additional opportunity to practice the skills and knowledge presented in the chapter and to prepare for the chapter exam. You will be allowed multiple attempts and the grade does not appear in the gradebook.

Chapter 2 Exam

The chapter exam assesses your knowledge of the chapter content.

Your Chapter Notes

Network Protocols and Communications

3.0 Introduction

3.0.1.1 Network Protocols and Communications

More and more, it is networks that connect us. People communicate online from everywhere. Conversations in classrooms spill into instant message chat sessions, and online debates continue at school. New services are being developed daily to take advantage of the network.

Rather than developing unique and separate systems for the delivery of each new service, the network industry as a whole has adopted a developmental framework that allows designers to understand current network platforms, and maintain them. At the same time, this framework is used to facilitate the development of new technologies to support future communications needs and technology enhancements.

Central to this developmental framework, is the use of generally-accepted models that describe network rules and functions.

Within this chapter, you will learn about these models, as well as the standards that make networks work, and how communication occurs over a network.

Refer to
Lab Activity
for this chapter

3.0.1.2 Class Activity - Designing a Communications System

You have just purchased a new automobile for your personal use. After driving the car for a week or so, you find that it is not working correctly.

After discussing the problem with several of your peers, you decide to take it to an automotive repair facility they highly recommend. It is the only repair facility located near you.

When you arrive at the repair facility, you find all of the mechanics speak another language. You are having difficulty explaining the automobile's performance problems, but the repairs really need to be done. You are not sure you can drive it back home to research other options.

You must find a way to work with the repair facility to ensure that your automobile is fixed correctly.

How will you communicate with the mechanics in this form? Design a communications model to ensure the car is properly repaired.

Refer to
Online Course
for Illustration

3.1   Rules of Communication

3.1.1   The Rules

3.1.1.1   Communication Fundamentals

A network can be as complex as devices connected across the Internet, or as simple as two computers directly connected to one another with a single cable, and anything in-between. Networks can vary in size, shape, and function. However, simply having a wired or wireless physical connection between end devices is not enough to enable communication. For communication to occur, devices must know "how" to communicate.

People exchange ideas using many different communication methods. However, regardless of the method chosen, all communication methods have three elements in common. The first of these elements is the message source, or sender. Message sources are people, or electronic devices, that need to send a message to other individuals or devices. The second element of communication is the destination, or receiver, of the message. The destination receives the message and interprets it. A third element, called a channel, consists of the media that provides the pathway over which the message travels from source to destination.

Communication begins with a message, or information, that must be sent from a source to a destination. The sending of this message, whether by face-to-face communication or over a network, is governed by rules called protocols. These protocols are specific to the type of communication method occurring. In our day-to-day personal communication, the rules we use to communicate over one medium, like a telephone call, are not necessarily the same as the protocols for using another medium, such as sending a letter.

For example, consider two people communicating face-to-face, as shown in Figure 1. Prior to communicating, they must agree on how to communicate. If the communication is using voice, they must first agree on the language. Next, when they have a message to share, they must be able to format that message in a way that is understandable. For example, if someone uses the English language, but poor sentence structure, the message can easily be misunderstood. Each of these tasks describe protocols put in place to accomplish communication. This is also true of computer communication, as shown in Figure 2.

Many different rules or protocols govern all methods of communication that exist in the world today.

Refer to
Online Course
for Illustration

3.1.1.2   Rule Establishment

Before communicating with one another, individuals must use established rules or agreements to govern the conversation. For example, consider Figure 1, protocols are necessary for effective communication. These rules, or protocols, must be followed in order for the message to be successfully delivered and understood. Protocols must account for the following requirements:

- An identified sender and receiver

- Common language and grammar

- Speed and timing of delivery

- Confirmation or acknowledgment requirements

The protocols that are used in network communications share many of these fundamental traits. In addition to identifying the source and destination, computer and network protocols define the details of how a message is transmitted across a network. Common computer protocols include the requirements shown in Figure 2. Each of these will be discussed in more detail.

Refer to
Online Course
for Illustration

3.1.1.3   Message Encoding

One of the first steps to sending a message is encoding. Encoding is the process of converting information into another acceptable form, for transmission. Decoding reverses this process in order to interpret the information.

Imagine a person planning a holiday trip with a friend, and calling the friend to discuss the details of where they want to go, as shown in Figure 1. To communicate the message, she converts her thoughts into an agreed upon language. She then speaks the words using the sounds and inflections of spoken language that convey the message. Her friend listens to the description and decodes the sounds to understand the message he received.

Encoding also occurs in computer communication, as shown in Figure 2. Encoding between hosts must be in an appropriate format for the medium. Messages sent across the network are first converted into bits by the sending host. Each bit is encoded into a pattern of sounds, light waves, or electrical impulses depending on the network media over which the bits are transmitted. The destination host receives and decodes the signals in order to interpret the message.

Refer to
Online Course
for Illustration

3.1.1.4   Message Formatting and Encapsulation

When a message is sent from source to destination, it must use a specific format or structure. Message formats depend on the type of message and the channel that is used to deliver the message.

Letter writing is one of the most common forms of written human communication. For centuries, the agreed format for personal letters has not changed. In many cultures, a personal letter contains the following elements:

- An identifier of the recipient
- A salutation or greeting
- The message content
- A closing phrase
- An identifier of the sender

In addition to having the correct format, most personal letters must also be enclosed in an envelope for delivery, as shown in Figure 1. The envelope has the address of the sender and receiver, each located at the proper place on the envelope. If the destination address and formatting are not correct, the letter is not delivered. The process of placing one message format (the letter) inside another message format (the envelope) is called encapsulation. De-encapsulation occurs when the process is reversed by the recipient and the letter is removed from the envelope.

A message that is sent over a computer network follows specific format rules for it to be delivered and processed. Just as a letter is encapsulated in an envelope for delivery, so too are computer messages. Each computer message is encapsulated in a specific format, called a frame, before it is sent over the network. A frame acts like an envelope; it provides the address of the destination and the address of the source host, as shown in Figure 2. Notice the frame has a source and destination in both the frame addressing portion and in the encapsulated message. The distinction between these two types of addresses will be explained later in this chapter.

The format and contents of a frame are determined by the type of message being sent and the channel over which it is communicated. Messages that are not correctly formatted are not successfully delivered to or processed by the destination host.

Refer to
Online Course
for Illustration

3.1.1.5 Message Size

Another rule of communication is size. When people communicate with each other, the messages that they send are usually broken into smaller parts or sentences. These sentences are limited in size to what the receiving person can process at one time, as shown in Figure 1. An individual conversation may be made up of many smaller sentences to ensure that each part of the message is received and understood. Imagine what it would be like to read this course if it all appeared as one long sentence; it would not be easy to read and comprehend.

Likewise, when a long message is sent from one host to another over a network, it is necessary to break the message into smaller pieces, as shown in Figure 2. The rules that govern the size of the pieces, or frames, communicated across the network are very strict. They can also be different, depending on the channel used. Frames that are too long or too short are not delivered.

The size restrictions of frames require the source host to break a long message into individual pieces that meet both the minimum and maximum size requirements. The long message will be sent in separate frames, with each frame containing a piece of the original message. Each frame will also have its own addressing information. At the receiving host, the individual pieces of the message are reconstructed into the original message.

Refer to
Online Course
for Illustration

3.1.1.6 Message Timing

These are the rules of engagement for message timing.

Access Method

Access method determines when someone is able to send a message. If two people talk at the same time, a collision of information occurs and it is necessary for the two to back off and start again, as shown in Figure 1. Likewise, it is necessary for computers to define an access method. Hosts on a network need an access method to know when to begin sending messages and how to respond when errors occur.

Flow Control

Timing also affects how much information can be sent and the speed that it can be delivered. If one person speaks too quickly, it is difficult for the other person to hear and understand the message, as shown in Figure 2. In network communication, source and destination hosts use flow control methods to negotiate correct timing for successful communication.

Response Timeout

If a person asks a question and does not hear a response within an acceptable amount of time, the person assumes that no answer is coming and reacts accordingly, as shown in

Figure 3. The person may repeat the question, or may go on with the conversation. Hosts on the network also have rules that specify how long to wait for responses and what action to take if a response timeout occurs.

Refer to
Online Course
for Illustration

3.1.1.7   Message Delivery Options

A message can be delivered in different ways, as shown in Figure 1. Sometimes, a person wants to communicate information to a single individual. At other times, the person may need to send information to a group of people at the same time, or even to all people in the same area.

There are also times when the sender of a message needs to be sure that the message is delivered successfully to the destination. In these cases, it is necessary for the recipient to return an acknowledgment to the sender. If no acknowledgment is required, the delivery option is referred to as unacknowledged.

Hosts on a network use similar delivery options to communicate, as shown in Figure 2.

A one-to-one delivery option is referred to as a unicast, meaning there is only a single destination for the message.

When a host needs to send messages using a one-to-many delivery option, it is referred to as a multicast. Multicasting is the delivery of the same message to a group of host destinations simultaneously.

If all hosts on the network need to receive the message at the same time, a broadcast may be used. Broadcasting represents a one-to-all message delivery option. Some protocols use a special multicast message that is sent to all devices, making it essentially the same as a broadcast. Additionally, hosts may be required to acknowledge the receipt of some messages while not needing to acknowledge others.

Refer to
Online Course
for Illustration

3.2   Network Protocols and Standards

3.2.1   Protocols

3.2.1.1   Rules that Govern Communications

A group of inter-related protocols necessary to perform a communication function is called a protocol suite. Protocol suites are implemented by hosts and networking devices in software, hardware or both.

One of the best ways to visualize how the protocols within a suite interact is to view the interaction as a stack. A protocol stack shows how the individual protocols within a suite are implemented. The protocols are viewed in terms of layers, with each higher level service depending on the functionality defined by the protocols shown in the lower levels. The lower layers of the stack are concerned with moving data over the network and providing services to the upper layers, which are focused on the content of the message being sent.

As the figure shows, we can use layers to describe the activity occurring in our face-to-face communication example. At the bottom, the physical layer, we have two people, each with a voice that can say words out loud. In the middle, the rules layer, we have an agreement to speak in a common language. At the top, the content layer, there are words that are actually spoken. This is the content of the communication.

Refer to
Online Course
for Illustration

3.2.1.2 Network Protocols

At the human level, some communication rules are formal and others are simply understood based on custom and practice. For devices to successfully communicate, a network protocol suite must describe precise requirements and interactions. Networking protocols define a common format and set of rules for exchanging messages between devices. Some common networking protocols are Hypertext Transfer Protocol (HTTP), Transmission Control Protocol (TCP), and Internet Protocol (IP).

Note IP in this course refers to both the IPv4 and IPv6 protocols. IPv6 is the most recent version of IP and the replacement for the more common IPv4.

The figures illustrate networking protocols that describe the following processes:

■ How the message is formatted or structured, as shown in Figure 1

■ The process by which networking devices share information about pathways with other networks, as shown in Figure 2

■ How and when error and system messages are passed between devices, as shown in Figure 3

■ The setup and termination of data transfer sessions, as shown in Figure 4.

Refer to
Online Course
for Illustration

3.2.1.3 Protocol Interaction

Communication between a web server and web client is an example of an interaction between several protocols. The protocols shown in the figure include:

■ **HTTP** – is an application protocol that governs the way a web server and a web client interact. HTTP defines the content and formatting of the requests and responses that are exchanged between the client and server. Both the client and the web server software implement HTTP as part of the application. HTTP relies on other protocols to govern how the messages are transported between the client and server.

■ **TCP** – is the transport protocol that manages the individual conversations. TCP divides the HTTP messages into smaller pieces, called segments. These segments are sent between the web server and client processes running at the destination host. TCP is also responsible for controlling the size and rate at which messages are exchanged between the server and the client.

■ **IP** - is responsible for taking the formatted segments from TCP, encapsulating them into packets, assigning them the appropriate addresses, and delivering them to the destination host.

■ **Ethernet** – is a network access protocol that describes two primary functions: communication over a data link and the physical transmission of data on the network media. Network access protocols are responsible for taking the packets from IP and formatting them to be transmitted over the media.

Refer to
Online Course
for Illustration

3.2.2   Protocol Suites

3.2.2.1   Protocol Suites and Industry Standards

A protocol suite is a set of protocols that work together to provide comprehensive network communication services. A protocol suite may be specified by a standards organization or developed by a vendor. Protocol suites, like the four shown in the figure, can be a bit overwhelming. However, this course will only cover the protocols of the TCP/IP protocol suite.

The TCP/IP protocol suite is an open standard, meaning these protocols are freely available to the public, and any vendor is able to implement these protocols on their hardware or in their software.

A standards-based protocol is a process that has been endorsed by the networking industry and approved by a standards organization. The use of standards in developing and implementing protocols ensures that products from different manufacturers can interoperate successfully. If a protocol is not rigidly observed by a particular manufacturer, their equipment or software may not be able to successfully communicate with products made by other manufacturers.

Some protocols are proprietary which means one company or vendor controls the definition of the protocol and how it functions. Examples of proprietary protocols are AppleTalk and Novell Netware, which are legacy protocol suites. It is not uncommon for a vendor (or group of vendors) to develop a proprietary protocol to meet the needs of its customers and later assist in making that proprietary protocol an open standard.

For example, click here to view a video presentation by Bob Metcalfe describing the story of how Ethernet was developed.

Refer to
Online Course
for Illustration

3.2.2.2   Development of TCP/IP

The first packet switching network and predecessor to today's Internet was the Advanced Research Projects Agency Network (ARPANET), which came to life in 1969 by connecting mainframe computers at four locations. ARPANET was funded by the U.S. Department of Defense for use by universities and research laboratories.

Click through the timeline in the figure to see details about the development of other network protocols and applications.

Refer to
Online Course
for Illustration

3.2.2.3   TCP/IP Protocol Suite

Today, the TCP/IP protocol suite includes many protocols, as shown in the figure. Click each protocol to view the acronym's translation and description. The individual protocols are organized in layers using the TCP/IP protocol model: Application, Transport, Internet, and Network Access Layers. TCP/IP protocols are specific to the Application, Transport, and Internet layers. The network access layer protocols are responsible for delivering the IP packet over the physical medium. These lower layer protocols are developed by various standards organizations.

The TCP/IP protocol suite is implemented as a TCP/IP stack on both the sending and receiving hosts to provide end-to-end delivery of applications over a network. The Ethernet protocols are used to transmit the IP packet over the physical medium used by the LAN.

Refer to
Online Course
for Illustration

3.2.2.4   TCP/IP Communication Process

Figures 1 and 2 demonstrate the complete communication process using an example of a web server transmitting data to a client. This process and these protocols will be covered in more detail in later chapters.

Click the **Play** button to view the animated demonstrations:

1. In Figure 1, the animation begins with the web server preparing the Hypertext Markup Language (HTML) page as data to be sent.

2. The application protocol HTTP header is added to the front of the HTML data. The header contains various information, including the HTTP version the server is using and a status code indicating it has information for the web client.

3. The HTTP application layer protocol delivers the HTML-formatted web page data to the transport layer. The TCP transport layer protocol is used to manage individual conversations, in this example between the web server and web client.

4. Next, the IP information is added to the front of the TCP information. IP assigns the appropriate source and destination IP addresses. This information is known as an IP packet.

5. The Ethernet protocol adds information to both ends of the IP packet, known as a data link frame. This frame is delivered to the nearest router along the path towards the web client. This router removes the Ethernet information, analyzes the IP packet, determines the best path for the packet, inserts the packet into a new frame, and sends it to the next neighboring router towards the destination. Each router removes and adds new data link information before forwarding the packet.

6. This data is now transported through the internetwork, which consists of media and intermediary devices.

7. In Figure 2, the animation begins with the client receiving the data link frames that contain the data. Each protocol header is processed and then removed in the opposite order it was added. The Ethernet information is processed and removed, followed by the IP protocol information, the TCP information, and finally the HTTP information.

8. The web page information is then passed on to the client's web browser software.

Refer to
Interactive Graphic
in online course

3.2.2.5   Activity - Mapping the Protocols of the TCP/IP Suite

Refer to
Online Course
for Illustration

3.2.3   Standard Organizations

3.2.3.1   Open Standards

Open standards encourage interoperability, competition, and innovation. They also guarantee that no single company's product can monopolize the market, or have an unfair advantage over its competition.

A good example of this is when purchasing a wireless router for the home. There are many different choices available from a variety of vendors, all of which incorporate standard protocols such as IPv4, DHCP, 802.3 (Ethernet), and 802.11 (Wireless LAN). These open standards also allow a client running Apple's OS X operating system to download a web page from a web server running the Linux operating system. This is because both operating systems implement the open standard protocols, such as those in the TCP/IP protocol suite.

Standards organizations are important in maintaining an open Internet with freely accessible specifications and protocols that can be implemented by any vendor. A standards organization may draft a set of rules entirely on its own or in other cases may select a proprietary protocol as the basis for the standard. If a proprietary protocol is used, it usually involves the vendor who created the protocol.

Standards organizations are usually vendor-neutral, non-profit organizations established to develop and promote the concept of open standards.

Click the logo in the figure to visit the website for each standards organization.

Refer to
Online Course
for Illustration

3.2.3.2   Internet Standards

Standards organizations are usually vendor-neutral, non-profit institutions established to develop and promote the concept of open standards. Various organizations have different responsibilities for promoting and creating standards for the TCP/IP protocol.

Standards organizations shown in Figure 1 include:

- **Internet Society (ISOC)** – Responsible for promoting the open development and evolution of Internet use throughout the world.

- **Internet Architecture Board (IAB)** – Responsible for the overall management and development of Internet standards.

- **Internet Engineering Task Force (IETF)** – Develops, updates, and maintains Internet and TCP/IP technologies. This includes the process and documents for developing new protocols and updating existing protocols know as Request for Comments (RFC) documents.

- **Internet Research Task Force (IRTF)** – Focused on long-term research related to Internet and TCP/IP protocols such as Anti-Spam Research Group (ASRG), Crypto Forum Research Group (CFRG), and Peer-to-Peer Research Group (P2PRG).

Standards organizations shown in Figure 2 include:

- **Internet Corporation for Assigned Names and Numbers (ICANN)** – Based in the United States, coordinates IP address allocation, the management of domain names, and assignment of other information used TCP/IP protocols.

- **Internet Assigned Numbers Authority (IANA)** – Responsible for overseeing and managing IP address allocation, domain name management, and protocol identifiers for ICANN.

Refer to
Online Course
for Illustration

3.2.3.3   Electronics and Communications Standard Organizations

Other standard organizations have responsibilities for promoting and creating the electronic and communication standards used to deliver the IP packets as electronic signals over a wired or wireless medium.

Institute of Electrical and Electronics Engineers (IEEE, pronounced "I-triple-E") – Organization of electrical engineering and electronics dedicated to advancing technological innovation and creating standards in a wide area of industries including power and energy, healthcare, telecommunications, and networking. Figure 1 shows several of the standards related to networking.

Electronic Industries Alliance (EIA) - Best known for its standards related to electrical wiring, connectors, and the 19-inch racks used to mount networking equipment.

Telecommunications Industry Association (TIA) - Responsible for developing communication standards in a variety of areas including radio equipment, cellular towers, Voice over IP (VoIP) devices, satellite communications, and more. Figure 2 shows an example of an Ethernet cable meeting TIA/EIA standards.

International Telecommunications Union-Telecommunication Standardization Sector (ITU-T) - One of the largest and oldest communication standard organizations. The ITU-T defines standards for video compression, Internet Protocol Television (IPTV), and broadband communications, such as a digital subscriber line (DSL).

Refer to **Lab Activity** for this chapter

3.2.3.4 Lab - Researching Networking Standards

In this lab, you will complete the following objectives:

- Part 1: Research Networking Standards Organizations
- Part 2: Reflect on Internet and Computer Networking Experience

Refer to **Online Course** for Illustration

3.2.4 Reference Models

3.2.4.1 The Benefits of Using a Layered Model

The benefits to using a layered model to describe network protocols and operations include:

- Assisting in protocol design because protocols that operate at a specific layer have defined information that they act upon and a defined interface to the layers above and below.

- Fostering competition because products from different vendors can work together.

- Preventing technology or capability changes in one layer from affecting other layers above and below.

- Providing a common language to describe networking functions and capabilities.

As shown in the figure, the TCP/IP model and the Open Systems Interconnection (OSI) model are the primary models used when discussing network functionality. They each represent a basic type of layered networking models:

- **Protocol model** – This type of model closely matches the structure of a particular protocol suite. The TCP/IP model is a protocol model because it describes the functions that occur at each layer of protocols within the TCP/IP suite. TCP/IP is also used as a reference model.

- **Reference model** – This type of model provides consistency within all types of network protocols and services by describing what has to be done at a particular layer, but not prescribing how it should be accomplished. The OSI model is a widely known internetwork reference model, but is also a protocol model for the OSI protocol suite.

Refer to
Online Course
for Illustration

3.2.4.2 The OSI Reference Model

The OSI model provides an extensive list of functions and services that can occur at each layer. It also describes the interaction of each layer with the layers directly above and below. The TCP/IP protocols discussed in this course are structured around both the OSI and TCP/IP models. Click each layer of the OSI model to view the details.

The functionality of each layer and the relationship between layers will become more evident throughout this course as the protocols are discussed in more detail.

Note Whereas the TCP/IP model layers are referred to only by name, the seven OSI model layers are more often referred to by number rather than by name. For instance, the physical layer is referred to as Layer 1 of the OSI model.

Refer to
Online Course
for Illustration

3.2.4.3 The TCP/IP Protocol Model

The TCP/IP protocol model for internetwork communications was created in the early 1970s and is sometimes referred to as the Internet model. As shown in the figure, it defines four categories of functions that must occur for communications to be successful. The architecture of the TCP/IP protocol suite follows the structure of this model. Because of this, the Internet model is commonly referred to as the TCP/IP model.

Most protocol models describe a vendor-specific protocol stack. Legacy protocol suites, such as Novell Netware and AppleTalk, are examples of vendor-specific protocol stacks. Because the TCP/IP model is an open standard, one company does not control the definition of the model. The definitions of the standard and the TCP/IP protocols are discussed in a public forum and defined in a publicly available set of RFCs.

Refer to
Online Course
for Illustration

3.2.4.4 OSI Model and TCP/IP Model Comparison

The protocols that make up the TCP/IP protocol suite can also be described in terms of the OSI reference model. In the OSI model, the network access layer and the application layer of the TCP/IP model are further divided to describe discrete functions that must occur at these layers.

At the network access layer, the TCP/IP protocol suite does not specify which protocols to use when transmitting over a physical medium; it only describes the handoff from the internet layer to the physical network protocols. OSI Layers 1 and 2 discuss the necessary procedures to access the media and the physical means to send data over a network.

OSI Layer 3, the network layer, maps directly to the TCP/IP Internet layer. This layer is used to describe protocols that address and route messages through an internetwork.

OSI Layer 4, the transport layer, maps directly to the TCP/IP Transport layer. This layer describes general services and functions that provide ordered and reliable delivery of data between source and destination hosts.

The TCP/IP application layer includes a number of protocols that provide specific functionality to a variety of end user applications. The OSI model Layers 5, 6, and 7 are used as references for application software developers and vendors to produce products that operate on networks.

Both the TCP/IP and OSI models are commonly used when referring to protocols at various layers. Because the OSI model separates the data link layer from the physical layer, it is commonly used when referring to these lower layers.

Refer to
Interactive Graphic
in online course

3.2.4.5   Activity - Identify Layers and Functions

Refer to **Packet
Tracer Activity**
for this chapter

3.2.4.6   Packet Tracer - Investigating the TCP/IP and OSI Models in Action

This simulation activity is intended to provide a foundation for understanding the TCP/IP protocol suite and the relationship to the OSI model. Simulation mode allows you to view the data contents being sent across the network at each layer.

As data moves through the network, it is broken down into smaller pieces and identified so that the pieces can be put back together when they arrive at the destination. Each piece is assigned a specific name (protocol data unit [PDU]) and associated with a specific layer of the TCP/IP and OSI models. Packet Tracer simulation mode enables you to view each of the layers and the associated PDU. The following steps lead the user through the process of requesting a web page from a web server by using the web browser application available on a client PC.

Even though much of the information displayed will be discussed in more detail later, this is an opportunity to explore the functionality of Packet Tracer and be able to visualize the encapsulation process.

Refer to
Online Course
for Illustration

3.3   Data Transfer in the Network

3.3.1   Data Encapsulation

3.3.1.1   Message Segmentation

In theory, a single communication, such as a music video or an email message, could be sent across a network from a source to a destination as one massive, uninterrupted stream of bits. If messages were actually transmitted in this manner, it would mean that no other device would be able to send or receive messages on the same network while this data transfer was in progress. These large streams of data would result in significant delays. Further, if a link in the interconnected network infrastructure failed during the transmission, the complete message would be lost and have to be retransmitted in full.

A better approach is to divide the data into smaller, more manageable pieces to send over the network. This division of the data stream into smaller pieces is called segmentation. Segmenting messages has two primary benefits:

- By sending smaller individual pieces from source to destination, many different conversations can be interleaved on the network, called multiplexing. Click each button in Figure 1, and then click the Play button to view the animations of segmentation and multiplexing.

- Segmentation can increase the efficiency of network communications. If part of the message fails to make it to the destination, due to failure in the network or network congestion, only the missing parts need to be retransmitted.

The challenge to using segmentation and multiplexing to transmit messages across a network is the level of complexity that is added to the process. Imagine if you had to send a 100-page letter, but each envelope would only hold one page. The process of addressing, labeling, sending, receiving, and opening the entire 100 envelopes would be time-consuming for both the sender and the recipient.

In network communications, each segment of the message must go through a similar process to ensure that it gets to the correct destination and can be reassembled into the content of the original message, as shown in Figure 2.

Refer to
Online Course
for Illustration

3.3.1.2   Protocol Data Units

As application data is passed down the protocol stack on its way to be transmitted across the network media, various protocol information is added at each level. This is known as the encapsulation process.

The form that a piece of data takes at any layer is called a protocol data unit (PDU). During encapsulation, each succeeding layer encapsulates the PDU that it receives from the layer above in accordance with the protocol being used. At each stage of the process, a PDU has a different name to reflect its new functions. Although there is no universal naming convention for PDUs, in this course, the PDUs are named according to the protocols of the TCP/IP suite, as shown in the figure. Click each PDU in the figure for more information.

Refer to
Online Course
for Illustration

3.3.1.3   Encapsulation Example

When sending messages on a network, the encapsulation process works from top to bottom. At each layer, the upper layer information is considered data within the encapsulated protocol. For example, the TCP segment is considered data within the IP packet.

Click Play in the figure to see the encapsulation process as a web server sends a web page to a web client.

Refer to
Online Course
for Illustration

3.3.1.4   De-encapsulation

This process is reversed at the receiving host, and is known as de-encapsulation. De-encapsulation is the process used by a receiving device to remove one or more of the protocol headers. The data is de-encapsulated as it moves up the stack toward the end-user application.

Click Play in the figure to see the de-encapsulation process.

Refer to
Interactive Graphic
in online course

3.3.1.5   Activity - Identify the PDU Layer

Refer to
Online Course
for Illustration

3.3.2   Data Access

3.3.2.1   Network Addresses

The network and data link layers are responsible for delivering the data from the source device to the destination device. As shown in Figure 1, protocols at both layers contain a source and destination address, but their addresses have different purposes.

- **Network layer source and destination addresses** – Responsible for delivering the IP packet from the original source to the final destination, either on the same network or to a remote network.

- **Data link layer source and destination addresses** – Responsible for delivering the data link frame from one network interface card (NIC) to another NIC on the same network.

An IP address is the network layer, or Layer 3, logical address used to deliver the IP packet from the original source to the final destination, as shown in Figure 2.

The IP packet contains two IP addresses:

- **Source IP address** – The IP address of the sending device, the original source of the packet.

- **Destination IP address** – The IP address of the receiving device, the final destination of the packet.

Refer to
Online Course
for Illustration

3.3.2.2   Data Link Addresses

The data link, or Layer 2, physical address has a different role. The purpose of the data link address is to deliver the data link frame from one network interface to another network interface on the same network. This process is illustrated in Figures 1 through 3.

Before an IP packet can be sent over a wired or wireless network, it must be encapsulated in a data link frame so it can be transmitted over the physical medium.

As the IP packet travels from host-to-router, router-to-router, and finally router-to-host, at each point along the way the IP packet is encapsulated in a new data link frame. Each data link frame contains the source data link address of the NIC card sending the frame, and the destination data link address of the NIC card receiving the frame.

The Layer 2, data link protocol is only used to deliver the packet from NIC-to-NIC on the same network. The router removes the Layer 2 information as it is received on one NIC and adds new data link information before forwarding out the exit NIC on its way towards the final destination.

The IP packet is encapsulated in a data link frame that contains data link information, including a:

- **Source data link address** – The physical address of the device's NIC that is sending the data link frame.

- **Destination data link address** – The physical address of the NIC that is receiving the data link frame. This address is either the next hop router or of the final destination device.

The data link frame also contains a trailer which will be discussed in later chapters.

Refer to
Online Course
for Illustration

3.3.2.3   Devices on the Same Network

To understand how devices communicate within a network, it is important to understand the roles of both the network layer addresses and the data link addresses.

Role of the Network Layer Addresses

The network layer addresses, or IP addresses, indicate the original source and final destination. An IP address contains two parts:

- **Network portion** – The left-most part of the address that indicates which network the IP address is a member. All devices on the same network will have the same network portion of the address.

- **Host portion** – The remaining part of the address that identifies a specific device on the network. The host portion is unique for each device on the network.

Note   The subnet mask is used to identify the network portion of an address from the host portion. The subnet mask is discussed in later chapters.

In this example we have a client computer, PC1, communicating with an FTP server on the same IP network.

- **Source IP address** – The IP address of the sending device, the client computer PC1: 192.168.1.110.

- **Destination IP address** – The IP address of the receiving device, FTP server: 192.168.1.9.

Notice in the figure that the network portion of both the source IP address and destination IP address are on the same network.

Role of the Data Link Layer Addresses

When the sender and receiver of the IP packet are on the same network, the data link frame is sent directly to the receiving device. On an Ethernet network, the data link addresses are known as Ethernet (Media Access Control) addresses. MAC addresses are physically embedded on the Ethernet NIC.

- **Source MAC address** – This is the data link address, or the Ethernet MAC address, of the device that sends the data link frame with the encapsulated IP packet. The MAC address of the Ethernet NIC of PC1 is AA-AA-AA-AA-AA-AA, written in hexadecimal notation.

- **Destination MAC address** – When the receiving device is on the same network as the sending device, this is the data link address of the receiving device. In this example, the destination MAC address is the MAC address of the FTP server: CC-CC-CC-CC-CC-CC, written in hexadecimal notation.

The frame with the encapsulated IP packet can now be transmitted from PC1 directly to the FTP server.

Refer to Online Course for Illustration

3.3.2.4   Devices on a Remote Network

But what are the roles of the network layer address and the data link layer address when a device is communicating with a device on a remote network? In this example we have a client computer, PC1, communicating with a server, named Web Server, on a different IP network.

Role of the Network Layer Addresses

When the sender of the packet is on a different network from the receiver, the source and destination IP addresses will represent hosts on different networks. This will be indicated by the network portion of the IP address of the destination host.

- **Source IP address** – The IP address of the sending device, the client computer PC1: 192.168.1.110.

■ **Destination IP address** – The IP address of the receiving device, the server, Web Server: 172.16.1.99.

Notice in the figure that the network portion of the source IP address and destination IP address are on different networks.

Role of the Data Link Layer Addresses

When the sender and receiver of the IP packet are on different networks, the Ethernet data link frame cannot be sent directly to the destination host because the host is not directly reachable in the network of the sender. The Ethernet frame must be sent to another device known as the router or default gateway. In our example, the default gateway is R1. R1 has an Ethernet data link address that is on the same network as PC1. This allows PC1 to reach the router directly.

■ **Source MAC address** – The Ethernet MAC address of the sending device, PC1. The MAC address of the Ethernet interface of PC1 is AA-AA-AA-AA-AA-AA.

■ **Destination MAC address** – When the receiving device, the destination IP address, is on a different network from the sending device, the sending device uses the Ethernet MAC address of the default gateway or router. In this example, the destination MAC address is the MAC address of R1's Ethernet interface, 11-11-11-11-11-11. This is the interface that is attached to the same network as PC1.

The Ethernet frame with the encapsulated IP packet can now be transmitted to R1. R1 forwards the packet to the destination, Web Server. This may mean that R1 forwards the packet to another router or directly to Web Server if the destination is on a network connected to R1.

It is important that the IP address of the default gateway be configured on each host on the local network. All packets to a destination on remote networks are sent to the default gateway. Ethernet MAC addresses and the default gateway are discussed in later chapters.

Refer to
Online Course
for Illustration

3.4 Summary

3.4.1 Conclusion

Refer to
Lab Activity
for this chapter

3.4.1.1 Lab - Installing Wireshark

Wireshark is a software protocol analyzer, or "packet sniffer" application, used for network troubleshooting, analysis, software and protocol development, and education. Wireshark is used throughout the course to demonstrate network concepts. In this lab, you will download and install Wireshark.

Refer to
Lab Activity
for this chapter

3.4.1.2 Lab - Using Wireshark to View Network Traffic

In this lab, you will use Wireshark to capture and analyze traffic.

Refer to
Lab Activity
for this chapter

3.4.1.3 Class Activity - Guaranteed to Work!

You have just completed the Chapter 3 content regarding network protocols and standards.

Assuming you resolved the beginning of this chapter's modeling activity, how would you compare the following steps taken to design a communications system to the networking models used for communications?

- Establishing a language to communicate

- Dividing the message into small steps, delivered a little at a time, to facilitate understanding of the problem

- Checking to see if the data has been delivered fully and correctly

- Timing needed to ensure quality data communication and delivery

Refer to
Online Course
for Illustration

3.4.1.4 Network Protocols and Communications

Data networks are systems of end devices, intermediary devices, and the media connecting them. For communication to occur, these devices must know how to communicate.

These devices must comply with communication rules and protocols. TCP/IP is an example of a protocol suite. Most protocols are created by a standards organization such as the IETF or IEEE. The Institute of Electrical and Electronics Engineers is a professional organization for those in the electrical engineering and electronics fields. ISO, the International Organization for Standardization, is the world's largest developer of international standards for a wide variety of products and services.

The most widely-used networking models are the OSI and TCP/IP models. Associating the protocols that set the rules of data communications with the different layers of these models is useful in determining which devices and services are applied at specific points as data passes across LANs and WANs.

Data that passes down the stack of the OSI model is segmented into pieces and encapsulated with addresses and other labels. The process is reversed as the pieces are de-encapsulated and passed up the destination protocol stack. The OSI model describes the processes of encoding, formatting, segmenting, and encapsulating data for transmission over the network.

The TCP/IP protocol suite is an open standard protocol that has been endorsed by the networking industry and ratified, or approved, by a standards organization. The Internet Protocol Suite is a suite of protocols required for transmitting and receiving information using the Internet.

Protocol Data Units (PDUs) are named according to the protocols of the TCP/IP suite: data, segment, packet, frame, and bits.

Applying models allows individuals, companies, and trade associations to analyze current networks and plan the networks of the future.

Go to the online course to take the quiz and exam.

Chapter 3 Quiz

This quiz is designed to provide an additional opportunity to practice the skills and knowledge presented in the chapter and to prepare for the chapter exam. You will be allowed multiple attempts and the grade does not appear in the gradebook.

Chapter 3 Exam

The chapter exam assesses your knowledge of the chapter content.

Your Chapter Notes

Network Access

4.0 Introduction

4.0.1.1 Network Access

To support our communication, the OSI model divides the functions of a data network into layers. Each layer works with the layers above and below to transmit data. Two layers of the OSI model are so closely tied, that according to the TCP/IP model they are in essence one layer. Those two layers are the data link layer and the physical layer.

On the sending device, it is the role of the data link layer to prepare data for transmission and control how that data accesses the physical media. However, the physical layer controls how the data is transmitted onto the physical media by encoding the binary digits that represent data into signals.

On the receiving end, the physical layer receives signals across the connecting media. After decoding the signal back into data, the physical layer passes the frame to the data link layer for acceptance and processing.

This chapter begins with the general functions of the physical layer and the standards and protocols that manage the transmission of data across local media. It also introduces the functions of the data link layer and the protocols associated with it.

Refer to **Lab Activity** for this chapter

4.0.1.2 Class Activity – Managing the Medium

You and your colleague are attending a networking conference. There are many lectures and presentations held during this event, and because they overlap, each of you can only choose a limited set of sessions to attend.

Therefore, you decide to split, each of you attending a separate set of presentations. Afterward, you share the slides and the knowledge each of you gained during the event.

Refer to **Online Course** for Illustration

4.1 Physical Layer Protocols

4.1.1 Physical Layer Connection

4.1.1.1 Types of Connections

Whether connecting to a local printer in the home or a web site in another country, before any network communications can occur, a physical connection to a local network must be established. A physical connection can be a wired connection using a cable or a wireless connection using radio waves.

The type of physical connection used is dependent upon the setup of the network. For example, in many corporate offices employees have desktop or laptop computers that are physically connected, via cable, to a shared switch. This type of setup is a wired network. Data is transmitted through a physical cable.

In addition to wired connections, some businesses may also offer wireless connections for laptops, tablets, and smartphones. With wireless devices, data is transmitted using radio waves. The use of wireless connectivity is becoming more common as individuals, and businesses alike, discover the advantages of offering this type of service. To offer wireless capability, devices on a wireless network must be connected to a wireless access point (AP).

Switch devices and wireless access points are often two separate dedicated devices within a network implementation. However, there are also devices that offer both wired and wireless connectivity. In many homes, for example, individuals are implementing home integrated service routers (ISRs), as shown in Figure 1. ISRs offer a switching component with multiple ports, allowing multiple devices to be connected to the local area network (LAN) using cables, as shown in Figure 2. Additionally, many ISRs also include an AP, which allows wireless devices to connect as well.

Refer to
Online Course
for Illustration

4.1.1.2   Network Interface Cards

Network Interface Cards (NICs) connect a device to the network. Ethernet NICs are used for a wired connection, as shown in Figure 1, whereas WLAN (Wireless Local Area Network) NICs are used for wireless. An end-user device may include one or both types of NICs. A network printer, for example, may only have an Ethernet NIC, and therefore, must connect to the network using an Ethernet cable. Other devices, such as tablets and smartphones, might only contain a WLAN NIC and must use a wireless connection.

Not all physical connections are equal, in terms of the performance level, when connecting to a network.

For example, a wireless device will experience degradation in performance based on its distance from a wireless access point. The further the device is from the access point, the weaker the wireless signal it receives. This can mean less bandwidth or no wireless connection at all. Figure 2 shows that a wireless range extender can be used to regenerate the wireless signal to other parts of the house that are too far from the wireless access point. Alternatively, a wired connection will not degrade in performance.

All wireless devices must share access to the airwaves connecting to the wireless access point. This means slower network performance may occur as more wireless devices access the network simultaneously. A wired device does not need to share its access to the network with other devices. Each wired device has a separate communications channel over its Ethernet cable. This is important when considering some applications, such as online gaming, streaming video, and video conferencing, which require more dedicated bandwidth than other applications.

Over the next couple of topics, you will learn more about the physical layer connections that occur and how those connections affect the transportation of data.

Refer to
Online Course
for Illustration

4.1.2   Purpose of the Physical Layer

4.1.2.1   The Physical Layer

The OSI physical layer provides the means to transport the bits that make up a data link layer frame across the network media. This layer accepts a complete frame from the data link layer and encodes it as a series of signals that are transmitted onto the local media. The encoded bits that comprise a frame are received by either an end device or an intermediate device.

The process that data undergoes from a source node to a destination node is:

- The user data is segmented by the transport layer, placed into packets by the network layer, and further encapsulated into frames by the data link layer.

- The physical layer encodes the frames and creates the electrical, optical, or radio wave signals that represent the bits in each frame.

- These signals are then sent on the media, one at a time.

- The destination node physical layer retrieves these individual signals from the media, restores them to their bit representations, and passes the bits up to the data link layer as a complete frame.

Refer to .
Online Course
for Illustration

4.1.2.2   Physical Layer Media

There are three basic forms of network media. The physical layer produces the representation and groupings of bits for each type of media as:

- **Copper cable:** The signals are patterns of electrical pulses.

- **Fiber-optic cable:** The signals are patterns of light.

- **Wireless:** The signals are patterns of microwave transmissions.

The figure displays signaling examples for copper, fiber-optic, and wireless.

To enable physical layer interoperability, all aspects of these functions are governed by standards organizations.

Refer to
Online Course
for Illustration

4.1.2.3   Physical Layer Standards

The protocols and operations of the upper OSI layers are performed in software designed by software engineers and computer scientists. The services and protocols in the TCP/IP suite are defined by the Internet Engineering Task Force (IETF).

The physical layer consists of electronic circuitry, media, and connectors developed by engineers. Therefore, it is appropriate that the standards governing this hardware are defined by the relevant electrical and communications engineering organizations.

There are many different international and national organizations, regulatory government organizations, and private companies involved in establishing and maintaining physical layer standards. For instance, the physical layer hardware, media, encoding, and signaling standards are defined and governed by the:

- International Organization for Standardization (ISO)
- Telecommunications Industry Association/Electronic Industries Association (TIA/EIA)
- International Telecommunication Union (ITU)
- American National Standards Institute (ANSI)
- Institute of Electrical and Electronics Engineers (IEEE)
- National telecommunications regulatory authorities including the Federal Communication Commission (FCC) in the USA and the European Telecommunications Standards Institute (ETSI)

In addition to these, there are often regional cabling standards groups such as CSA (Canadian Standards Association), CENELEC (European Committee for Electrotechnical Standardization), and JSA/JIS (Japanese Standards Association), developing local specifications.

Refer to
Lab Activity
for this chapter

4.1.2.4   Lab - Identifying Network Devices and Cabling
In this lab, you will complete the following objectives:

- Part 1: Identify Network Devices
- Part 2: Identify Network Media

Refer to
Online Course
for Illustration

4.1.3   Physical Layer Characteristics

4.1.3.1   Functions

The physical layer standards address three functional areas:

Physical Components

The physical components are the electronic hardware devices, media, and other connectors that transmit and carry the signals to represent the bits. Hardware components such as NICs, interfaces and connectors, cable materials, and cable designs are all specified in standards associated with the physical layer. The various ports and interfaces on a Cisco 1941 router are also examples of physical components with specific connectors and pinouts resulting from standards.

Encoding

Encoding or line encoding is a method of converting a stream of data bits into a predefined "code". Codes are groupings of bits used to provide a predictable pattern that can be recognized by both the sender and the receiver. In the case of networking, encoding is a pattern of voltage or current used to represent bits; the 0s and 1s.

For example, Manchester encoding represents a 0 bit by a high to low voltage transition, and a 1 bit is represented as a low to high voltage transition. An example of Manchester encoding is illustrated in Figure 1. The transition occurs at the middle of each bit period. This type of encoding is used in 10 b/s Ethernet. Faster data rates require more complex encoding.

Signaling

The physical layer must generate the electrical, optical, or wireless signals that represent the "1" and "0" on the media. The method of representing the bits is called the signaling method. The physical layer standards must define what type of signal represents a "1" and what type of signal represents a "0". This can be as simple as a change in the level of an electrical signal or optical pulse. For example, a long pulse might represent a 1 whereas a short pulse represents a 0.

This is similar to how Morse code is used for communication. Morse code is another signaling method that uses a series of on-off tones, lights, or clicks to send text over telephone wires or between ships at sea.

There are many ways to transmit signals. A common method to send data is using modulation techniques. Modulation is the process by which the characteristic of one wave (the signal) modifies another wave (the carrier).

The nature of the actual signals representing the bits on the media will depend on the signaling method in use.

Figure 2 illustrates the how AM and FM techniques are used to send a signal.

Refer to the Chapter Appendix for more information on encoding and signaling.

Refer to
Online Course
for Illustration

4.1.3.2   Bandwidth

Different physical media support the transfer of bits at different rates. Data transfer is usually discussed in terms of bandwidth and throughput.

Bandwidth is the capacity of a medium to carry data. Digital bandwidth measures the amount of data that can flow from one place to another in a given amount of time. Bandwidth is typically measured in kilobits per second (kb/s), megabits per second (Mb/s), or gigabits per second (Gb/s). Bandwidth is sometimes thought of as the speed that bits travel, however this is not accurate. For example, in both 10Mb/s and 100Mb/s Ethernet, the bits are sent at the speed of electricity. The difference is the number of bits that are transmitted per second.

A combination of factors determines the practical bandwidth of a network:

■ The properties of the physical media

■ The technologies chosen for signaling and detecting network signals

Physical media properties, current technologies, and the laws of physics all play a role in determining the available bandwidth.

The table shows the commonly used units of measure for bandwidth.

Refer to
Online Course
for Illustration

4.1.3.3   Throughput

Throughput is the measure of the transfer of bits across the media over a given period of time.

Due to a number of factors, throughput usually does not match the specified bandwidth in physical layer implementations. Many factors influence throughput, including:

- The amount of traffic
- The type of traffic
- The latency created by the number of network devices encountered between source and destination

Latency refers to the amount of time, to include delays, for data to travel from one given point to another.

In an internetwork or network with multiple segments, throughput cannot be faster than the slowest link in the path from source to destination. Even if all or most of the segments have high bandwidth, it will only take one segment in the path with low throughput to create a bottleneck to the throughput of the entire network.

There are many online speed tests that can reveal the throughput of an Internet connection. The figure provides sample results from a speed test.

There is a third measurement to assess the transfer of usable data that is known as goodput. Goodput is the measure of usable data transferred over a given period of time. Goodput is throughput minus traffic overhead for establishing sessions, acknowledgments, and encapsulation.

Refer to
Online Course
for Illustration

4.1.3.4   Types of Physical Media

The physical layer produces the representation and groupings of bits as voltages, radio frequencies, or light pulses. Various standards organizations have contributed to the definition of the physical, electrical, and mechanical properties of the media available for different data communications. These specifications guarantee that cables and connectors will function as anticipated with different data link layer implementations.

As an example, standards for copper media are defined for the:

- Type of copper cabling used
- Bandwidth of the communication
- Type of connectors used
- Pinout and color codes of connections to the media
- Maximum distance of the media

The figure shows different types of interfaces and ports available on a 1941 router.

Refer to
Interactive Graphic
in online course

4.1.3.5   Activity - Physical Layer Terminology

Refer to
Online Course
for Illustration

4.2   Network Media

4.2.1   Copper Cabling

4.2.1.1   Characteristics of Copper Cabling

Networks use copper media because it is inexpensive, easy to install and has low resistance to electrical current. However, copper media is limited by distance and signal interference.

Data is transmitted on copper cables as electrical pulses. A detector in the network interface of a destination device must receive a signal that can be successfully decoded to match the signal sent. However, the longer the signal travels, the more it deteriorates. This is referred to as signal attenuation. For this reason, all copper media must follow strict distance limitations as specified by the guiding standards.

The timing and voltage values of the electrical pulses are also susceptible to interference from two sources:

- **Electromagnetic interference (EMI) or radio frequency interference (RFI)** – EMI and RFI signals can distort and corrupt the data signals being carried by copper media. Potential sources of EMI and RFI include radio waves and electromagnetic devices, such as fluorescent lights or electric motors as shown in the figure.

- **Crosstalk** – Crosstalk is a disturbance caused by the electric or magnetic fields of a signal on one wire to the signal in an adjacent wire. In telephone circuits, crosstalk can result in hearing part of another voice conversation from an adjacent circuit. Specifically, when an electrical current flows through a wire, it creates a small, circular magnetic field around the wire, which can be picked up by an adjacent wire.

Play the animation in the figure to see how data transmission can be affected by interference.

To counter the negative effects of EMI and RFI, some types of copper cables are wrapped in metallic shielding and require proper grounding connections.

To counter the negative effects of crosstalk, some types of copper cables have opposing circuit wire pairs twisted together, which effectively cancels the crosstalk.

The susceptibility of copper cables to electronic noise can also be limited by:

- Selecting the cable type or category most suited to a given networking environment.

- Designing a cable infrastructure to avoid known and potential sources of interference in the building structure.

- Using cabling techniques that include the proper handling and termination of the cables.

Refer to
Online Course
for Illustration

4.2.1.2   Copper Media

There are three main types of copper media used in networking:

- **Unshielded Twisted-Pair (UTP)**

- **Shielded Twisted-Pair (STP)**

- **Coaxial**

These cables are used to interconnect nodes on a LAN and infrastructure devices such as switches, routers, and wireless access points. Each type of connection and the accompanying devices has cabling requirements stipulated by physical layer standards.

Different physical layer standards specify the use of different connectors. These standards specify the mechanical dimensions of the connectors and the acceptable electrical properties of each type. Networking media use modular jacks and plugs to provide easy connection and disconnection. Also, a single type of physical connector may be used for multiple types of connections. For example, the RJ-45 connector is widely used in LANs with one type of media and in some WANs with another media type.

Refer to **Online Course** for Illustration

4.2.1.3   Unshielded Twisted-Pair Cable

Unshielded twisted-pair (UTP) cabling is the most common networking media. UTP cabling, terminated with RJ-45 connectors, is used for interconnecting network hosts with intermediate networking devices, such as switches and routers.

In LANs, UTP cable consists of four pairs of color-coded wires that have been twisted together and then encased in a flexible plastic sheath that protects from minor physical damage. The twisting of wires helps protect against signal interference from other wires.

As seen in the figure, the color codes identify the individual pairs and wires and aid in cable termination.

Refer to **Online Course** for Illustration

4.2.1.4   Shielded Twisted-Pair Cable

Shielded twisted-pair (STP) provides better noise protection than UTP cabling. However, compared to UTP cable, STP cable is significantly more expensive and difficult to install. Like UTP cable, STP uses an RJ-45 connector.

STP cables combine the techniques of shielding to counter EMI and RFI, and wire twisting to counter crosstalk. To gain the full benefit of the shielding, STP cables are terminated with special shielded STP data connectors. If the cable is improperly grounded, the shield may act as an antenna and pick up unwanted signals.

The STP cable shown uses four pairs of wires, each wrapped in a foil shield, which are then wrapped in an overall metallic braid or foil.

Refer to **Online Course** for Illustration

4.2.1.5   Coaxial Cable

Coaxial cable, or coax for short, gets its name from the fact that there are two conductors that share the same axis. As shown in the figure, coaxial cable consists of:

- A copper conductor used to transmit the electronic signals.

- A layer of flexible plastic insulation surrounding a copper conductor.

- The insulating material is surrounded in a woven copper braid, or metallic foil, that acts as the second wire in the circuit and as a shield for the inner conductor. This second layer, or shield, also reduces the amount of outside electromagnetic interference.

- The entire cable is covered with a cable jacket to prevent minor physical damage.

There are different types of connectors used with coax cable.

Although UTP cable has essentially replaced coaxial cable in modern Ethernet installations, the coaxial cable design is used in:

- **Wireless installations:** Coaxial cables attach antennas to wireless devices. The coaxial cable carries radio frequency (RF) energy between the antennas and the radio equipment.

- **Cable Internet installations:** Cable service providers provide Internet connectivity to their customers by replacing portions of the coaxial cable and supporting amplification elements with fiber-optic cable. However, the wiring inside the customer's premises is still coax cable.

Refer to
Online Course
for Illustration

4.2.1.6 Copper Media Safety

All three types of copper media are susceptible to fire and electrical hazards.

Fire hazards exist because cable insulation and sheaths may be flammable, or produce toxic fumes when heated or burned. Building authorities or organizations may stipulate related safety standards for cabling and hardware installations.

Electrical hazards are a potential problem because copper wires can conduct electricity in undesirable ways. This could subject personnel and equipment to a range of electrical hazards. For example, a defective network device could conduct currents to the chassis of other network devices. Additionally, network cabling could present undesirable voltage levels when used to connect devices that have power sources with different ground potentials. Such situations are possible when copper cabling is used to connect networks in different buildings or on separate floors that use disparate power facilities. Finally, copper cabling may conduct voltages caused by lightning strikes to network devices.

The result of undesirable voltages and currents can include damage to network devices and connected computers, or injury to personnel. It is important that copper cabling be installed appropriately, and according to the relevant specifications and building codes, in order to avoid potentially dangerous and damaging situations.

The figure displays proper cabling practices that help to prevent potential fire and electrical hazards.

Refer to
Interactive Graphic
in online course

4.2.1.7 Activity - Copper Media Characteristics

Refer to
Online Course
for Illustration

4.2.2 UTP Cabling

4.2.2.1 Properties of UTP Cabling

When used as a networking medium, unshielded twisted-pair (UTP) cabling consists of four pairs of color-coded copper wires that have been twisted together and then encased in a flexible plastic sheath. Its small size can be advantageous during installation.

UTP cable does not use shielding to counter the effects of EMI and RFI. Instead, cable designers have discovered that they can limit the negative effect of crosstalk by:

- **Cancellation:** Designers now pair wires in a circuit. When two wires in an electrical circuit are placed close together, their magnetic fields are the exact opposite of each other. Therefore, the two magnetic fields cancel each other and also cancel out any outside EMI and RFI signals.

- **Varying the number of twists per wire pair:** To further enhance the cancellation effect of paired circuit wires, designers vary the number of twists of each wire pair in a cable. UTP cable must follow precise specifications governing how many twists or braids are permitted per meter (3.28 feet) of cable. Notice in the figure that the orange/orange white pair is twisted less than the blue/blue white pair. Each colored pair is twisted a different number of times.

UTP cable relies solely on the cancellation effect produced by the twisted wire pairs to limit signal degradation and effectively provide self-shielding for wire pairs within the network media.

Refer to **Online Course** for Illustration

4.2.2.2   UTP Cabling Standards

UTP cabling conforms to the standards established jointly by the TIA/EIA. Specifically, TIA/EIA-568 stipulates the commercial cabling standards for LAN installations and is the standard most commonly used in LAN cabling environments. Some of the elements defined are:

- Cable types
- Cable lengths
- Connectors
- Cable termination
- Methods of testing cable

The electrical characteristics of copper cabling are defined by the Institute of Electrical and Electronics Engineers (IEEE). IEEE rates UTP cabling according to its performance. Cables are placed into categories based on their ability to carry higher bandwidth rates. For example, Category 5 (Cat5) cable is used commonly in 100BASE-TX Fast Ethernet installations. Other categories include Enhanced Category 5 (Cat5e) cable, Category 6 (Cat6), and Category 6a.

Cables in higher categories are designed and constructed to support higher data rates. As new gigabit speed Ethernet technologies are being developed and adopted, Cat5e is now the minimally acceptable cable type, with Cat6 being the recommended type for new building installations.

Click each category of cable in the figure to learn more about their properties.

Some manufacturers are making cables exceeding the TIA/EIA Category 6a specifications and refer to these as Category 7.

Refer to **Online Course** for Illustration

4.2.2.3   UTP Connectors

UTP cable is usually terminated with an RJ-45 connector. This connector is used for a range of physical layer specifications, one of which is Ethernet. The TIA/EIA-568 standard describes the wire color codes to pin assignments (pinouts) for Ethernet cables.

As shown in Figure1, the RJ-45 connector is the male component, crimped at the end of the cable. The socket is the female component of a network device, wall, cubicle partition outlet, or patch panel.

Each time copper cabling is terminated; there is the possibility of signal loss and the introduction of noise into the communication circuit. When terminated improperly, each cable is a potential source of physical layer performance degradation. It is essential that all copper media terminations be of high quality to ensure optimum performance with current and future network technologies.

Figure 2 displays an example of a badly terminated UTP cable and a well terminated UTP cable.

Refer to **Online Course** for Illustration

4.2.2.4   Types of UTP Cable

Different situations may require UTP cables to be wired according to different wiring conventions. This means that the individual wires in the cable have to be connected in different orders to different sets of pins in the RJ-45 connectors.

The following are the main cable types that are obtained by using specific wiring conventions:

- **Ethernet Straight-through:** The most common type of networking cable. It is commonly used to interconnect a host to a switch and a switch to a router.

- **Ethernet Crossover:** A cable used to interconnect similar devices. For example to connect a switch to a switch, a host to a host, or a router to a router.

- **Rollover:** A Cisco proprietary cable used to connect a workstation to a router or switch console port.

The figure shows the UTP cable type, related standards, and typical application of these cables. It also identifies the individual wire pairs for the TIA-568A and TIA-568B standards.

Using a crossover or straight-through cable incorrectly between devices may not damage the devices, but connectivity and communication between the devices will not take place. This is a common error in the lab and checking that the device connections are correct should be the first troubleshooting action if connectivity is not achieved.

Refer to **Online Course** for Illustration

4.2.2.5   Testing UTP Cables

After installation, a UTP cable tester, like the one shown in the figure, should be used to test for the following parameters:

- Wire map
- Cable length
- Signal loss due to attenuation
- Crosstalk

It is recommended to check thoroughly that all UTP installation requirements have been met.

Refer to
Online Course
for Illustration

4.2.2.6   Cable Pinouts

Refer to
Lab Activity
for this chapter

4.2.2.7   Lab - Building an Ethernet Crossover Cable

In this lab, you will complete the following objectives:

- Part 1: Analyze Ethernet Cabling Standards and Pinouts
- Part 2: Build an Ethernet Crossover Cable
- Part 3: Test an Ethernet Crossover Cable

Refer to
Online Course
for Illustration

4.2.3   Fiber-Optic Cabling

4.2.3.1   Properties of Fiber-Optic Cabling

Optical fiber cable transmits data over longer distances and at higher bandwidths than any other networking media. Unlike copper wires, fiber-optic cable can transmit signals with less attenuation and is completely immune to EMI and RFI. Optical fiber is commonly used to interconnect network devices.

Optical fiber is a flexible, but extremely thin, transparent strand of very pure glass, not much bigger than a human hair. Bits are encoded on the fiber as light impulses. The fiber-optic cable acts as a waveguide, or "light pipe," to transmit light between the two ends with minimal loss of signal.

As an analogy, consider an empty paper towel roll with the inside coated like a mirror. It is a thousand meters in length, and a small laser pointer is used to send Morse code signals at the speed of light. Essentially that is how a fiber-optic cable operates, except that it is smaller in diameter and uses sophisticated light technologies.

Fiber-optic cabling is now being used in four types of industry:

- **Enterprise Networks:** Used for backbone cabling applications and interconnecting infrastructure devices.
- **Fiber-to-the-Home (FTTH):** Used to provide always-on broadband services to homes and small businesses.
- **Long-Haul Networks:** Used by service providers to connect countries and cities.
- **Submarine Networks:** Used to provide reliable high-speed, high-capacity solutions capable of surviving in harsh undersea environments up to transoceanic distances. Click here to view a telegeography map that depicts the location of submarine cables.

Our focus in this course is the use of fiber within the enterprise.

Refer to
Online Course
for Illustration

4.2.3.2   Fiber Media Cable Design

Optical fiber is composed of two kinds of glass (core and cladding) and a protective outer shield (jacket). Click each component in the figure to learn more information.

Although the optical fiber is very thin and susceptible to sharp bends, the properties of the core and cladding make it very strong. Optical fiber is durable and is deployed in harsh environmental conditions in networks all around the world.

Refer to
Online Course
for Illustration

4.2.3.3   Types of Fiber Media

Light pulses representing the transmitted data as bits on the media are generated by either:

- Lasers

- Light emitting diodes (LEDs)

Electronic semiconductor devices called photodiodes detect the light pulses and convert them to voltages. The laser light transmitted over fiber-optic cabling can damage the human eye. Care must be taken to avoid looking into the end of an active optical fiber.

Fiber-optic cables are broadly classified into two types:

- **Single-mode fiber (SMF):** Consists of a very small core and uses expensive laser technology to send a single ray of light, as shown in Figure 1. Popular in long-distance situations spanning hundreds of kilometers, such as those required in long haul telephony and cable TV applications.

- **Multimode fiber (MMF):** Consists of a larger core and uses LED emitters to send light pulses. Specifically, light from an LED enters the multimode fiber at different angles, as shown in Figure 2. Popular in LANs because they can be powered by low-cost LEDs. It provides bandwidth up to 10 Gb/s over link lengths of up to 550 meters.

One of the highlighted differences between multimode and single-mode fiber is the amount of dispersion. Dispersion refers to the spreading out of a light pulse over time. The more dispersion there is, the greater the loss of signal strength.

Refer to
Online Course
for Illustration

4.2.3.4   Fiber-Optic Connectors

An optical fiber connector terminates the end of an optical fiber. A variety of optical fiber connectors are available. The main differences among the types of connectors are dimensions and methods of coupling. Businesses decide on the types of connectors that will be used, based on their equipment.

Click each connector in Figure 1 to learn about the three most popular types of fiber-optic connectors, ST, SC, and LC.

Because light can only travel in one direction over optical fiber, two fibers are required to support the full duplex operation. Therefore, fiber-optic patch cables bundle together two optical fiber cables and terminate them with a pair of standard single fiber connectors. Some fiber connectors accept both the transmitting and receiving fibers in a single connector known as a duplex connector, as shown in the Duplex Multimode LC Connector in Figure 1.

Fiber patch cords are required for interconnecting infrastructure devices. Figure 2 displays various common patch cords. The use of color distinguishes between single-mode and multimode patch cords. A yellow jacket is for single-mode fiber cables and orange (or aqua) for multimode fiber cables.

Fiber cables should be protected with a small plastic cap when not in use.

Refer to
Online Course
for Illustration

4.2.3.5   Testing Fiber Cables

Terminating and splicing fiber-optic cabling requires special training and equipment. Incorrect termination of fiber-optic media will result in diminished signaling distances or complete transmission failure.

Three common types of fiber-optic termination and splicing errors are:

■ **Misalignment:** The fiber-optic media are not precisely aligned to one another when joined.

■ **End gap:** The media does not completely touch at the splice or connection.

■ **End finish:** The media ends are not well polished, or dirt is present at the termination.

A quick and easy field test can be performed by shining a bright flashlight into one end of the fiber while observing the other end. If light is visible, the fiber is capable of passing light. Although this does not ensure performance, it is a quick and inexpensive way to find a broken fiber.

As shown in the figure, an Optical Time Domain Reflectometer (OTDR) can be used to test each fiber-optic cable segment. This device injects a test pulse of light into the cable and measures backscatter and reflection of light detected as a function of time. The OTDR will calculate the approximate distance at which these faults are detected along the length of the cable.

Refer to
Online Course
for Illustration

4.2.3.6   Fiber versus Copper

There are many advantages to using fiber-optic cable compared to copper cables. The figure highlights some of these differences.

Given that the fibers used in fiber-optic media are not electrical conductors, the media is immune to electromagnetic interference and will not conduct unwanted electrical currents due to grounding issues. Optical fibers are thin and have a relatively low signal loss and can be operated at much greater lengths than copper media. Some optical fiber physical layer specifications allow lengths that can reach multiple kilometers.

At present, in most enterprise environments, optical fiber is primarily used as backbone cabling for high-traffic point-to-point connections between data distribution facilities and for the interconnection of buildings in multi-building campuses. Because optical fiber does not conduct electricity and has a low signal loss, it is well suited for these uses.

Refer to
Interactive Graphic
in online course

4.2.3.7   Activity - Fiber Optics Terminology

Refer to
Online Course
for Illustration

4.2.4   Wireless Media

4.2.4.1   Properties of Wireless Media

Wireless media carry electromagnetic signals that represent the binary digits of data communications using radio or microwave frequencies.

Wireless media provides the greatest mobility options of all media, and the number of wireless-enabled devices continues to increase. As network bandwidth options increase, wireless is quickly gaining in popularity in enterprise networks.

The figure highlights various wireless-related symbols.

Wireless does have some areas of concern, including:

- **Coverage area:** Wireless data communication technologies work well in open environments. However, certain construction materials used in buildings and structures, and the local terrain, will limit the effective coverage.

- **Interference:** Wireless is susceptible to interference and can be disrupted by such common devices as household cordless phones, some types of fluorescent lights, microwave ovens, and other wireless communications.

- **Security:** Wireless communication coverage requires no access to a physical strand of media. Therefore, devices and users, not authorized for access to the network, can gain access to the transmission. Network security is a major component of wireless network administration.

- **Shared medium:** WLANs operate in half-duplex, which means only one device can send or receive at a time. The wireless medium is shared amongst all wireless users. The more users needing to access the WLAN simultaneously, results in less bandwidth for each user. Half-duplex is discussed later in this chapter.

Although wireless is increasing in popularity for desktop connectivity, copper and fiber are the most popular physical layer media for network deployments.

Refer to
Online Course
for Illustration

4.2.4.2   Types of Wireless Media

The IEEE and telecommunications industry standards for wireless data communications cover both the data link and physical layers. Click on each standard in the figure for more information.

Note   Other wireless technologies such as cellular and satellite communications can also provide data network connectivity. However, these wireless technologies are out of scope for this chapter.

In each of these standards, physical layer specifications are applied to areas that include:

- Data to radio signal encoding
- Frequency and power of transmission
- Signal reception and decoding requirements
- Antenna design and construction

Wi-Fi is a trademark of the Wi-Fi Alliance. Wi-Fi is used with certified products that belong to WLAN devices that are based on the IEEE 802.11 standards. Refer to the Chapter Appendix for more information on 802.11 wireless standards.

Refer to
Online Course
for Illustration

4.2.4.3   Wireless LAN

A common wireless data implementation is enabling devices to connect wirelessly via a LAN. In general, a wireless LAN requires the following network devices:

- **Wireless Access Point (AP):** Concentrates the wireless signals from users and connects to the existing copper-based network infrastructure, such as Ethernet. Home and small business wireless routers integrate the functions of a router, switch, and access point into one device as shown in the figure.

- **Wireless NIC adapters:** Provide wireless communication capability to each network host.

As the technology has developed, a number of WLAN Ethernet-based standards have emerged. Care needs to be taken in purchasing wireless devices to ensure compatibility and interoperability.

The benefits of wireless data communications technologies are evident, especially the savings on costly premises wiring and the convenience of host mobility. Network administrators need to develop and apply stringent security policies and processes to protect wireless LANs from unauthorized access and damage.

Refer to **Packet Tracer Activity** for this chapter

4.2.4.4   Packet Tracer – Connecting a Wired and Wireless LAN

When working in Packet Tracer, a lab environment, or a corporate setting, you should know how to select the appropriate cable and how to properly connect devices. This activity will examine device configurations in Packet Tracer, selecting the proper cable based on the configuration, and connecting the devices. This activity will also explore the physical view of the network in Packet Tracer.

Refer to **Lab Activity** for this chapter

4.2.4.5   Lab - Viewing Wired and Wireless NIC Information

In this lab, you will complete the following objectives:

- Part 1: Identify and Work with PC NICs

- Part 2: Identify and Use the System Tray Network Icons

Refer to
Online Course
for Illustration

4.3   Data Link Layer Protocols

4.3.1   Purpose of the Data Link Layer

4.3.1.1   The Data Link Layer

The data link layer of the OSI model (Layer 2), as shown in Figure 1, is responsible for:

- Allowing the upper layers to access the media

- Accepting Layer 3 packets and packaging them into frames

- Preparing network data for the physical network

- Controlling how data is placed and received on the media

- Exchanging frames between nodes over a physical network media, such as UTP or fiber-optic

- Receiving and directing packets to an upper layer protocol

- Performing error detection

The Layer 2 notation for network devices connected to a common media is called a node. Nodes build and forward frames. As shown in Figure 2, the OSI data link layer is responsible for the exchange of Ethernet frames between source and destination nodes over a physical network media.

The data link layer effectively separates the media transitions that occur as the packet is forwarded from the communication processes of the higher layers. The data link layer receives packets from and directs packets to an upper layer protocol, in this case IPv4 or IPv6. This upper layer protocol does not need to be aware of which media the communication will use.

Refer to
Online Course
for Illustration

4.3.1.2   Data Link Sublayers

The data link layer is divided into two sublayers:

- **Logical Link Control (LLC)** – This upper sublayer communicates with the network layer. It places information in the frame that identifies which network layer protocol is being used for the frame. This information allows multiple Layer 3 protocols, such as IPv4 and IPv6, to utilize the same network interface and media.

- **Media Access Control (MAC)** – This lower sublayer defines the media access processes performed by the hardware. It provides data link layer addressing and access to various network technologies.

The figure illustrates how the data link layer is separated into the LLC and MAC sublayers. The LLC communicates with the network layer while the MAC sublayer allows various network access technologies. For instance, the MAC sublayer communicates with Ethernet LAN technology to send and receive frames over copper or fiber-optic cable. The MAC sublayer also communicates with wireless technologies such as Wi-Fi and Bluetooth to send and receive frames wirelessly.

Refer to
Online Course
for Illustration

4.3.1.3   Media Access Control

Layer 2 protocols specify the encapsulation of a packet into a frame and the techniques for getting the encapsulated packet on and off each medium. The technique used for getting the frame on and off the media is called the media access control method.

As packets travel from the source host to the destination host, they typically traverse over different physical networks. These physical networks can consist of different types of physical media such as copper wires, optical fibers, and wireless consisting of electromagnetic signals, radio and microwave frequencies, and satellite links.

Without the data link layer, network layer protocols such as IP, would have to make provisions for connecting to every type of media that could exist along a delivery path. Moreover, IP would have to adapt every time a new network technology or medium was developed. This process would hamper protocol and network media innovation and development. This is a key reason for using a layered approach to networking.

The animation in the figure provides an example of a PC in Paris connecting to a laptop in Japan. Although the two hosts are communicating using IP exclusively, it is likely that numerous data link layer protocols are being used to transport the IP packets over various types of LANs and WANs. Each transition at a router may require a different data link layer protocol for transport on a new medium.

Refer to **Online Course** for Illustration

4.3.1.4   Providing Access to Media

Different media access control methods may be required during a single communication. Each network environment that packets encounter as they travel from a local host to a remote host can have different characteristics. For example, an Ethernet LAN consists of many hosts contending to access the network medium. Serial links consist of a direct connection between only two devices.

Router interfaces encapsulate the packet into the appropriate frame, and a suitable media access control method is used to access each link. In any given exchange of network layer packets, there may be numerous data link layers and media transitions.

At each hop along the path, a router:

- Accepts a frame from a medium

- De-encapsulates the frame

- Re-encapsulates the packet into a new frame

- Forwards the new frame appropriate to the medium of that segment of the physical network

The router in the figure has an Ethernet interface to connect to the LAN and a serial interface to connect to the WAN. As the router processes frames, it will use data link layer services to receive the frame from one medium, de-encapsulate it to the Layer 3 PDU, re-encapsulate the PDU into a new frame, and place the frame on the medium of the next link of the network.

Refer to **Online Course** for Illustration

4.3.1.5   Data Link Layer Standards

Unlike the protocols of the upper layers of the TCP/IP suite, data link layer protocols are generally not defined by Request for Comments (RFCs). Although the Internet Engineering Task Force (IETF) maintains the functional protocols and services for the TCP/IP protocol suite in the upper layers, the IETF does not define the functions and operation of that model's network access layer.

Engineering organizations that define open standards and protocols that apply to the network access layer include:

- Institute of Electrical and Electronics Engineers (IEEE)

- International Telecommunication Union (ITU)

- International Organization for Standardization (ISO)

- American National Standards Institute (ANSI)

Refer to
Online Course
for Illustration

4.4   Media Access Control

4.4.1   Topologies

4.4.1.1   Controlling Access to the Media

Regulating the placement of data frames onto the media is controlled by the media access control sublayer.

Media access control is the equivalent of traffic rules that regulate the entrance of motor vehicles onto a roadway. The absence of any media access control would be the equivalent of vehicles ignoring all other traffic and entering the road without regard to the other vehicles. However, not all roads and entrances are the same. Traffic can enter the road by merging, by waiting for its turn at a stop sign, or by obeying signal lights. A driver follows a different set of rules for each type of entrance.

In the same way, there are different methods to regulate placing frames onto the media. The protocols at the data link layer define the rules for access to different media. These media access control techniques define if and how the nodes share the media.

The actual media access control method used depends on:

- **Topology** – How the connection between the nodes appears to the data link layer.

- **Media sharing** – How the nodes share the media. The media sharing can be point-to-point, such as in WAN connections, or shared such as in LAN networks.

Refer to
Online Course
for Illustration

4.4.1.2   Physical and Logical Topologies

The topology of a network is the arrangement or relationship of the network devices and the interconnections between them. LAN and WAN topologies can be viewed in two ways:

- **Physical topology** – Refers to the physical connections and identifies how end devices and infrastructure devices such as routers, switches, and wireless access points are interconnected. Physical topologies are usually point-to-point or star. See Figure 1.

- **Logical topology** – Refers to the way a network transfers frames from one node to the next. This arrangement consists of virtual connections between the nodes of a network. These logical signal paths are defined by data link layer protocols. The logical topology of point-to-point links is relatively simple while shared media offers different access control methods. See Figure 2.

The data link layer "sees" the logical topology of a network when controlling data access to the media. It is the logical topology that influences the type of network framing and media access control used.

Refer to
Online Course
for Illustration

4.4.2   WAN Topologies

4.4.2.1   Common Physical WAN Topologies

WANs are commonly interconnected using the following physical topologies:

- **Point-to-Point** – This is the simplest topology that consists of a permanent link between two endpoints. For this reason, this is a very popular WAN topology.

- **Hub and Spoke** – A WAN version of the star topology in which a central site interconnects branch sites using point-to-point links.

- **Mesh** – This topology provides high availability, but requires that every end system be interconnected to every other system. Therefore the administrative and physical costs can be significant. Each link is essentially a point-to-point link to the other node. Variations of this topology include a partial mesh where some but not all of end devices are interconnected.

The three common physical WAN topologies are illustrated in the figure.

Refer to
Online Course
for Illustration

4.4.2.2   Physical Point-to-Point Topology

Physical point-to-point topologies directly connect two nodes as shown in the figure.

In this arrangement, two nodes do not have to share the media with other hosts. Additionally, a node does not have to make any determination about whether an incoming frame is destined for it or another node. Therefore, the logical data link protocols can be very simple, as all frames on the media can only travel to or from the two nodes. The frames are placed on the media by the node at one end and taken from the media by the node at the other end of the point-to-point circuit.

Refer to
Online Course
for Illustration

4.4.2.3   Logical Point-to-Point Topology

The end nodes communicating in a point-to-point network can be physically connected via a number of intermediate devices. However, the use of physical devices in the network does not affect the logical topology.

As shown in Figure 1, the source and destination node may be indirectly connected to each other over some geographical distance. In some cases, the logical connection between nodes forms what is called a virtual circuit. A virtual circuit is a logical connection created within a network between two network devices. The two nodes on either end of the virtual circuit exchange the frames with each other. This occurs even if the frames are directed through intermediary devices, as shown in Figure 2. Virtual circuits are important logical communication constructs used by some Layer 2 technologies.

The media access method used by the data link protocol is determined by the logical point-to-point topology, not the physical topology. This means that the logical point-to-point connection between two nodes may not necessarily be between two physical nodes at each end of a single physical link.

Refer to
Online Course
for Illustration

4.4.3   LAN Topologies

4.4.3.1   Physical LAN Topologies

Physical topology defines how the end systems are physically interconnected. In shared media LANs, end devices can be interconnected using the following physical topologies:

- **Star** – End devices are connected to a central intermediate device. Early star topologies interconnected end devices using Ethernet hubs. However, star topologies now use Ethernet switches. The star topology is easy to install, very scalable (easy to add and remove end devices), and easy to troubleshoot.

- **Extended Star** – In an extended star topology, additional Ethernet switches interconnect other star topologies.

- **Bus** – All end systems are chained to each other and terminated in some form on each end. Infrastructure devices such as switches are not required to interconnect the end devices. Bus topologies using coax cables were used in legacy Ethernet networks because it was inexpensive and easy to set up.

- **Ring** – End systems are connected to their respective neighbor forming a ring. Unlike the bus topology, the ring does not need to be terminated. Ring topologies were used in legacy Fiber Distributed Data Interface (FDDI) and Token Ring networks.

The figure illustrates how end devices are interconnected on LANs. It is common for a straight line in networking graphics to represent an Ethernet LAN including a simple star and an extended star.

Refer to
Online Course
for Illustration

4.4.3.2   Half and Full Duplex

Duplex communications refer to the direction of data transmission between two devices. Half-duplex communications restrict the exchange of data to one direction at a time while full-duplex allows the sending and receiving of data to happen simultaneously.

- **Half-duplex communication** – Both devices can transmit and receive on the media but cannot do so simultaneously. The half-duplex mode is used in legacy bus topologies and with Ethernet hubs. WLANs also operate in half-duplex. Half-duplex allows only one device to send or receive at a time on the shared medium and is used with contention-based access methods. Figure 1 shows half-duplex communication.

- **Full-duplex communication** – Both devices can transmit and receive on the media at the same time. The data link layer assumes that the media is available for transmission for both nodes at any time. Ethernet switches operate in full-duplex mode by default, but can operate in half-duplex if connecting to a device such as an Ethernet hub. Figure 2 shows full-duplex communication.

It is important that two interconnected interfaces, such as a host's NIC and an interface on an Ethernet switch operate using the same duplex mode. Otherwise, there will be a duplex mismatch creating inefficiency and latency on the link.

Refer to
Online Course
for Illustration

4.4.3.3   Media Access Control Methods

Some network topologies share a common medium with multiple nodes. These are called multi-access networks. Ethernet LANs and WLANs are examples of a multi-access network. At any one time, there may be a number of devices attempting to send and receive data using the same network media.

Some multi-access networks require rules to govern how devices share the physical media. There are two basic access control methods for shared media:

- **Contention-based access** – All nodes operating in half-duplex compete for the use of the medium, but only one device can send at a time. However, there is a process if more than one device transmits at the same time. Ethernet LANs using hubs and WLANs are examples of this type of access control. Figure 1 shows contention-based access.

- **Controlled access** – Each node has its own time to use the medium. These deterministic types of networks are inefficient because a device must wait its turn to access the medium. Legacy Token Ring LANs are an example of this type of access control. Figure 2 shows controlled access. Refer to the Chapter Appendix to learn more about controlled access.

By default, Ethernet switches operate in full-duplex mode. This allows the switch and the full-duplex connected device to send and receive simultaneously.

Refer to
Online Course
for Illustration

4.4.3.4   Contention-Based Access – CSMA/CD

WLANs, Ethernet LANs with hubs, and legacy Ethernet bus networks are all examples of contention-based access networks. All of these networks operate in half-duplex mode. This requires a process to govern when a device can send and what happens when multiple devices send at the same time.

The Carrier Sense Multiple Access/Collision Detection (CSMA/CD) process is used in half-duplex Ethernet LANs. Figure 1 shows an Ethernet LAN using a hub. The CSMA process is as follows:

1. PC1 has an Ethernet frame to send to PC3.

2. PC1's NIC needs to determine if anyone is transmitting on the medium. If it does not detect a carrier signal, in other words, it is not receiving transmissions from another device, it will assume the network is available to send.

3. PC1's NIC sends the Ethernet Frame, as shown in Figure 1.

4. The Ethernet hub receives the frame. An Ethernet hub is also known as a multiport repeater. Any bits received on an incoming port are regenerated and sent out all other ports, as shown in Figure 2.

5. If another device, such as PC2, wants to transmit, but is currently receiving a frame, it must wait until the channel is clear.

6. All devices attached to the hub will receive the frame. Because the frame has a destination data link address for PC3, only that device will accept and copy in the entire frame. All other devices' NICs will ignore the frame, as shown in Figure 3.

If two devices transmit at the same time, a collision will occur. Both devices will detect the collision on the network. This is done by the NIC comparing data transmitted with data received, or by recognizing the signal amplitude is higher than normal on the media. The data sent by both devices will be corrupted and will need to be resent.

Refer to
Online Course
for Illustration

4.4.3.5 Contention-Based Access – CSMA/CA

Another form of CSMA that is used by IEEE 802.11 WLANs is Carrier Sense Multiple Access/Collision Avoidance (CSMA/CA). CMSA/CA uses a method similar to CSMA/CD to detect if the media is clear. CMSA/CA also uses additional techniques. CMSA/CA does not detect collisions but attempts to avoid them by waiting before transmitting. Each device that transmits includes the time duration that it needs for the transmission. All other wireless devices receive this information and know how long the medium will be unavailable, as shown in the figure. After a wireless device sends an 802.11 frame, the receiver returns an acknowledgment so that the sender knows the frame arrived.

Whether it is an Ethernet LAN using hubs, or a WLAN, contention-based systems do not scale well under heavy media use. It is important to note that Ethernet LANs using switches do not use a contention-based system because the switch and the host NIC operate in full-duplex mode.

Refer to
Online Course
for Illustration

4.4.4 Data Link Frame

4.4.4.1 The Frame

The data link layer prepares a packet for transport across the local media by encapsulating it with a header and a trailer to create a frame. The description of a frame is a key element of each data link layer protocol. Although there are many different data link layer protocols that describe data link layer frames, each frame type has three basic parts:

- Header
- Data
- Trailer

All data link layer protocols encapsulate the Layer 3 PDU within the data field of the frame. However, the structure of the frame and the fields contained in the header and trailer vary according to the protocol.

There is no one frame structure that meets the needs of all data transportation across all types of media. Depending on the environment, the amount of control information needed in the frame varies to match the access control requirements of the media and logical topology.

As shown in the figure, a fragile environment requires more control.

Refer to
Online Course
for Illustration

4.4.4.2 Frame Fields

Framing breaks the stream into decipherable groupings, with control information inserted in the header and trailer as values in different fields. This format gives the physical signals a structure that can be received by nodes and decoded into packets at the destination.

As shown in the figure, generic frame field types include:

- **Frame start and stop indicator flags** – Used to identify the beginning and end limits of the frame.

- **Addressing** – Indicates the source and destination nodes on the media.

- **Type** – Identifies the Layer 3 protocol in the data field.

- **Control** – Identifies special flow control services such as quality of service (QoS). QoS is used to give forwarding priority to certain types of messages. Data link frames carrying voice over IP (VoIP) packets normally receive priority because they are sensitive to delay.

- **Data** – Contains the frame payload (i.e., packet header, segment header, and the data).

- **Error Detection** – These frame fields are used for error detection and are included after the data to form the trailer.

Not all protocols include all of these fields. The standards for a specific data link protocol define the actual frame format.

Data link layer protocols add a trailer to the end of each frame. The trailer is used to determine if the frame arrived without error. This process is called error detection and is accomplished by placing a logical or mathematical summary of the bits that comprise the frame in the trailer. Error detection is added at the data link layer because the signals on the media could be subject to interference, distortion, or loss that would substantially change the bit values that those signals represent.

A transmitting node creates a logical summary of the contents of the frame, known as the cyclic redundancy check (CRC) value. This value is placed in the Frame Check Sequence (FCS) field to represent the contents of the frame. In the Ethernet trailer, the FCS provides a method for the receiving node to determine whether the frame experienced transmission errors. Refer to the Chapter Appendix to learn more about the frame trailer.

Refer to
Interactive Graphic
in online course

4.4.4.3   Activity – Generic Frame Fields

Refer to
Online Course
for Illustration

4.4.4.4   Layer 2 Address

The data link layer provides addressing that is used in transporting a frame across a shared local media. Device addresses at this layer are referred to as physical addresses. Data link layer addressing is contained within the frame header and specifies the frame destination node on the local network. The frame header may also contain the source address of the frame.

Unlike Layer 3 logical addresses, which are hierarchical, physical addresses do not indicate on what network the device is located. Rather, the physical address is unique to the specific device. If the device is moved to another network or subnet, it will still function with the same Layer 2 physical address.

Figures 1 through 3 illustrate the function of the Layer 2 and Layer 3 addresses. As the IP packet travels from host-to-router, router-to-router, and finally router-to-host, at each point along the way the IP packet is encapsulated in a new data link frame. Each data link frame contains the source data link address of the NIC card sending the frame, and the destination data link address of the NIC card receiving the frame.

An address that is device-specific and non-hierarchical cannot be used to locate a device on large networks or the Internet. This would be like trying to find a single house within the entire world, with nothing more than a house number and street name. The physical address, however, can be used to locate a device within a limited area. For this reason, the data link layer address is only used for local delivery. Addresses at this layer have no meaning beyond the local network. Compare this to Layer 3, where addresses in the packet header are carried from the source host to the destination host, regardless of the number of network hops along the route.

If the data must pass onto another network segment, an intermediate device, such as a router, is necessary. The router must accept the frame based on the physical address and de-encapsulate the frame in order to examine the hierarchical address, or IP address. Using the IP address, the router is able to determine the network location of the destination device and the best path to reach it. When it knows where to forward the packet, the router then creates a new frame for the packet, and the new frame is sent on to the next network segment toward its final destination.

4.4.4.5 LAN and WAN Frames

In a TCP/IP network, all OSI Layer 2 protocols work with IP at OSI Layer 3. However, the Layer 2 protocol used depends on the logical topology and the physical media.

Each protocol performs media access control for specified Layer 2 logical topologies. This means that a number of different network devices can act as nodes that operate at the data link layer when implementing these protocols. These devices include the NICs on computers as well as the interfaces on routers and Layer 2 switches.

The Layer 2 protocol used for a particular network topology is determined by the technology used to implement that topology. The technology is, in turn, determined by the size of the network - in terms of the number of hosts and the geographic scope - and the services to be provided over the network.

A LAN typically uses a high bandwidth technology that is capable of supporting large numbers of hosts. A LAN's relatively small geographic area (a single building or a multi-building campus) and its high density of users, make this technology cost-effective.

However, using a high bandwidth technology is usually not cost-effective for WANs that cover large geographic areas (cities or multiple cities, for example). The cost of the long distance physical links and the technology used to carry the signals over those distances typically results in lower bandwidth capacity.

The difference in bandwidth normally results in the use of different protocols for LANs and WANs.

Data link layer protocols include:

- Ethernet
- 802.11 Wireless
- Point-to-Point Protocol (PPP)
- HDLC
- Frame Relay

Click Play to see examples of Layer 2 protocols.

Refer to the Chapter Appendix for more information on different frame types including the Ethernet frame, PPP frame, and wireless frame.

Refer to Online Course for Illustration

Refer to
Online Course
for Illustration

4.5   Summary

4.5.1   Conclusion

Refer to
Lab Activity
for this chapter

4.5.1.1   Class Activity – Linked In!

Note   This activity is best completed in groups of 2-3 students.

Your small business is moving to a new location! Your building is brand new, and you must come up with a physical topology so that network port installation can begin.

Your instructor will provide you with a blueprint created for this activity. The area on the blueprint, indicated by Number 1, is the reception area and the area numbered RR is the restroom area.

All rooms are within Category 6 UTP specifications (100 meters), so you have no concerns about hard-wiring the building to code. Each room in the diagram must have at least one network connection available for users/intermediary devices.

Do not go into excessive detail on your design. Just use the content from the chapter to be able to justify your decisions to the class.

Refer to
Online Course
for Illustration

4.5.1.2   Network Access

The TCP/IP network access layer is the equivalent of the OSI data link layer (Layer 2) and the physical layer (Layer 1).

The OSI physical layer provides the means to transport the bits that make up a data link layer frame across the network media. The physical components are the electronic hardware devices, media, and other connectors that transmit and carry the signals to represent the bits. Hardware components such as network adapters (NICs), interfaces and connectors, cable materials, and cable designs are all specified in standards associated with the physical layer. The physical layer standards address three functional areas: physical components, frame encoding technique, and signaling method.

Using the proper media is an important part of network communications. Without the proper physical connection, either wired or wireless, communications between any two devices will not occur.

Wired communication consists of copper media and fiber cable:

- There are three main types of copper media used in networking: unshielded-twisted pair (UTP), shielded-twisted pair (STP), and coaxial cable. UTP cabling is the most common copper networking media.

- Optical fiber cable has become very popular for interconnecting infrastructure network devices. It permits the transmission of data over longer distances and at higher bandwidths (data rates) than any other networking media. Unlike copper wires, fiber-optic cable can transmit signals with less attenuation and is completely immune to EMI and RFI.

Wireless media carry electromagnetic signals that represent the binary digits of data communications using radio or microwave frequencies.

The number of wireless-enabled devices continues to increase. For this reason, wireless has become the medium of choice for home networks and is quickly gaining in popularity in enterprise networks.

The data link layer handles the exchange of frames between nodes over a physical network media. It allows the upper layers to access the media and controls how data is placed and received on the media.

Among the different implementations of the data link layer protocols, there are different methods of controlling access to the media. These media access control techniques define if and how the nodes share the media. The actual media access control method used depends on the topology and media sharing. LAN and WAN topologies can be physical or logical. It is the logical topology that influences the type of network framing and media access control used. WANs are commonly interconnected using the point-to-point, hub and spoke, or mesh physical topologies. In shared media LANs, end devices can be interconnected using the star, bus, ring, or extended star physical topologies.

All data link layer protocols encapsulate the Layer 3 PDU within the data field of the frame. However, the structure of the frame and the fields contained in the header and trailer vary according to the protocol.

Go to the online course to take the quiz and exam.

Chapter 4 Quiz

This quiz is designed to provide an additional opportunity to practice the skills and knowledge presented in the chapter and to prepare for the chapter exam. You will be allowed multiple attempts and the grade does not appear in the gradebook.

Chapter 4 Exam

The chapter exam assesses your knowledge of the chapter content.

Your Chapter Notes

Ethernet

5.0 Introduction

5.0.1.1 Ethernet

The OSI physical layer provides the means to transport the bits that make up a data link layer frame across the network media.

Ethernet is now the predominant LAN technology in the world. Ethernet operates in the data link layer and the physical layer. The Ethernet protocol standards define many aspects of network communication including frame format, frame size, timing, and encoding. When messages are sent between hosts on an Ethernet network, the hosts format the messages into the frame layout that is specified by the standards.

Because Ethernet is comprised of standards at these lower layers, it may best be understood in reference to the OSI model. The OSI model separates the data link layer functionalities of addressing, framing, and accessing the media from the physical layer standards of the media. Ethernet standards define both the Layer 2 protocols and the Layer 1 technologies. Although Ethernet specifications support different media, bandwidths, and other Layer 1 and 2 variations, the basic frame format and address scheme is the same for all varieties of Ethernet.

This chapter examines the characteristics and operation of Ethernet as it has evolved from a shared media, contention-based data communications technology to today's high bandwidth, full-duplex technology.

Refer to **Lab Activity** for this chapter

5.0.1.2 Class Activity - Join My Social Circle!

Much of our network communication takes the form of messaging (text or instant), video contact, social media postings, etc.

For this activity, choose one of the communication networks you use most:

■ Text (or instant) messaging

■ Audio/video conferencing

■ Emailing

■ Gaming

Now that you have selected a network communication type, record your answers to the following questions:

■ Is there a procedure you must follow to register others and yourself so that you form a communications group?

- How do you initiate contact with the person/people with whom you wish to communicate?

- How do you limit your conversations so they are received by only those with whom you wish to communicate?

Be prepared to discuss your recorded answers in class.

Refer to
Online Course
for Illustration

5.1   Ethernet Protocol

5.1.1   Ethernet Frame

5.1.1.1   Ethernet Encapsulation

Ethernet is the most widely used LAN technology today.

Ethernet operates in the data link layer and the physical layer. It is a family of networking technologies that are defined in the IEEE 802.2 and 802.3 standards. Ethernet supports data bandwidths of:

- 10 Mb/s

- 100 Mb/s

- 1000 Mb/s (1 Gb/s)

- 10,000 Mb/s (10 Gb/s)

- 40,000 Mb/s (40 Gb/s)

- 100,000 Mb/s (100 Gb/s)

As shown in Figure 1, Ethernet standards define both the Layer 2 protocols and the Layer 1 technologies. For the Layer 2 protocols, as with all 802 IEEE standards, Ethernet relies on the two separate sublayers of the data link layer to operate, the Logical Link Control (LLC) and the MAC sublayers.

LLC sublayer

The Ethernet LLC sublayer handles the communication between the upper layers and the lower layers. This is typically between the networking software and the device hardware. The LLC sublayer takes the network protocol data, which is typically an IPv4 packet, and adds control information to help deliver the packet to the destination node. The LLC is used to communicate with the upper layers of the application, and transition the packet to the lower layers for delivery.

LLC is implemented in software, and its implementation is independent of the hardware. In a computer, the LLC can be considered the driver software for the NIC. The NIC driver is a program that interacts directly with the hardware on the NIC to pass the data between the MAC sublayer and the physical media.

MAC sublayer

MAC constitutes the lower sublayer of the data link layer. MAC is implemented by hardware, typically in the computer NIC. The specifics are listed in the IEEE 802.3 standards. Figure 2 lists common IEEE Ethernet standards.

Refer to
Online Course
for Illustration

5.1.1.2   MAC Sublayer

As shown in the figure, the Ethernet MAC sublayer has two primary responsibilities:

■ Data encapsulation

■ Media access control

Data encapsulation

The data encapsulation process includes frame assembly before transmission, and frame disassembly upon reception of a frame. In forming the frame, the MAC layer adds a header and trailer to the network layer PDU.

Data encapsulation provides three primary functions:

■ **Frame delimiting** – The framing process provides important delimiters that are used to identify a group of bits that make up a frame. These delimiting bits provide synchronization between the transmitting and receiving nodes.

■ **Addressing** – The encapsulation process contains the Layer 3 PDU and also provides for data link layer addressing.

■ **Error detection** – Each frame contains a trailer used to detect any errors in transmissions.

The use of frames aids in the transmission of bits as they are placed on the media and in the grouping of bits at the receiving node.

Media Access Control

The second responsibility of the MAC sublayer is media access control. Media access control is responsible for the placement of frames on the media and the removal of frames from the media. As its name implies, it controls access to the media. This sublayer communicates directly with the physical layer.

The underlying logical topology of Ethernet is a multi-access bus; therefore, all nodes (devices) on a single network segment share the medium. Ethernet is a contention-based method of networking. A contention-based method means that any device can try to transmit data across the shared medium whenever it has data to send. The Carrier Sense Multiple Access/Collision Detection (CSMA/CD) process is used in half-duplex Ethernet LANs to detect and resolve collisions. Today's Ethernet LANs use full-duplex switches, which allow multiple devices to send and receive simultaneously with no collisions.

Refer to
Online Course
for Illustration

5.1.1.3   Ethernet Evolution

Since the creation of Ethernet in 1973, standards have evolved for specifying faster and more flexible versions of the technology. This ability for Ethernet to improve over time is one of the main reasons it has become so popular. Early versions of Ethernet were relatively slow at 10 Mbps. The latest versions of Ethernet operate at 10 Gigabits per second and faster. Scroll through the timeline in Figure 1 to view the various versions of Ethernet.

At the data link layer, the frame structure is nearly identical for all speeds of Ethernet. The Ethernet frame structure adds headers and trailers around the Layer 3 PDU to encapsulate the message being sent, as shown in Figure 2.

Ethernet II is the Ethernet frame format used in TCP/IP networks.

Refer to
Online Course
for Illustration

5.1.1.4   Ethernet Frame Fields

The minimum Ethernet frame size is 64 bytes and the maximum is 1518 bytes. This includes all bytes from the Destination MAC Address field through the Frame Check Sequence (FCS) field. The Preamble field is not included when describing the size of a frame.

Any frame less than 64 bytes in length is considered a "collision fragment" or "runt frame" and is automatically discarded by receiving stations. Frames with more than 1500 bytes of data are considered "jumbo" or "baby giant frames".

If the size of a transmitted frame is less than the minimum or greater than the maximum, the receiving device drops the frame. Dropped frames are likely to be the result of collisions or other unwanted signals and are therefore considered invalid.

In the figure, click each field in the Ethernet frame to read more about its function.

Refer to
Interactive Graphic
in online course

5.1.1.5   Activity - MAC and LLC Sublayers

Refer to
Interactive Graphic
in online course

5.1.1.6   Activity - Ethernet Frame Fields

Refer to
Lab Activity
for this chapter

5.1.1.7   Lab - Using Wireshark to Examine Ethernet Frames

In this lab, you will complete the following objectives:

- Part 1: Examine the Header Fields in an Ethernet II Frame
- Part 2: Use Wireshark to Capture and Analyze Ethernet Frames

Refer to
Online Course
for Illustration

5.1.2   Ethernet MAC Addresses

5.1.2.1   MAC Address and Hexadecimal

An Ethernet MAC address is a 48-bit binary value expressed as 12 hexadecimal digits (4 bits per hexadecimal digit).

Just as decimal is a base ten number system, hexadecimal is a base sixteen system. The base sixteen number system uses the numbers 0 to 9 and the letters A to F. Figure 1 shows the equivalent decimal and hexadecimal values for binary 0000 to 1111. It is easier to express a value as a single hexadecimal digit than as four binary bits.

Given that 8 bits (one byte) is a common binary grouping, binary 00000000 to 11111111 can be represented in hexadecimal as the range 00 to FF, as shown in Figure 2. Leading zeroes are always displayed to complete the 8-bit representation. For example, the binary value 0000 1010 is shown in hexadecimal as 0A.

Note   It is important to distinguish hexadecimal values from decimal values regarding the characters 0 to 9, as shown in the figure.

Representing Hexadecimal Values

Hexadecimal is usually represented in text by the value preceded by 0x (for example 0x73) or a subscript 16. Less commonly, it may be followed by an H(for example 73H). However, because subscript text is not recognized in command line or programming environments, the technical representation of hexadecimal is preceded with "0x" (zero X). Therefore, the examples above would be shown as 0x0A and 0x73 respectively.

Hexadecimal is used to represent Ethernet MAC addresses and IP Version 6 addresses.

Hexadecimal Conversions

Number conversions between decimal and hexadecimal values are straightforward, but quickly dividing or multiplying by 16 is not always convenient. If such conversions are required, it is usually easier to convert the decimal or hexadecimal value to binary, and then to convert the binary value to either decimal or hexadecimal as appropriate.

5.1.2.2   MAC Address: Ethernet Identity

Refer to **Online Course** for Illustration

In Ethernet, every network device is connected to the same, shared media. Ethernet was once predominantly a half-duplex topology using a multi-access bus or later Ethernet hubs. This meant that all nodes would receive every frame transmitted. To prevent the excessive overhead involved in the processing of every frame, MAC addresses were created to identify the actual source and destination. MAC addressing provides a method for device identification at the lower level of the OSI model. Although Ethernet has now transitioned to full-duplex NICs and switches, it is still possible that a device that is not the intended destination will receive an Ethernet frame.

MAC Address Structure

The MAC address value is a direct result of IEEE-enforced rules for vendors to ensure globally unique addresses for each Ethernet device. The rules established by IEEE require any vendor that sells Ethernet devices to register with IEEE. The IEEE assigns the vendor a 3-byte (24-bit) code, called the Organizationally Unique Identifier (OUI).

IEEE requires a vendor to follow two simple rules, as shown in the figure:

- All MAC addresses assigned to a NIC or other Ethernet device must use that vendor's assigned OUI as the first 3 bytes.

- All MAC addresses with the same OUI must be assigned a unique value in the last 3 bytes.

Note   It is possible for duplicate MAC addresses to exist due to mistakes during manufacturing or in some virtual machine implementation methods. In either case, it will be necessary to modify the MAC address with a new NIC or in software.

5.1.2.3   Frame Processing

Refer to **Online Course** for Illustration

The MAC address is often referred to as a burned-in address (BIA) because, historically, this address is burned into ROM (Read-Only Memory) on the NIC. This means that the address is encoded into the ROM chip permanently.

Note   On modern PC operating systems and NICs, it is possible to change the MAC address in software. This is useful when attempting to gain access to a network that filters based on BIA. Consequently, filtering or controlling traffic based on the MAC address is no longer as secure.

When the computer starts up, the first thing the NIC does is copy the MAC address from ROM into RAM. When a device is forwarding a message to an Ethernet network, it attaches header information to the packet. The header information contains the source and destination MAC address.

Click Play in the animation to view the frame forwarding process. When a NIC receives an Ethernet frame, it examines the destination MAC address to see if it matches the device's physical MAC address stored in RAM. If there is no match, the device discards the frame. If there is a match, it passes the frame up the OSI layers, where the de-encapsulation process takes place.

Note   Ethernet NICs will also accept frames if the destination MAC address is a broadcast or a multicast group of which the host is a member.

Any device that can be the source or destination of an Ethernet frame must be assigned a MAC address. This includes workstations, servers, printers, mobile devices, and routers.

Refer to
Online Course
for Illustration

5.1.2.4   MAC Address Representations

Different hardware and software manufacturers might represent the MAC address in different hexadecimal formats, as shown in the following:

- 00-05-9A-3C-78-00

- 00:05:9A:3C:78:00

- 0005.9A3C.7800

On a Windows host, the **ipconfig /all** command can be used to identify the MAC address of an Ethernet adapter. In Figure 1, notice the display indicates the Physical Address (MAC) of the computer to be 00-18-DE-DD-A7-B2. If you have access, you may wish to try this on your own computer. On a MAC or Linux host, the **ifconfig** command is used.

Depending on the device and the operating system, you will see various representations of MAC addresses, as displayed in Figure 2. Cisco routers and switches use the form XXXX.XXXX.XXXX where X is a hexadecimal character.

Refer to
Online Course
for Illustration

5.1.2.5   Unicast MAC Address

In Ethernet, different MAC addresses are used for Layer 2 unicast, broadcast, and multicast communications.

A unicast MAC address is the unique address used when a frame is sent from a single transmitting device to a single destination device.

In the example shown in the animation, a host with IPv4 address 192.168.1.5 (source) requests a web page from the server at IPv4 unicast address 192.168.1.200. For a unicast packet to be sent and received, a destination IP address must be in the IP packet header.

A corresponding destination MAC address must also be present in the Ethernet frame header. The IP address and MAC address combine to deliver data to one specific destination host.

The process that a source host uses to determine the destination MAC address is known as Address Resolution Protocol (ARP). ARP is discussed later in this chapter.

Although the destination MAC address can be a unicast, broadcast, or multicast address, the source MAC address must always be a unicast.

Refer to
Online Course
for Illustration

5.1.2.6   Broadcast MAC Address

A broadcast packet contains a destination IPv4 address that has all ones (1s) in the host portion. This numbering in the address means that all hosts on that local network (broadcast domain) will receive and process the packet. Many network protocols, such as DHCP and ARP, use broadcasts.

As shown in the animation, the source host sends an IPv4 broadcast packet to all devices on its network. The IPv4 destination address is a broadcast address, 192.168.1.255. When the IPv4 broadcast packet is encapsulated in the Ethernet frame, the destination MAC address is the broadcast MAC address of FF-FF-FF-FF-FF-FF in hexadecimal (48 ones in binary).

Refer to
Online Course
for Illustration

5.1.2.7   Multicast MAC Address

Multicast addresses allow a source device to send a packet to a group of devices. Devices that belong to a multicast group are assigned a multicast group IP address. The range of IPv4 multicast addresses is 224.0.0.0 to 239.255.255.255. Because multicast addresses represent a group of addresses (sometimes called a host group), they can only be used as the destination of a packet. The source will always be a unicast address.

Multicast addresses would be used in remote gaming, where many players are connected remotely but playing the same game. Another use of multicast addresses is in distance learning through video conferencing, where many students are connected to the same class.

As with the unicast and broadcast addresses, the multicast IP address requires a corresponding multicast MAC address to actually deliver frames on a local network. The multicast MAC address is a special value that begins with 01-00-5E in hexadecimal. The remaining portion of the multicast MAC address is created by converting the lower 23 bits of the IP multicast group address into 6 hexadecimal characters.

An example, as shown in the animation, is the multicast hexadecimal address 01-00-5E-00-00-C8. The last byte, or eight bits, of the IP address 224.0.0.200, is the decimal value 200. The easiest way to see the hexadecimal equivalent is to first convert it to binary with a space between each four bits, 200 (decimal) = 1100 1000 (binary). Using the binary to hexadecimal conversion chart shown earlier, 1100 1000 (binary) = 0xC8.

Refer to
Lab Activity
for this chapter

5.1.2.8   Lab - Viewing Network Device MAC Addresses

In this lab, you will complete the following objectives:

■ Part 1: Set Up the Topology and Initialize Devices

■ Part 2: Configure Devices and Verify Connectivity

■ Part 3: Display, Describe, and Analyze Ethernet MAC Addresses

Refer to
Online Course
for Illustration

5.2   LAN Switches

5.2.1   The MAC Address Table

5.2.1.1   Switch Fundamentals

An Ethernet switch is a Layer 2 device, which means it uses MAC addresses to make forwarding decisions. It is completely unaware of the protocol being carried in the data portion of the frame, such as an IPv4 packet. The switch makes its forwarding decisions based only on the Layer 2 Ethernet MAC addresses.

Unlike an Ethernet hub that repeats bits out all ports except the incoming port, an Ethernet switch consults a MAC address table to make a forwarding decision for each frame. In the figure, the four-port switch was just powered on. It has not yet learned the MAC addresses for the four attached PCs.

Note   The MAC address table is sometimes referred to as a content addressable memory (CAM) table. While the term CAM table is fairly common, for the purposes of this course, we will refer to it as a MAC address table.

Refer to
Online Course
for Illustration

5.2.1.2   Learning MAC Addresses

The switch dynamically builds the MAC address table by examining the source MAC address of the frames received on a port. The switch forwards frames by searching for a match between the destination MAC address in the frame and an entry in the MAC address table.

The following process is performed on every Ethernet frame that enters a switch.

Learn – Examining the Source MAC Address

Every frame that enters a switch is checked for new information to learn. It does this by examining the frame's source MAC address and port number where the frame entered the switch.

- If the source MAC address does not exist, it is added to the table along with the incoming port number. In Figure 1, PC-A is sending an Ethernet frame to PC-D. The switch adds the MAC address for PC-A to the table.

- If the source MAC address does exist, the switch updates the refresh timer for that entry. By default, most Ethernet switches keep an entry in the table for 5 minutes.

Note   If the source MAC address does exist in the table but on a different port, the switch treats this as a new entry. The entry is replaced using the same MAC address but with the more current port number.

Forward – Examining the Destination MAC Address

Next, if the destination MAC address is a unicast address, the switch will look for a match between the destination MAC address of the frame and an entry in its MAC address table.

- If the destination MAC address is in the table, it will forward the frame out the specified port.

- If the destination MAC address is not in the table, the switch will forward the frame out all ports except the incoming port. This is known as an unknown unicast. As shown in Figure 2, the switch does not have the destination MAC address in its table for PC-D, so it sends the frame out all ports except port 1.

Note   If the destination MAC address is a broadcast or a multicast, the frame is also flooded out all ports except the incoming port.

Refer to
Online Course
for Illustration

5.2.1.3   Filtering Frames

As a switch receives frames from different devices, it is able to populate its MAC address table by examining the source MAC address of every frame. When the switch's MAC address table contains the destination MAC address, it is able to filter the frame and forward out a single port.

Figures 1 and 2 show PC-D sending a frame back to PC-A. The switch will first learn PC-D's MAC address. Next, because the switch has PC-A's MAC address in its table, it will send the frame only out port 1.

Figure 3 shows PC-A sending another frame to PC-D. The MAC address table already contains PC-A's MAC address, so the five-minute refresh timer for that entry is reset. Next, because the switch's table contains PC-D's MAC address, it sends the frame only out port 4.

Refer to **Video**
in online course

5.2.1.4   Video Demonstration - MAC Address Tables on Connected Switches

A switch can have multiple MAC addresses associated with a single port. This is common when the switch is connected to another switch. The switch will have a separate MAC address table entry for each frame received with a different source MAC address.

Click Play in the figure to view a demonstration of how two connected switches build MAC address tables.

Click here to download video slides from the demonstration.

Click here to read the transcript of this video.

Refer to **Video**
in online course

5.2.1.5   Video Demonstration - Sending a Frame to the Default Gateway

When a device has an IP address that is on a remote network, the Ethernet frame cannot be sent directly to the destination device. Instead, the Ethernet frame is sent to the MAC address of the default gateway, the router.

Click Play in the figure to view a demonstration of how PC-A communicates with its default gateway.

Note   In the video, the IP packet that is sent from PC-A to a destination on a remote network has a source IP address of PC-A and a destination IP address of the remote host. The returning IP packet will have the source IP address of remote host and the destination IP address will be that of PC-A.

Click here to download video slides from the demonstration.

Click here to read the transcript of this video.

Refer to
Interactive Graphic
in online course

5.2.1.6   Activity - Switch It!

Refer to
Lab Activity
for this chapter

5.2.1.7   Lab - Viewing the Switch MAC Address Table

In this lab, you will complete the following objectives:

- Part 1: Build and Configure the Network
- Part 2: Examine the Switch MAC Address Table

Refer to
Online Course
for Illustration

5.2.2   Switch Forwarding Methods

5.2.2.1   Frame Forwarding Methods on Cisco Switches

Switches use one of the following forwarding methods for switching data between network ports:

- Store-and-forward switching
- Cut-through switching

Figure 1 highlights differences between these two methods.

Note: Cut-through switching is the predominant switching method used on Cisco switches.

In store-and-forward switching, when the switch receives the frame, it stores the data in buffers until the complete frame has been received. During the storage process, the switch analyzes the frame for information about its destination. In this process, the switch also performs an error check using the Cyclic Redundancy Check (CRC) trailer portion of the Ethernet frame.

CRC uses a mathematical formula, based on the number of bits (1s) in the frame, to determine whether the received frame has an error. After confirming the integrity of the frame, the frame is forwarded out the appropriate port, toward its destination. When an error is detected in a frame, the switch discards the frame. Discarding frames with errors reduces the amount of bandwidth consumed by corrupt data. Store-and-forward switching is required for Quality of Service (QoS) analysis on converged networks where frame classification for traffic prioritization is necessary. For example, voice over IP data streams need to have priority over web-browsing traffic.

In Figure 2, play the animation for a demonstration of the store-and-forward process.

Click here to learn more about store-and-forward and cut-through switching.

Refer to
Online Course
for Illustration

5.2.2.2 Cut-Through Switching

In cut-through switching, the switch acts upon the data as soon as it is received, even if the transmission is not complete. The switch buffers just enough of the frame to read the destination MAC address so that it can determine to which port to forward the data. The destination MAC address is located in the first 6 bytes of the frame following the preamble. The switch looks up the destination MAC address in its switching table, determines the outgoing interface port, and forwards the frame onto its destination through the designated switch port. The switch does not perform any error checking on the frame.

Play the animation for a demonstration of the cut-through switching process.

There are two variants of cut-through switching:

■ **Fast-forward switching** – Fast-forward switching offers the lowest level of latency. Fast-forward switching immediately forwards a packet after reading the destination address. Because fast-forward switching starts forwarding before the entire packet has been received, there may be times when packets are relayed with errors. This occurs infrequently, and the destination network adapter discards the faulty packet upon receipt. In fast-forward mode, latency is measured from the first bit received to the first bit transmitted. Fast-forward switching is the typical cut-through method of switching.

■ **Fragment-free switching** – In fragment-free switching, the switch stores the first 64 bytes of the frame before forwarding. Fragment-free switching can be viewed as a compromise between store-and-forward switching and fast-forward switching. The reason fragment-free switching stores only the first 64 bytes of the frame is that most network errors and collisions occur during the first 64 bytes. Fragment-free switching tries to enhance fast-forward switching by performing a small error check on the first 64 bytes of the frame to ensure that a collision has not occurred before forwarding the frame. Fragment-free switching is a compromise between the high latency and high integrity of store-and-forward switching, and the low latency and reduced integrity of fast-forward switching.

Some switches are configured to perform cut-through switching on a per-port basis until a user-defined error threshold is reached, and then they automatically change to store-and-forward. When the error rate falls below the threshold, the port automatically changes back to cut-through switching.

Refer to
Online Course
for Illustration

5.2.2.3 Memory Buffering on Switches

An Ethernet switch may use a buffering technique to store frames before forwarding them. Buffering may also be used when the destination port is busy due to congestion and the switch stores the frame until it can be transmitted.

As shown in the figure, there are two methods of memory buffering: port-based and shared memory.

Port-based Memory Buffering

In port-based memory buffering, frames are stored in queues that are linked to specific incoming and outgoing ports. A frame is transmitted to the outgoing port only when all the frames ahead of it in the queue have been successfully transmitted. It is possible for a single frame to delay the transmission of all the frames in memory because of a busy destination port. This delay occurs even if the other frames could be transmitted to open destination ports.

Shared Memory Buffering

Shared memory buffering deposits all frames into a common memory buffer that all the ports on the switch share. The amount of buffer memory required by a port is dynamically allocated. The frames in the buffer are linked dynamically to the destination port. This allows the packet to be received on one port and then transmitted on another port, without moving it to a different queue.

The switch keeps a map of frame to port links showing where a packet needs to be transmitted. The map link is cleared after the frame has been successfully transmitted. The number of frames stored in the buffer is restricted by the size of the entire memory buffer and not limited to a single port buffer. This permits larger frames to be transmitted with fewer dropped frames. This is especially important to asymmetric switching. Asymmetric switching allows for different data rates on different ports. This allows more bandwidth to be dedicated to certain ports, such as a port connected to a server.

Refer to the Chapter Appendix for more information on LAN switches including fixed and modular switches, Layer 3 switching, and Cisco Express Forwarding.

Refer to
Interactive Graphic
in online course

5.2.2.4   Activity - Frame Forwarding Methods

Refer to
Online Course
for Illustration

5.2.3   Switch Port Settings

5.2.3.1   Duplex and Speed Settings

Two of the most basic settings on a switch are the bandwidth and duplex settings for each individual switch port. It is critical that the duplex and bandwidth settings match between the switch port and the connected devices, such as a computer or another switch.

There are two types of duplex settings used for communications on an Ethernet network: half duplex and full duplex.

- **Full-duplex** – Both ends of the connection can send and receive simultaneously.
- **Half-duplex** – Only one end of the connection can send at a time.

Autonegotiation is an optional function found on most Ethernet switches and NICs. Autonegotiation enables two devices to automatically exchange information about speed and duplex capabilities. The switch and the connected device will choose the highest performance mode. Full-duplex is chosen if both devices have the capability along with their highest common bandwidth.

For example, in Figure 1 PC-A's Ethernet NIC can operate in full-duplex or half-duplex, and in 10 Mb/s or 100 Mb/s. PC-A is connected to switch S1 on port 1, which can operate in full-duplex or half-duplex, and in 10 Mb/s, 100 Mb/s or 1000 Mb/s (1 Gb/s). If both devices are using autonegotiation, the operating mode will be full-duplex and 100 Mb/s.

Note   Most Cisco switches and Ethernet NICs default to autonegotiation for speed and duplex. Gigabit Ethernet ports only operate in full-duplex.

Duplex Mismatch

One of the most common causes of performance issues on 10/100 Mb/s Ethernet links occurs when one port on the link operates at half-duplex while the other port operates at full-duplex, as shown in Figure 2. This occurs when one or both ports on a link are reset, and the autonegotiation process does not result in both link partners having the same configuration. It also can occur when users reconfigure one side of a link and forget to reconfigure the other. Both sides of a link should have autonegotiation on, or both sides should have it off.

> Refer to
> **Online Course**
> for Illustration

5.2.3.2   Auto-MDIX

In addition to having the correct duplex setting, it is also necessary to have the correct cable type defined for each port. Connections between specific devices, such as switch-to-switch, switch-to-router, switch-to-host, and router-to-host devices, once required the use of specific cable types (crossover or straight-through). Most switch devices now support the mdix auto interface configuration command in the CLI to enable the automatic medium-dependent interface crossover (auto-MDIX) feature.

When the auto-MDIX feature is enabled, the switch detects the type of cable attached to the port, and configures the interfaces accordingly. Therefore, you can use either a crossover or a straight-through cable for connections to a copper 10/100/1000 port on the switch, regardless of the type of device on the other end of the connection.

Note   The auto-MDIX feature is enabled by default on switches running Cisco IOS Release 12.2(18)SE or later. For releases between Cisco IOS Release 12.1(14)EA1 and 12.2(18) SE, the auto-MDIX feature is disabled by default.

> Refer to
> **Online Course**
> for Illustration

5.3   Address Resolution Protocol

5.3.1   MAC and IP

5.3.1.1   Destination on Same Network

There are two primary addresses assigned to a device on an Ethernet LAN:

- **Physical address (the MAC address)** – Used for Ethernet NIC to Ethernet NIC communications on the same network.
- **Logical address (the IP address)** – Used to send the packet from the original source to the final destination.

IP addresses are used to identify the address of the original source and the final destination. The destination IP address may be on the same IP network as the source or may be on a remote network.

Note Most applications use DNS (Domain Name System) to determine the IP address when given a domain name such as www.cisco.com. DNS is discussed in a later chapter.

Layer 2 or physical addresses, like Ethernet MAC addresses, have a different purpose. These addresses are used to deliver the data link frame with the encapsulated IP packet from one NIC to another NIC on the same network. If the destination IP address is on the same network, the destination MAC address will be that of the destination device.

The figure shows the Ethernet MAC addresses and IP address for PC-A sending an IP packet to the file server on the same network.

The Layer 2 Ethernet frame contains:

■ **Destination MAC address** – This is the MAC address of the file server's Ethernet NIC.

■ **Source MAC address** – This is the MAC address of PC-A's Ethernet NIC.

The Layer 3 IP packet contains:

■ **Source IP address** – This is the IP address of the original source, PC-A.

■ **Destination IP address** – This is the IP address of the final destination, the file server.

Refer to
Online Course
for Illustration

5.3.1.2 Destination Remote Network

When the destination IP address is on a remote network, the destination MAC address will be the address of the host's default gateway, the router's NIC, as shown in the figure. Using a postal analogy, this would be similar to a person taking a letter to their local post office. All they need to do is take the letter to the post office and then it becomes the responsibility of the post office to forward the letter on towards its final destination.

The figure shows the Ethernet MAC addresses and IP addresses for PC-A sending an IP packet to a web server on a remote network. Routers examine the destination IP address to determine the best path to forward the IP packet. This is similar to how the postal service forwards mail based on the address of the recipient.

When the router receives the Ethernet frame, it de-encapsulates the Layer 2 information. Using the destination IP address, it determines the next-hop device, and then encapsulates the IP packet in a new data link frame for the outgoing interface. Along each link in a path, an IP packet is encapsulated in a frame specific to the particular data link technology associated with that link, such as Ethernet. If the next-hop device is the final destination, the destination MAC address will be that of the device's Ethernet NIC.

How are the IP addresses of the IP packets in a data flow associated with the MAC addresses on each link along the path to the destination? This is done through a process called Address Resolution Protocol (ARP).

Refer to **Packet Tracer Activity** for this chapter

5.3.1.3   Packet Tracer – Identify MAC and IP Addresses

This activity is optimized for viewing PDUs. The devices are already configured. You will gather PDU information in simulation mode and answer a series of questions about the data you collect.

Refer to **Online Course** for Illustration

5.3.2   ARP

5.3.2.1   Introduction to ARP

Recall that every device with an IP address on an Ethernet network also has an Ethernet MAC address. When a device sends an Ethernet frame, it contains these two addresses:

- **Destination MAC address** – The MAC address of the Ethernet NIC, which will be either the MAC address of the final destination device or the router.

- **Source MAC address** – The MAC address of the sender's Ethernet NIC.

To determine the destination MAC address, the device uses ARP. ARP provides two basic functions:

- Resolving IPv4 addresses to MAC addresses

- Maintaining a table of mappings

Refer to **Online Course** for Illustration

5.3.2.2   ARP Functions

Resolving IPv4 Addresses to MAC Addresses

When a packet is sent to the data link layer to be encapsulated into an Ethernet frame, the device refers to a table in its memory to find the MAC address that is mapped to the IPv4 address. This table is called the ARP table or the ARP cache. The ARP table is stored in the RAM of the device.

The sending device will search its ARP table for a destination IPv4 address and a corresponding MAC address.

- If the packet's destination IPv4 address is on the same network as the source IPv4 address, the device will search the ARP table for the destination IPv4 address.

- If the destination IPv4 address is on a different network than the source IPv4 address, the device will search the ARP table for the IPv4 address of the default gateway.

In both cases, the search is for an IPv4 address and a corresponding MAC address for the device.

Each entry, or row, of the ARP table binds an IPv4 address with a MAC address. We call the relationship between the two values a map - it simply means that you can locate an IPv4 address in the table and discover the corresponding MAC address. The ARP table temporarily saves (caches) the mapping for the devices on the LAN.

If the device locates the IPv4 address, its corresponding MAC address is used as the destination MAC address in the frame. If there is no entry is found, then the device sends an ARP request.

Refer to **Video** in online course

5.3.2.3   Video Demonstration – ARP Request

An ARP request is sent when a device needs a MAC address associated with an IPv4 address, and it does not have an entry for the IPv4 address in its ARP table.

ARP messages are encapsulated directly within an Ethernet frame. There is no IPv4 header. The ARP request message includes:

■ **Target IPv4 address** – This is the IPv4 address that requires a corresponding MAC address.

■ **Target MAC address** – This is the unknown MAC address and will be empty in the ARP request message.

The ARP request is encapsulated in an Ethernet frame using the following header information:

■ **Destination MAC address** – This is a broadcast address requiring all Ethernet NICs on the LAN to accept and process the ARP request.

■ **Source MAC address** – This is the sender of the ARP request's MAC address.

■ **Type** – ARP messages have a type field of 0x806. This informs the receiving NIC that the data portion of the frame needs to be passed to the ARP process.

Because ARP requests are broadcasts, they are flooded out all ports by the switch except the receiving port. All Ethernet NICs on the LAN process broadcasts. Every device must process the ARP request to see if the target IPv4 address matches its own. A router will not forward broadcasts out other interfaces.

Only one device on the LAN will have an IPv4 address that matches the target IPv4 address in the ARP request. All other devices will not reply.

Click Play in the figure to view a demonstration of an ARP request for a destination IPv4 address that is on the local network.

Click here to download video slides from the demonstration.

Click here to read the transcript of this video.

Refer to **Video** in online course

5.3.2.4   Video Demonstration – ARP Reply

Only the device with an IPv4 address associated with the target IPv4 address in the ARP request will respond with an ARP reply. The ARP reply message includes:

■ **Sender's IPv4 address** – This is the IPv4 address of the sender, the device whose MAC address was requested.

■ **Sender's MAC address** – This is the MAC address of the sender, the MAC address needed by the sender of the ARP request.

The ARP reply is encapsulated in an Ethernet frame using the following header information:

■ **Destination MAC address** – This is the MAC address of the sender of the ARP request.

■ **Source MAC address** – This is the sender of the ARP reply's MAC address.

■ **Type** – ARP messages have a type field of 0x806. This informs the receiving NIC that the data portion of the frame needs to be passed to the ARP process.

Only the device that originally sent the ARP request will receive the unicast ARP reply. Once the ARP reply is received, the device will add the IPv4 address and the corresponding MAC address to its ARP table. Packets destined for that IPv4 address can now be encapsulated in frames using its corresponding MAC address.

Click Play in the figure to view a demonstration of an ARP reply.

Click here to download video slides from the demonstration.

If no device responds to the ARP request, the packet is dropped because a frame cannot be created.

Entries in the ARP table are time stamped. If a device does not receive a frame from a particular device by the time the timestamp expires, the entry for this device is removed from the ARP table.

Additionally, static map entries can be entered in an ARP table, but this is rarely done. Static ARP table entries do not expire over time and must be manually removed.

Note   IPv6 uses a similar process to ARP for IPv4, known as ICMPv6 neighbor discovery. IPv6 uses neighbor solicitation and neighbor advertisement messages, similar to IPv4 ARP requests and ARP replies.

Click here to read the transcript of this video.

Refer to **Video** in online course

5.3.2.5   Video Demonstration – ARP Role in Remote Communication

When the destination IPv4 address is not on the same network as the source IPv4 address, the source device needs to send the frame to its default gateway. This is the interface of the local router. Whenever a source device has a packet with an IPv4 address on another network, it will encapsulate that packet in a frame using the destination MAC address of the router.

The IPv4 address of the default gateway address is stored in the IPv4 configuration of the hosts. When a host creates a packet for a destination, it compares the destination IPv4 address and its own IPv4 address to determine if the two IP addresses are located on the same Layer 3 network. If the destination host is not on its same network, the source checks its ARP table for an entry with the IPv4 address of the default gateway. If there is not an entry, it uses the ARP process to determine a MAC address of the default gateway.

Click Play to view a demonstration of an ARP request and ARP reply associated with the default gateway.

Click here to download video slides from the demonstration.

Click here to read the transcript of this video.

Refer to
Online Course
for Illustration

5.3.2.6   Removing Entries from an ARP Table

For each device, an ARP cache timer removes ARP entries that have not been used for a specified period of time. The times differ depending on the device's operating system. For example, some Windows operating systems store ARP cache entries for 2 minutes, as shown in the figure.

Commands may also be used to manually remove all or some of the entries in the ARP table. After an entry has been removed, the process for sending an ARP request and receiving an ARP reply must occur again to enter the map in the ARP table.

Refer to
Online Course
for Illustration

5.3.2.7   ARP Tables

On a Cisco router, the **show ip arp** command is used to display the ARP table, as shown in Figure 1.

On a Windows 7 PC, the **arp –a** command is used to display the ARP table, as shown in Figure 2.

Refer to **Packet
Tracer Activity**
for this chapter

5.3.2.8   Packet Tracer - Examine the ARP Table

This activity is optimized for viewing PDUs. The devices are already configured. You will gather PDU information in simulation mode and answer a series of questions about the data you collect.

Refer to
Online Course
for Illustration

5.3.3   ARP Issues

5.3.3.1   ARP Broadcasts

As a broadcast frame, an ARP request is received and processed by every device on the local network. On a typical business network, these broadcasts would probably have minimal impact on network performance. However, if a large number of devices were to be powered up and all start accessing network services at the same time, there could be some reduction in performance for a short period of time, as shown in the figure. After the devices send out the initial ARP broadcasts and have learned the necessary MAC addresses, any impact on the network will be minimized

Refer to
Online Course
for Illustration

5.3.3.2   ARP Spoofing

In some cases, the use of ARP can lead to a potential security risk known as ARP spoofing or ARP poisoning. This is a technique used by an attacker to reply to an ARP request for an IPv4 address belonging to another device, such as the default gateway, as shown in the figure. The attacker sends an ARP reply with its own MAC address. The receiver of the ARP reply will add the wrong MAC address to its ARP table and send these packets to the attacker.

Enterprise level switches include mitigation techniques known as dynamic ARP inspection (DAI). DAI is beyond the scope of this course.

Refer to
Online Course
for Illustration

5.4   Summary

5.4.1   Conclusion

Refer to
Lab Activity
for this chapter

5.4.1.1   Class Activity - MAC and Choose...

Note   This activity can be completed individually, in small groups, or in a full-classroom learning environment.

Please view the video located at the following link:http://www.netevents.tv/video/bob-metcalfe-the-history-of-ethernet

Topics discussed include not only where we have come from in Ethernet development, but where we are going with Ethernet technology (a futuristic approach).

After viewing the video and comparing its contents to Chapter 5, go to the web and search for information about Ethernet. Use a constructivist approach:

- What did Ethernet look like when it was first developed?

- How has Ethernet stayed the same over the past 25 years or so, and what changes are being made to make it more useful/applicable to today's data transmission methods?

Collect three pictures of old, current, and future Ethernet physical media and devices (focus on switches) – share these pictures with the class and discuss:

- How have Ethernet physical media and intermediary devices changed?

- How have Ethernet physical media and intermediary devices stayed the same?

- How will Ethernet change in the future?

Refer to
Online Course
for Illustration

5.4.1.2   Chapter 5: Ethernet

Ethernet is the most widely used LAN technology today. It is a family of networking technologies that are defined in the IEEE 802.2 and 802.3 standards. Ethernet standards define both the Layer 2 protocols and the Layer 1 technologies. For the Layer 2 protocols, as with all 802 IEEE standards, Ethernet relies on the two separate sublayers of the data link layer to operate, the Logical Link Control (LLC) and the MAC sublayers.

At the data link layer, the frame structure is nearly identical for all bandwidths of Ethernet. The Ethernet frame structure adds headers and trailers around the Layer 3 PDU to encapsulate the message being sent.

There are two styles of Ethernet framing: IEEE 802.3 Ethernet standard and the DIX Ethernet standard which is now referred to Ethernet II. The most significant difference between the two standards is the addition of a Start Frame Delimiter (SFD) and the change of the Type field to a Length field in the 802.3. Ethernet II is the Ethernet frame format used in TCP/IP networks. As an implementation of the IEEE 802.2/3 standards, the Ethernet frame provides MAC addressing and error checking.

The Layer 2 addressing provided by Ethernet supports unicast, multicast, and broadcast communications. Ethernet uses the Address Resolution Protocol to determine the MAC addresses of destinations and map them against known IPv4 addresses.

Each node on an IPv4 network has both a MAC address and an IPv4 address. The IP addresses are used to identify the original source and final destination of the packet. The Ethernet MAC addresses are used to send the packet from one Ethernet NIC to another Ethernet NIC on the same IP network. ARP is used to map a known IPv4 address to a MAC address, so the packet can be encapsulated in an Ethernet frame with the correct Layer 2 address.

ARP relies on certain types of Ethernet broadcast messages and Ethernet unicast messages, called ARP requests and ARP replies. The ARP protocol resolves IPv4 addresses to MAC addresses and maintains a table of mappings.

On most Ethernet networks, end devices are typically connected on a point-to-point basis to a Layer 2, full-duplex switch. A Layer 2 LAN switch performs switching and filtering based only on the OSI data link layer (Layer 2) MAC address. A Layer 2 switch builds a MAC address table that it uses to make forwarding decisions. Layer 2 switches depend on routers to pass data between independent IP subnetworks.

Go to the online course to take the quiz and exam.

Chapter 5 Quiz

This quiz is designed to provide an additional opportunity to practice the skills and knowledge presented in the chapter and to prepare for the chapter exam. You will be allowed multiple attempts and the grade does not appear in the gradebook.

Chapter 5 Exam

The chapter exam assesses your knowledge of the chapter content.

Your Chapter Notes

Network Layer

6.0 Introduction

6.0.1.1 Network Layer

Network applications and services on one end device can communicate with applications and services running on another end device. How is this data communicated across the network in an efficient way?

The protocols of the OSI model network layer specify addressing and processes that enable transport layer data to be packaged and transported. The network layer encapsulation enables data to be passed to a destination within a network (or on another network) with minimum overhead.

This chapter focuses on the role of the network layer. It examines how it divides networks into groups of hosts to manage the flow of data packets within a network. It also covers how communication between networks is facilitated. This communication between networks is called routing.

Refer to Lab Activity for this chapter

6.0.1.2 Class Activity - The Road Less Traveled...

During the upcoming weekend, you decide to visit a schoolmate who is currently at home sick. You know his street address, but you have never been to his town before. Instead of looking up the address on the map, you decide to ask town residents for directions after you arrive by train. The citizens you ask for directions are very helpful. However, they all have an interesting habit. Instead of explaining the entire route to your destination, they all tell you, "Take this road and as soon as you arrive at the nearest crossroad, ask somebody there again."

Somewhat bemused at this apparent oddity, you follow these instructions and finally arrive, crossroad by crossroad, and road by road, at your friend's house.

Answer the following questions:

- Would it have made a significant difference if you were told about the whole route or a larger part of the route instead of just being directed to the nearest crossroad?

- Would it have been more helpful to ask about the specific street address or just about the street name? What would happen if the person you asked for directions did not know where the destination street was, or directed you through an incorrect road?

- Assume that on your way back home, you again choose to ask residents for directions. Would it be guaranteed that you would be directed via the same route you took to get to your friend's home? Explain your answer.

- Is it necessary to explain where you depart from when asking directions to an intended destination?

Refer to
Online Course
for Illustration

6.1 Network Layer Protocols

6.1.1 Network Layer in Communications

6.1.1.1 The Network Layer

The network layer, or OSI Layer 3, provides services to allow end devices to exchange data across the network. To accomplish this end-to-end transport, the network layer uses four basic processes:

- **Addressing end devices** – End devices must be configured with a unique IP address for identification on the network.

- **Encapsulation** – The network layer encapsulates the protocol data unit (PDU) from the transport layer into a packet. The encapsulation process adds IP header information, such as the IP address of the source (sending) and destination (receiving) hosts.

- **Routing** – The network layer provides services to direct packets to a destination host on another network. To travel to other networks, the packet must be processed by a router. The role of the router is to select the best path and direct packets toward the destination host in a process known as routing. A packet may cross many intermediary devices before reaching the destination host. Each router a packet crosses to reach the destination host is called a hop.

- **De-encapsulation** – When the packet arrives at the network layer of the destination host, the host checks the IP header of the packet. If the destination IP address within the header matches its own IP address, the IP header is removed from the packet. After the packet is de-encapsulated by the network layer, the resulting Layer 4 PDU is passed up to the appropriate service at the transport layer.

Unlike the transport layer (OSI Layer 4), which manages the data transport between the processes running on each host, network layer protocols specify the packet structure and processing used to carry the data from one host to another host. Operating without regard to the data carried in each packet allows the network layer to carry packets for multiple types of communications between multiple hosts.

Click Play in the figure to view an animation that demonstrates the exchange of data.

Refer to
Online Course
for Illustration

6.1.1.2 Network Layer Protocols

There are several network layer protocols in existence. However, only the following two are commonly implemented:

- Internet Protocol version 4 (IPv4)

- Internet Protocol version 6 (IPv6)

Note Legacy network layer protocols are not shown in the figure and are not discussed in this course.

Refer to
Online Course
for Illustration

6.1.2   Characteristics of the IP Protocol

6.1.2.1   Encapsulating IP

IP encapsulates the transport layer segment by adding an IP header. This header is used to deliver the packet to the destination host. The IP header remains in place from the time the packet leaves the source host until it arrives at the destination host.

Figure 1 shows the process to create the transport layer PDU. Figure 2 illustrates how the transport layer PDU is then encapsulated by the network layer PDU to create an IP packet.

The process of encapsulating data layer by layer enables the services at the different layers to develop and scale without affecting the other layers. This means the transport layer segments can be readily packaged by IPv4 or IPv6 or by any new protocol that might be developed in the future.

Routers can implement these different network layer protocols to operate concurrently over a network. The routing performed by these intermediate devices only considers the contents of the network layer packet header. In all cases, the data portion of the packet, that is, the encapsulated transport layer PDU, remains unchanged during the network layer processes.

Refer to
Online Course
for Illustration

6.1.2.2   Characteristics of IP

IP was designed as a protocol with low overhead. It provides only the functions that are necessary to deliver a packet from a source to a destination over an interconnected system of networks. The protocol was not designed to track and manage the flow of packets. These functions, if required, are performed by other protocols at other layers.

The basic characteristics of IP are described in the figure.

Refer to
Online Course
for Illustration

6.1.2.3   IP - Connectionless

IP is connectionless, meaning that no dedicated end-to-end connection is created before data is sent. As shown in Figure 1, connectionless communication is conceptually similar to sending a letter to someone without notifying the recipient in advance.

Connectionless data communications work on the same principle. As shown in Figure 2, IP requires no initial exchange of control information to establish an end-to-end connection before packets are forwarded. IP also does not require additional fields in the header to maintain an established connection. This process greatly reduces the overhead of IP. However, with no pre-established end-to-end connection, senders are unaware whether destination devices are present and functional when sending packets, nor are they aware if the destination receives the packet, or if they are able to access and read the packet.

Refer to
Online Course
for Illustration

6.1.2.4   IP - Best Effort Delivery

The figure illustrates the unreliable or best-effort delivery characteristic of the IP protocol. The IP protocol does not guarantee that all packets that are delivered are, in fact, received.

Unreliable means that IP does not have the capability to manage and recover from undelivered or corrupt packets. This is because while IP packets are sent with information about the location of delivery, they contain no information that can be processed to inform the sender whether delivery was successful. Packets may arrive at the destination corrupted, out of sequence, or not at all. IP provides no capability for packet retransmissions if errors occur.

If out-of-order packets are delivered, or packets are missing, then applications using the data, or upper layer services, must resolve these issues. This allows IP to function very efficiently. In the TCP/IP protocol suite, reliability is the role of the transport layer.

Refer to
Online Course
for Illustration

6.1.2.5 IP - Media Independent

IP operates independently of the media that carry the data at lower layers of the protocol stack. As shown in the figure, IP packets can be communicated as electronic signals over copper cable, as optical signals over fiber, or wirelessly as radio signals.

It is the responsibility of the OSI data link layer to take an IP packet and prepare it for transmission over the communications medium. This means that the transport of IP packets is not limited to any particular medium.

There is, however, one major characteristic of the media that the network layer considers: the maximum size of the PDU that each medium can transport. This characteristic is referred to as the maximum transmission unit (MTU). Part of the control communication between the data link layer and the network layer is the establishment of a maximum size for the packet. The data link layer passes the MTU value up to the network layer. The network layer then determines how large packets can be.

In some cases, an intermediate device, usually a router, must split up a packet when forwarding it from one medium to another medium with a smaller MTU. This process is called fragmenting the packet or fragmentation.

Refer to
Interactive Graphic
in online course

6.1.2.6 Activity - IP Characteristics

Refer to
Online Course
for Illustration

6.1.3 IPv4 Packet

6.1.3.1 IPv4 Packet Header

An IPv4 packet header consists of fields containing important information about the packet. These fields contain binary numbers which are examined by the Layer 3 process. The binary values of each field identify various settings of the IP packet. Protocol header diagrams, like the one shown in the figure, are read left to right, and top down.

Significant fields in the IPv4 header include:

- **Version** – Contains a 4-bit binary value set to 0100 that identifies this as an IP version 4 packet.

- **Differentiated Services (DS)** – Formerly called the Type of Service (ToS) field, the DS field is an 8-bit field used to determine the priority of each packet.

- **Time-to-Live (TTL)** – Contains an 8-bit binary value that is used to limit the lifetime of a packet. The packet sender sets the initial TTL value, and it is decreased by one each time the packet is processed by a router. If the TTL field decrements to zero, the router discards the packet and sends an Internet Control Message Protocol (ICMP) Time Exceeded message to the source IP address.

- **Protocol** – This 8-bit binary value indicates the data payload type that the packet is carrying, which enables the network layer to pass the data to the appropriate upper-layer protocol. Common values include ICMP (1), TCP (6), and UDP (17).

- **Source IP Address** – Contains a 32-bit binary value that represents the source IP address of the packet.

- **Destination IP Address** – Contains a 32-bit binary value that represents the destination IP address of the packet.

The two most commonly referenced fields are the source and destination IP addresses. These fields identify where the packet is coming from and where it is going. Typically these addresses do not change while travelling from the source to the destination.

The Internet Header Length (IHL), Total Length, and Header Checksum fields are used to identify and validate the packet.

Other fields are used to reorder a fragmented packet. Specifically, the IPv4 packet uses Identification, Flags, and Fragment Offset fields to keep track of the fragments. A router may have to fragment a packet when forwarding it from one medium to another with a smaller MTU.

The Options and Padding fields are rarely used and are beyond the scope of this chapter.

Refer to **Video** in online course

6.1.3.2 Video Demonstration - Sample IPv4 Headers in Wireshark

Click Play in the figure to view a demonstration of examining IPv4 headers in a Wireshark capture.

Click here to download a PDF file of the Wireshark captures and notes used during the demonstration.

Click here to read the transcript of this video.

Refer to **Interactive Graphic** in online course

6.1.3.3 Activity - IPv4 Header Fields

Refer to **Online Course** for Illustration

6.1.4 IPv6 Packet

6.1.4.1 Limitations of IPv4

Through the years, IPv4 has been updated to address new challenges. However, even with changes, IPv4 still has three major issues:

- **IP address depletion** – IPv4 has a limited number of unique public IPv4 addresses available. Although there are approximately 4 billion IPv4 addresses, the increasing number of new IP-enabled devices, always-on connections, and the potential growth of less-developed regions have increased the need for more addresses.

- **Internet routing table expansion** – A routing table is used by routers to make best path determinations. As the number of servers connected to the Internet increases, so too does the number of network routes. These IPv4 routes consume a great deal of memory and processor resources on Internet routers.

- **Lack of end-to-end connectivity** – Network Address Translation (NAT) is a technology commonly implemented within IPv4 networks. NAT provides a way for multiple devices to share a single public IPv4 address. However, because the public IPv4 address is shared, the IPv4 address of an internal network host is hidden. This can be problematic for technologies that require end-to-end connectivity.

Refer to **Online Course** for Illustration

6.1.4.2   Introducing IPv6

In the early 1990s, the Internet Engineering Task Force (IETF) grew concerned about the issues with IPv4 and began to look for a replacement. This activity led to the development of IP version 6 (IPv6). IPv6 overcomes the limitations of IPv4 and is a powerful enhancement with features that better suit current and foreseeable network demands.

Improvements that IPv6 provides include:

- **Increased address space** – IPv6 addresses are based on 128-bit hierarchical addressing as opposed to IPv4 with 32 bits.

- **Improved packet handling** – The IPv6 header has been simplified with fewer fields.

- **Eliminates the need for NAT** – With such a large number of public IPv6 addresses, NAT between a private IPv4 address and a public IPv4 is not needed. This avoids some of the NAT-induced application problems experienced by applications requiring end-to-end connectivity.

The 32-bit IPv4 address space provides approximately 4,294,967,296 unique addresses. IPv6 address space provides 340,282,366,920,938,463,463,374,607,431,768,211,456, or 340 undecillion addresses, which is roughly equivalent to every grain of sand on Earth.

The figure provides a visual to compare the IPv4 and IPv6 address space.

Refer to **Online Course** for Illustration

6.1.4.3   Encapsulating IPv6

One of the major design improvements of IPv6 over IPv4 is the simplified IPv6 header.

For instance, the IPv4 header shown in Figure 1 consists of 20 octets (up to 60 bytes if the Options field is used) and 12 basic header fields, not including the Options field and Padding field. As highlighted in the figure, for IPv6, some fields have remained the same, some fields have changed names and positions, and some IPv4 fields are no longer required.

In contrast, the simplified IPv6 header shown in Figure 2 consists of 40 octets (largely due to the length of the source and destination IPv6 addresses) and 8 header fields (3 IPv4 basic header fields and 5 additional header fields). As highlighted in this figure, some fields have kept the same names as IPv4, some fields have changed names or positions, and a new field has been added.

The IPv6 simplified header offers several advantages over IPv4 as listed in Figure 3.

Refer to **Online Course** for Illustration

6.1.4.4   IPv6 Packet Header

The fields in the IPv6 packet header include:

- **Version** – This field contains a 4-bit binary value set to 0110 that identifies this as an IP version 6 packet.

- **Traffic Class** – This 8-bit field is equivalent to the IPv4 Differentiated Services (DS) field.

- **Flow Label** – This 20-bit field suggests that all packets with the same flow label receive the same type of handling by routers.

- **Payload Length** – This 16-bit field indicates the length of the data portion or payload of the IPv6 packet.

- **Next Header** – This 8-bit field is equivalent to the IPv4 Protocol field. It indicates the data payload type that the packet is carrying, enabling the network layer to pass the data to the appropriate upper-layer protocol.

- **Hop Limit** – This 8-bit field replaces the IPv4 TTL field. This value is decremented by a value of 1 by each router that forwards the packet. When the counter reaches 0, the packet is discarded, and an ICMPv6 Time Exceeded message is forwarded to the sending host, indicating that the packet did not reach its destination because the hop limit was exceeded.

- **Source Address** – This 128-bit field identifies the IPv6 address of the sending host.

- **Destination Address** – This 128-bit field identifies the IPv6 address of the receiving host.

An IPv6 packet may also contain extension headers (EH), which provide optional network layer information. Extension headers are optional and are placed between the IPv6 header and the payload. EHs are used for fragmentation, security, to support mobility and more.

Refer to **Video** in online course

6.1.4.5   Video Demonstration - Sample IPv6 Headers and Wireshark

Click Play in the figure to view a demonstration of examining IPv6 headers in a Wireshark capture.

Click here to download a PDF file of the Wireshark captures and notes used during the demonstration.

Click here to read the transcript of this video.

Refer to **Interactive Graphic** in online course

6.1.4.6   Activity - IPv6 Header Fields

Refer to **Online Course** for Illustration

6.2   Routing

6.2.1   How a Host Routes

6.2.1.1   Host Forwarding Decision

Another role of the network layer is to direct packets between hosts. A host can send a packet to:

- **Itself** – A host can ping itself by sending a packet to a special IPv4 address of 127.0.0.1, which is referred to as the loopback interface. Pinging the loopback interface tests the TCP/IP protocol stack on the host.

- **Local host** – This is a host on the same local network as the sending host. The hosts share the same network address.

■ **Remote host** – This is a host on a remote network. The hosts do not share the same network address.

Whether a packet is destined for a local host or a remote host is determined by the IPv4 address and subnet mask combination of the source (or sending) device compared to the IPv4 address and subnet mask of the destination device.

In a home or business network, you may have several wired and wireless devices interconnected together using an intermediate device, such as a LAN switch and/or a wireless access point (WAP). This intermediate device provides interconnections between local hosts on the local network. Local hosts can reach each other and share information without the need for any additional devices. If a host is sending a packet to a device that is configured with the same IP network as the host device, the packet is simply forwarded out of the host interface, through the intermediate device, and to the destination device directly.

Of course, in most situations we want our devices to be able to connect beyond the local network segment, such as out to other homes, businesses, and the Internet. Devices that are beyond the local network segment are known as remote hosts. When a source device sends a packet to a remote destination device, then the help of routers and routing is needed. Routing is the process of identifying the best path to a destination. The router connected to the local network segment is referred to as the **default gateway.**

Refer to
Online Course
for Illustration

6.2.1.2   Default Gateway

The default gateway is the network device that can route traffic to other networks. It is the router that can route traffic out of the local network.

If you use the analogy that a network is like a room, then the default gateway is like a doorway. If you want to get to another room or network you need to find the doorway.

Alternatively, a PC or computer that does not know the IP address of the default gateway is like a person, in a room, that does not know where the doorway is. They can talk to other people in the room or network, but if they do not know the default gateway address, or there is no default gateway, then there is no way out.

The figure lists functions provided by the default gateway.

Refer to
Online Course
for Illustration

6.2.1.3   Using the Default Gateway

A host's routing table will typically include a default gateway. The host receives the IPv4 address of the default gateway either dynamically from Dynamic Host Configuration Protocol (DHCP) or configured manually. In the figure, PC1 and PC2 are configured with the default gateway's IPv4 address of 192.168.10.1. Having a default gateway configured creates a default route in the routing table of the PC. A default route is the route or pathway your computer will take when it tries to contact a remote network.

The default route is derived from the default gateway configuration and is placed in the host computer's routing table. Both PC1 and PC2 will have a default route to send all traffic destined to remote networks to R1.

Refer to
Online Course
for Illustration

6.2.1.4   Host Routing Tables

On a Windows host, the **route print** or **netstat -r** command can be used to display the host routing table. Both commands generate the same output. The output may seem overwhelming at first, but is fairly simple to understand.

Entering the **netstat -r** command or the equivalent **route print** command, displays three sections related to the current TCP/IP network connections:

- **Interface List** – Lists the Media Access Control (MAC) address and assigned interface number of every network-capable interface on the host, including Ethernet, Wi-Fi, and Bluetooth adapters.

- **IPv4 Route Table** – Lists all known IPv4 routes, including direct connections, local network, and local default routes.

- **IPv6 Route Table** – Lists all known IPv6 routes, including direct connections, local network, and local default routes.

Refer to the Chapter Appendix for more information on the host routing table.

Refer to
Online Course
for Illustration

6.2.2   Router Routing Tables

6.2.2.1   Router Packet Forwarding Decision

When a host sends a packet to another host, it will use its routing table to determine where to send the packet. If the destination host is on a remote network, the packet is forwarded to the default gateway.

What happens when a packet arrives at the default gateway, which is usually a router? The router looks at its routing table to determine where to forward packets.

The routing table of a router can store information about:

- **Directly-connected routes** – These routes come from the active router interfaces. Routers add a directly connected route when an interface is configured with an IP address and is activated. Each of the router's interfaces is connected to a different network segment.

- **Remote routes** – These routes come from remote networks connected to other routers. Routes to these networks can be manually configured on the local router by the network administrator or dynamically configured by enabling the local router to exchange routing information with other routers using a dynamic routing protocol.

- **Default route** – Like a host, routers also use a default route as a last resort if there is no other route to the desired network in the routing table.

The figure identifies the directly connected networks and remote networks of router R1.

Refer to
Online Course
for Illustration

6.2.2.2   IPv4 Router Routing Table

On a Cisco IOS router, the **show ip route** command can be used to display the router's routing table, as shown in the figure.

In addition to providing routing information for directly-connected networks and remote networks, the routing table also has information on how the route was learned, the trustworthiness and rating of the route, when the route was last updated, and which interface to use to reach the requested destination.

When a packet arrives at the router interface, the router examines the packet header to determine the destination network. If the destination network matches a route in the routing table, the router forwards the packet using the information specified in the routing table. If there are two or more possible routes to the same destination, the metric is used to decide which route appears in the routing table.

The figure shows the routing table of R1 depicted in the network diagram.

Refer to **Video** in online course

6.2.2.3   Video Demonstration - Introducing the IPv4 Routing Table

Unlike a host computer's routing table, there are no column headings identifying the information contained in a router's routing table. It is important to learn the meaning of the different items included in each entry of the routing table.

Click Play in the figure to view an introduction to the IPv4 routing table.

Click here to read the transcript of this video.

Refer to **Online Course** for Illustration

6.2.2.4   Directly Connected Routing Table Entries

When a router interface is configured with an IPv4 address, a subnet mask, and is activated, the following two routing table entries are automatically created:

- C – Identifies a directly-connected network. Directly-connected networks are automatically created when an interface is configured with an IP address and activated.

- L – Identifies that this is a local interface. This is the IPv4 address of the interface on the router.

The figure describes the routing table entries on R1 for the directly-connected network 192.168.10.0. These entries were automatically added to the routing table when the GigabitEthernet 0/0 interface was configured and activated. Click each plus sign to view more information about directly-connected routing table entries.

Note   Local interface entries did not appear in routing tables prior to IOS Release 15.

Refer to **Online Course** for Illustration

6.2.2.5   Remote Network Routing Table Entries

A router typically has multiple interfaces configured. The routing table stores information about both directly-connected networks and remote networks.

The figure describes the R1 route to remote network 10.1.1.0. Click each plus sign to view more information about directly-connected routing table entries.

Refer to **Online Course** for Illustration

6.2.2.6   Next-Hop Address

When a packet destined for a remote network arrives at the router, the router matches the destination network to a route in the routing table. If a match is found, the router forwards the packet to the next hop address out of the identified interface.

Refer to the sample network topology in Figure 1. Assume that either PC1 or PC2 has sent a packet destined for either the 10.1.1.0 or 10.1.2.0 network. When the packet arrives on the R1 Gigabit interface, R1 will compare the packet's destination IPv4 address to entries in its routing table. The routing table is displayed in Figure 2. Based on the content of its routing, R1 will forward the packet out of its Serial 0/0/0 interface to the next hop address 209.165.200.226.

Notice how directly connected networks with a route source of **C** and **L** have no next-hop address. This is because a router can forward packets directly to hosts on these networks using the designated interface.

It is also important to understand that packets cannot be forwarded by the router without a route for the destination network in the routing table. If a route representing the destination network is not in the routing table, the packet is dropped (that is, not forwarded). However, just as a host can use a default gateway to forward a packet to an unknown destination, a router can also be configured to use a default static route to create a Gateway of Last Resort.

Refer to **Video** in online course

6.2.2.7 Video Demonstration – Explaining the IPv4 Routing Table

Hosts and routers make packet routing decisions by consulting their respective routing tables.

Click Play in the figure to view a detailed explanation of the IPv4 routing table.

Click here to read the transcript of this video.

Refer to **Interactive Graphic** in online course

6.2.2.8 Activity - Identify Elements of a Router Routing Table Entry

Refer to **Online Course** for Illustration

6.3 Routers

6.3.1 Anatomy of a Router

6.3.1.1 A Router is a Computer

There are many types of infrastructure routers available. In fact, Cisco routers are designed to address the needs of many different types of businesses and networks:

- **Branch** – Teleworkers, small businesses, and medium-size branch sites. Includes Cisco Integrated Services Routers (ISR) G2 (2nd generation).

- **WAN** – Large businesses, organizations, and enterprises. Includes the Cisco Catalyst Series Switches and the Cisco Aggregation Services Routers (ASR).

- **Service Provider** – Large service providers. Includes Cisco ASR, Cisco CRS-3 Carrier Routing System, and 7600 Series routers.

The focus of CCNA certification is on the branch family of routers. The figure displays the Cisco 1900, 2900, and 3900 G2 Integrated Services Routers.

Regardless of their function, size or complexity, all router models are essentially computers. Just like computers, tablets, and smart devices, routers also require:

- Central processing units (CPU)

- Operating systems (OS)

- Memory consisting of random-access memory (RAM), read-only memory (ROM), nonvolatile random-access memory (NVRAM), and flash.

Refer to **Online Course** for Illustration

6.3.1.2   Router CPU and OS

Like all computers, tablets, gaming consoles, and smart devices, Cisco devices require a CPU to execute OS instructions, such as system initialization, routing functions, and switching functions.

The highlighted component in the figure is the CPU of a Cisco 1941 router with the heatsink attached. The heatsink helps dissipate the heat generated by the CPU.

The CPU requires an OS to provide routing and switching functions. The Cisco Internetwork Operating System (IOS) is the system software used for most Cisco devices regardless of the size and type of the device. It is used for routers, LAN switches, small wireless access points, large routers with dozens of interfaces, and many other devices.

Refer to **Online Course** for Illustration

6.3.1.3   Router Memory

A router has access to volatile or non-volatile memory storage. Volatile memory requires continual power to maintain its information. When the router is powered down or restarted, the content is erased and lost. Non-volatile memory retains its information even when a device is rebooted.

Specifically, Cisco router uses four types of memory:

- **RAM** – This is volatile memory used in Cisco routers to store applications, processes, and data needed to be executed by the CPU. Cisco routers use a fast type of RAM called synchronous dynamic random access memory (SDRAM). Click RAM in the figure to view more information.

- **ROM** – This non-volatile memory is used to store crucial operational instructions and a limited IOS. Specifically, ROM is firmware embedded on an integrated circuit inside the router which can only be altered by Cisco. Click ROM in the figure to view more information.

- **NVRAM** – This memory is used as the permanent storage for the startup configuration file (startup-config).

- **Flash** – Flash memory is non-volatile computer memory used as permanent storage for the IOS and other system related files such as log files, voice configuration files, HTML files, backup configurations, and more. When a router is rebooted, the IOS is copied from flash into RAM.

All router platforms have default settings and components. For instance, the Cisco 1941 comes with 512 MB of SDRAM but is upgradable up to 2.0 GB. The Cisco 1941 routers also come with 256 MB of flash but are upgradable using two external Compact Flash slots. Each slot can support high-speed storage cards upgradable to 4GB. Click here to learn more about the Cisco 1941 Integrated Services Router.

6.3.1.4   Inside a Router

Although there are several different types and models of routers, every router has the same general hardware components.

The figure shows the inside of a Cisco 1841 first generation ISR. Click the components to see a brief description of each. The figure also includes images of other components found in a router, such as the power supply, cooling fan, heat shields, and an advanced integration module (AIM), which are beyond the scope of this chapter.

Note A networking professional should be familiar with and understand the function of the main internal components of a router, rather than the exact location of those components inside a specific router. Depending on the model, those components are located in different places inside the router. ⟩

6.3.1.5   Connect to a Router

Cisco devices, routers, and switches typically interconnect many devices. For this reason, these devices have several types of ports and interfaces that are used to connect to the device. For example, a Cisco 1941 router backplane includes the connections and ports described in the figure. Click each highlighted area to view more information

Like many networking devices, Cisco devices use light emitting diode (LED) indicators to provide status information. An interface LED indicates the activity of the corresponding interface. If an LED is off when the interface is active, and the interface is correctly connected, this may be an indication of a problem with that interface. If an interface is extremely busy, its LED is always on.

6.3.1.6   LAN and WAN Interfaces

The connections on a Cisco router can be grouped into two categories: In-band router interfaces and management ports. Click the highlighted areas in Figure 1 to view more information.

Similar to a Cisco switch, there are several ways to access user EXEC mode in the CLI environment on a Cisco router. These are the most common:

- **Console** – This is a physical management port that provides out-of-band access to a Cisco device. Out-of-band access refers to access via a dedicated management channel that is used for device maintenance purposes only.

- **Secure Shell (SSH)** – SSH is a method for remotely establishing a secure CLI connection through a virtual interface, over a network. Unlike a console connection, SSH connections require active networking services on the device including an active interface configured with an address.

- **Telnet** – Telnet is an insecure method of remotely establishing a CLI session through a virtual interface, over a network. Unlike SSH, Telnet does not provide a securely encrypted connection. User authentication, passwords, and commands are sent over the network in plaintext.

Refer to
Online Course
for Illustration

Refer to
Online Course
for Illustration

Refer to
Online Course
for Illustration

Note Some devices, such as routers, may also support a legacy auxiliary port that was used to establish a CLI session remotely using a modem. Similar to a console connection, the AUX port is out-of-band and does not require networking services to be configured or available.

Telnet and SSH require an inband network connection which means that an administrator must access the router through one of the WAN or LAN interfaces. Click the highlighted areas in Figure 2 to view more information.

Inband interfaces receive and forward IP packets. Every configured and active interface on the router is a member or host on a different IP network. Each interface must be configured with an IPv4 address and subnet mask of a different network. The Cisco IOS does not allow two active interfaces on the same router to belong to the same network.

Refer to **Interactive Graphic** in online course

6.3.1.7   Activity - Identify Router Components

Refer to **Packet Tracer Activity** for this chapter

6.3.1.8   Packet Tracer - Exploring Internetworking Devices

In this activity, you will explore the different options available on internetworking devices. You will also be required to determine which options provide the necessary connectivity when connecting multiple devices. Finally, you will add the correct modules and connect the devices.

Refer to **Online Course** for Illustration

6.3.2   Router Boot-up

6.3.2.1   Bootset Files

Both Cisco routers and switches load the IOS image and startup configuration file into RAM when they are booted, as shown in the figure.

The running configuration is modified when the network administrator performs device configurations. Changes made to the running-config file should be saved to the startup configuration file in NVRAM, in case the router is restarted or loses power.

Refer to **Online Course** for Illustration

6.3.2.2   Router Bootup Process

There are three major phases to the bootup process. As shown in Figure 1, they are:

1. Perform the POST and load the bootstrap program.

2. Locate and load the Cisco IOS software.

3. Locate and load the startup configuration file or enter setup mode.

1. Performing POST and Load Bootstrap Program (Figure 2)

During the Power-On Self-Test (POST), the router executes diagnostics from ROM on several hardware components, including the CPU, RAM, and NVRAM. After the POST, the bootstrap program is copied from ROM into RAM. The main task of the bootstrap program is to locate the Cisco IOS and load it into RAM.

Note At this point, if you have a console connection to the router, you begin to see the output on the screen.

2. Locating and Loading Cisco IOS (Figure 3)

The IOS is typically stored in flash memory and is copied into RAM for execution by the CPU. If the IOS image is not located in flash, then the router may look for it using a Trivial File Transfer Protocol (TFTP) server. If a full IOS image cannot be located, a limited IOS is copied into RAM, which can be used to diagnose problems and transfer a full IOS into Flash memory.

3. Locating and Loading the Configuration File (Figure 4)

The bootstrap program then copies the startup configuration file from NVRAM into RAM. This becomes the running configuration. If the startup configuration file does not exist in NVRAM, the router may be configured to search for a TFTP server. If a TFTP server is not found, then the router displays the setup mode prompt.

Note Setup mode is not used in this course to configure the router. When prompted to enter setup mode, always answer **no**. If you answer yes and enter setup mode, press **Ctrl+C** at any time to terminate the setup process.

Refer to **Video**
in online course

6.3.2.3 Video Demonstration – Router Bootup Process

Click Play in the figure to view a demonstration of the router bootup process.

Click here to read the transcript of this video.

Refer to
Online Course
for Illustration

6.3.2.4 Show Version Output

As highlighted in the figure, the **show version** command displays information about the version of the Cisco IOS software currently running on the router, the version of the bootstrap program, and information about the hardware configuration, including the amount of system memory.

Refer to **Video**
in online course

6.3.2.5 Video Demonstration - The show version Command

Click Play in the figure to view an explanation of the **show version** command.

Click here to read the transcript of this video.

Refer to
Interactive Graphic
in online course

6.3.2.6 Activity - The Router Boot Process

Refer to
Lab Activity
for this chapter

6.3.2.7 Lab - Exploring Router Physical Characteristics

In this lab, you will complete the following objectives:

- Part 1: Examine Router External Characteristics
- Part 2: Examine Router Internal Characteristics Using Show Commands

Refer to
Online Course
for Illustration

6.4   Configure a Cisco Router

6.4.1   Configure Initial Settings

6.4.1.1   Basic Switch Configuration Steps

Cisco routers and Cisco switches have many similarities. They support a similar operating system, support similar command structures and support many of the same commands. In addition, both devices have identical initial configuration steps when implemented in a network.

Before we begin configuring a router, review the initial switch configuration tasks listed in Figure 1. Figure 2 displays a sample configuration.

Refer to
Online Course
for Illustration

6.4.1.2   Basic Router Configuration Steps

Similar to configuring a switch, the tasks listed in Figure 1 should be completed when configuring initial settings on a router.

Figures 2 through 5 provide an example of these tasks being configured on a router. In Figure 2, the router is assigned a hostname. In Figure 3, the privileged EXEC, user EXEC, and remote access lines are secured with a password and all passwords in the configuration file are encrypted. Providing legal notification is configured in Figure 4. And finally, the configuration is being saved in Figure 5.

Use the Syntax Checker in Figure 6 to practice these configuration steps.

Refer to **Packet
Tracer Activity**
for this chapter

6.4.1.3   Packet Tracer - Configure Initial Router Settings

In this activity, you will perform basic router configurations. You will secure access to the CLI and console port using encrypted and plaintext passwords. You will also configure messages for users logging into the router. These banners also warn unauthorized users that access is prohibited. Finally, you will verify and save your running configuration.

Refer to
Online Course
for Illustration

6.4.2   Configure Interfaces

6.4.2.1   Configure Router Interfaces

For routers to be reachable, the in-band router interfaces must be configured. There are many different types of interfaces available on Cisco routers. In this example, the Cisco 1941 router is equipped with:

- **Two Gigabit Ethernet interfaces** – GigabitEthernet 0/0 (G0/0) and GigabitEthernet 0/1 (G0/1)

- **A serial WAN interface card (WIC) consisting of two interfaces** – Serial 0/0/0 (S0/0/0) and Serial 0/0/1 (S0/0/1)

Note   Click here for more information on the abbreviations and numbering of interfaces.

The tasks to configure a router interface are listed in Figure 1. Notice how they are very similar to configuring a management SVI on a switch.

Although not required, it is good practice to configure a description on each interface to help document the network information. The description text is limited to 240 characters. On production networks, a description can be helpful in troubleshooting by providing information about the type of network that the interface is connected to and if there are any other routers on that network. If the interface connects to an ISP or service carrier, it is helpful to enter the third party connection and contact information.

Using the **no shutdown** command activates the interface and is similar to powering on the interface. The interface must also be connected to another device (a hub, a switch, or another router) for the physical layer to be active.

Figure 2 shows the configuration of the LAN interfaces connected to R1.

Use the Syntax Checker in Figure 3 to practice configuring a LAN interface.

Refer to
Online Course
for Illustration

6.4.2.2   Verify Interface Configuration

There are several commands that can be used to verify interface configuration. The most useful of these is the **show ip interface brief** command. The output generated displays all interfaces, their IPv4 address, and their current status. The configured and connected interfaces should display a Status of "up" and Protocol of "up". Anything else would indicate a problem with either the configuration or the cabling.

You can verify connectivity from the interface using the **ping** command. Cisco routers send five consecutive pings and measure minimal, average, and maximum round trip times. Exclamation marks verify connectivity.

Figure 1 displays the output of the **show ip interface brief** command, which reveals that the LAN interfaces and the WAN link are all activated and operational. Notice that the **ping** command generated five exclamation marks verifying connectivity to R2.

Other interface verification commands include:

- **show ip route** – Displays the contents of the IPv4 routing table stored in RAM.
- **show interfaces** – Displays statistics for all interfaces on the device.
- **show ip interface** – Displays the IPv4 statistics for all interfaces on a router.

Figure 2 displays the output of the **show ip route** command. Notice the three directly connected network entries with their local interface IPv4 addresses.

Remember to save the configuration using the **copy running-config startup-config** command.

Refer to
Online Course
for Illustration

6.4.3   Configure the Default Gateway

6.4.3.1   Default Gateway for a Host

For an end device to communicate over the network, it must be configured with the correct IP address information, including the default gateway address. The default gateway is only used when the host wants to send a packet to a device on another network. The default gateway address is generally the router interface address attached to the local network of the host. The IP address of the host device and the router interface address must be in the same network.

The figures display a topology of a router with two separate interfaces. Each interface is connected to a separate network. G0/0 is connected to network 192.168.10.0, while G0/1 is connected to network 192.168.11.0. Each host device is configured with the appropriate default gateway address.

In Figure 1, PC1 sends a packet to PC2. In this example, the default gateway is not used; rather, PC1 addresses the packet with the IP address of PC2 and forwards the packet directly to PC2 through the switch.

In Figure 2, PC1 sends a packet to PC3. In this example, PC1 addresses the packet with the IP address of PC3, but then forwards the packet to the router. The router accepts the packet, accesses its routing table to determine the appropriate exit interface based on the destination address, and then forwards the packet out of the appropriate interface to reach PC3.

> Refer to
> **Online Course**
> for Illustration

6.4.3.2   Default Gateway for a Switch

Typically a workgroup switch that interconnects client computers is a Layer 2 device. As such, a Layer 2 switch does not require an IP address to function properly. However, if you wish to connect to the switch and administratively manage it over multiple networks, you will need to configure the SVI with an IPv4 address, subnet mask, and default gateway address.

The default gateway address is typically configured on all devices that wish to communicate beyond just their local network. In other words, to remotely access the switch from another network using SSH or Telnet, the switch must have an SVI with an IPv4 address, subnet mask, and default gateway address configured. If the switch is accessed from a host within the local network, then the default gateway IPv4 address is not required.

To configure a default gateway on a switch use the **ip default-gateway** global configuration command. The IP address configured is that of the router interface of the connected switch.

Figure 1 shows an administrator connecting to a switch on a remote network. For the switch to forward response packets to the administrator, the default gateway must be configured.

A common misconception is that the switch uses its configured default gateway address to determine where to forward packets originating from hosts connected to the switch and destined for hosts on remote networks. Actually, the IP address and default gateway information is only used for packets that originate from the switch. Packets originating from host computers connected to the switch must already have the default gateway address configured on their host computer operating systems.

Use the Syntax Checker in Figure 2 to practice configuring a default gateway on a switch.

> Refer to **Packet
> Tracer Activity**
> for this chapter

6.4.3.3   Packet Tracer - Connect a Router to a LAN

In this activity, you will use various **show** commands to display the current state of the router. You will then use the Addressing Table to configure router Ethernet interfaces. Finally, you will use commands to verify and test your configurations.

Refer to **Packet Tracer Activity** for this chapter

6.4.3.4   Packet Tracer - Troubleshooting Default Gateway Issues

For a device to communicate across multiple networks, it must be configured with an IP address, subnet mask, and a default gateway. The default gateway is used when the host wants to send a packet to a device on another network. The default gateway address is generally the router interface address attached to the local network to which the host is connected. In this activity, you will finish documenting the network. You will then verify the network documentation by testing end-to-end connectivity and troubleshooting issues. The troubleshooting method you will use consists of the following steps:

Step 1.   Verify the network documentation and use tests to isolate problems.

Step 2.   Determine an appropriate solution for a given problem.

Step 3.   Implement the solution.

Step 4.   Test to verify the problem is resolved.

Step 5.   Document the solution.

6.5   Summary

6.5.1   Conclusion

Refer to **Lab Activity** for this chapter

6.5.1.1   Class Activity - Can You Read This Map?

Note   It is suggested that students work in pairs; however, if preferred, students can complete this activity individually.

Your instructor will provide you with output generated by a router's **show ip route** command. Use Packet Tracer to build a topology model using this routing information.

At a minimum, the following should be used in your topology model:

■ 1 Catalyst 2960 switch

■ 1 Cisco Series 1941 Router with one HWIC-4ESW switching port modular card and IOS version 15.1 or higher

■ 3 PCs (can be servers, generic PCs, laptops, etc.)

Use the note tool in Packet Tracer to indicate the addresses of the router interfaces and possible addresses for the end devices you chose for your model. Label all end devices, ports, and addresses ascertained from the **show ip route** output/routing table information in your Packet Tracer file. Save your work in hard or soft copy to share with the class.

Refer to
Lab Activity
for this chapter

6.5.1.2   Lab - Building a Switch and Router Network

In this lab, you will complete the following objectives:

- Part 1: Set Up the Topology and Initialize Devices

- Part 2: Configure Devices and Verify Connectivity

- Part 3: Display Device Information

Refer to **Packet
Tracer Activity**
for this chapter

6.5.1.3   Packet Tracer - Skills Integration Challenge

Your network manager is impressed with your performance in your job as a LAN technician. She would like you to now demonstrate your ability to configure a router connecting two LANs. Your tasks include configuring basic settings on a router and a switch using the Cisco IOS. You will then verify your configurations, as well as configurations on existing devices by testing end-to-end connectivity.

Refer to
Online Course
for Illustration

6.5.1.4   Network Layer

The network layer, or OSI Layer 3, provides services to allow end devices to exchange data across the network. To accomplish this end-to-end transport, the network layer uses four basic processes: IP addressing for end devices, encapsulation, routing, and de-encapsulation.

The Internet is largely based on IPv4, which is still the most widely-used network layer protocol. An IPv4 packet contains the IP header and the payload. However, IPv4 has a limited number of unique public IP addresses available. This led to the development of IP version 6 (IPv6). The IPv6 simplified header offers several advantages over IPv4, including better routing efficiency, simplified extension headers, and capability for per-flow processing. Plus, IPv6 addresses are based on 128-bit hierarchical addressing as opposed to IPv4 with 32 bits. This dramatically increases the number of available IP addresses.

In addition to hierarchical addressing, the network layer is also responsible for routing.

Hosts require a local routing table to ensure that packets are directed to the correct destination network. The local table of a host typically contains the direct connection, the local network route, and the local default route. The local default route is the route to the default gateway.

The default gateway is the IP address of a router interface connected to the local network. When a host needs to forward a packet to a destination address that is not on the same network as the host, the packet is sent to the default gateway for further processing.

When a router, such as the default gateway, receives a packet, it examines the destination IP address to determine the destination network. The routing table of a router stores information about directly-connected routes and remote routes to IP networks. If the router has an entry in its routing table for the destination network, the router forwards the packet. If no routing entry exists, the router may forward the packet to its own default route if one is configured, or it will drop the packet.

Routing table entries can be configured manually on each router to provide static routing, or the routers may communicate route information dynamically between each other using a routing protocol.

In order for routers to be reachable, the router interface must be configured. To enable a specific interface, enter interface configuration mode using the **interface** *type-and-number* global configuration mode command.

Go to the online course to take the quiz and exam.

Chapter 6 Quiz

This quiz is designed to provide an additional opportunity to practice the skills and knowledge presented in the chapter and to prepare for the chapter exam. You will be allowed multiple attempts and the grade does not appear in the gradebook.

Chapter 6 Exam

The chapter exam assesses your knowledge of the chapter content.

Your Chapter Notes

IP Addressing

7.0 Introduction

7.0.1.1 IP Addressing

Addressing is a critical function of network layer protocols. Addressing enables data communication between hosts, regardless of whether the hosts are on the same network, or on different networks. Both Internet Protocol version 4 (IPv4) and Internet Protocol version 6 (IPv6) provide hierarchical addressing for packets that carry data.

Designing, implementing and managing an effective IP addressing plan ensures that networks can operate effectively and efficiently.

This chapter examines in detail the structure of IP addresses and their application to the construction and testing of IP networks and subnetworks.

Refer to **Lab Activity** for this chapter

7.0.1.2 Class Activity – The Internet of Everything (IoE)

If nature, traffic, transportation, networking, and space exploration depend on digital information sharing, how will that information be identified from source to destination?

In this activity, you will begin to think about not only what will be identified in the IoE world, but how everything will be addressed in the same world!

- Navigate to the IoE main page located at http://www.cisco.com/c/r/en/us/internet-of-everything-ioe.

- Next, watch some videos or read through some content from the IoE main page that interests you.

- Write 5 comments or questions about what you saw or read. Be prepared to share with the class.

Refer to **Online Course** for Illustration

7.1 IPv4 Network Addresses

7.1.1 Binary and Decimal Conversion

7.1.1.1 IPv4 Addresses

Binary is a numbering system that consists of the numbers 0 and 1 called *bits*. In contrast, the decimal numbering system consists of 10 digits consisting of the numbers 0 – 9.

Binary is important for us to understand because hosts, servers, and network devices use binary addressing. Specifically, they use binary IPv4 addresses, as shown in Figure 1, to identify each other.

Each address consists of a string of 32 bits, divided into four sections called *octets*. Each octet contains 8 bits (or 1 byte) separated with a dot. For example, PC1 in the figure is assigned IPv4 address 11000000.10101000.00001010.00001010. Its default gateway address would be that of R1 Gigabit Ethernet interface 11000000.10101000.00001010.000 00001.

Working with binary numbers can be challenging. For ease of use by people, IPv4 addresses are commonly expressed in dotted decimal notation as shown in Figure 2. PC1 is assigned IPv4 address 192.168.10.10, and its default gateway address is 192.168.10.1.

Figure 3 contrasts the dotted decimal address and 32-bit binary address of PC1.

For a solid understanding of network addressing, it is necessary to know binary addressing and gain practical skills converting between binary and dotted decimal IPv4 addresses.

This section will cover how to convert between base two and base 10 numbering systems.

Refer to **Video** in online course

7.1.1.2   Video Demonstration – Converting Between Binary and Decimal Numbering Systems

Click Play to view a demonstration of converting between the binary and decimal numbering systems.

Click here to read the transcript of this video.

Refer to **Online Course** for Illustration

7.1.1.3   Positional Notation

Learning to convert binary to decimal requires an understanding of *positional notation*. Positional notation means that a digit represents different values depending on the "position" the digit occupies in the sequence of numbers. You already know the most common numbering system, the decimal (base 10) notation system.

The decimal positional notation system operates as described in Figure 1. Click the row titles for a description of each row. To use the positional system, match a given number to its positional value. The example in Figure 2 illustrates how positional notation is used with the decimal number 1234.

In contrast, the binary positional notation operates as described in Figure 3. Click the row titles for a description of each row.

The example in Figure 4 illustrates how a binary number 11000000 corresponds to the number 192. If the binary number had been 10101000, then the corresponding decimal number would be 168.

Refer to **Online Course** for Illustration

7.1.1.4   Binary to Decimal Conversion

To convert a binary IPv4 address to its dotted decimal equivalent, divide the IPv4 address into four 8-bit octets. Next apply the binary positional value to the first octet binary number and calculate accordingly.

For example, consider that 11000000.10101000.00001011.00001010 is the binary IPv4 address of a host. To convert the binary address to decimal, start with the first octet as shown in Figure 1. Enter the 8-bit binary number under the positional value of row 1 and then calculate to produce the decimal number 192. This number goes into the first octet of the dotted decimal notation.

Next convert the second octet as shown in Figure 2. The resulting decimal value is 168, and it goes into the second octet.

Convert the third octet as shown in Figure 4 and the fourth octet as shown in Figure 5 which completes the IP address and produces **192.168.11.10**.

Refer to **Interactive Graphic** in online course

7.1.1.5   Activity – Binary to Decimal Conversion

Refer to **Online Course** for Illustration

7.1.1.6   Decimal to Binary Conversion

It is also necessary to understand how to convert a dotted decimal IPv4 address to binary. A useful tool is the binary positional value table. The following illustrates how to use the table to convert decimal to binary:

- Figure 1 questions if the decimal number of the octet (n) is equal to or greater than the most-significant bit (128). If no, then enter binary 0 in the 128 positional value. If yes, then add a binary 1 in the 128 positional value and subtract 128 from the decimal number.

- Figure 2 questions if the remainder (n) is equal to or greater than the next most-significant bit (64). If no, then add a binary 0 in the 64 positional value, otherwise add binary 1 and subtract 64 from the decimal.

- Figure 3 questions if the remainder (n) is equal to or greater than the next most-significant bit (32). If no, then add a binary 0 in the 32 positional value, otherwise add binary 1 and subtract 32 from the decimal.

Figures 4 through 8 continue to evaluate the decimal until all positional values have been entered resulting in the equivalent binary value.

Refer to **Online Course** for Illustration

7.1.1.7   Decimal to Binary Conversion Examples

To help understand the process, consider the IP address 192.168.11.10. Using the previously explained process, start with the binary positional value table and the first decimal number 192.

Figure 1 illustrates how 192 is compared to see if it is equal to or greater than the high-order bit 128. Because 192 is greater than 128, add a 1 to the high-order positional value to represent 128. Then subtract 128 from 192 to produce a remainder of 64. Figure 2 then compares 64 to the next high-order bit 64. Because they are equal, add a 1 to next high-order positional value. Enter binary 0 in the remainder of the positional values as shown in Figure 3. The binary value of the first octet is 11000000.

The next octet is 168. Figure 4 compares 168 to the 128 high-order bit. Because 168 is greater than 128, add a 1 to the high-order positional value. Then subtract 128 from 168 to produce a remainder of 40. Figure 5 then compares 40 to the next high-order bit 64. Because 40 is less, add a 0 to the next high-order positional value of 64. Figure 6 compares the next high-order bit 32. Because 40 is greater than 32, add a 1 to the positional value, and subtract 32 from 40 to produce a remainder of 8. Eight matches a specific positional value. Therefore, enter a 0 for the positional value of 16 and add a 1 to the positional value of 8, as shown in Figure 7. Add 0s to all remaining positional values. As shown in Figure 8, the binary value of the third octet is **10101000**.

The third octet is 11. It is possible to bypass the process of subtraction with easier or smaller decimal numbers. For instance, Figure 9 displays the converted binary number. Notice that it would be fairly easy to calculate this number without actually going through the subtraction process (8 + 2 + 1 = 11). The binary value of the second octet is 00001011.

The fourth octet is 10 (8 + 2). As shown in Figure 10, the binary value of the fourth octet is 00001010.

Converting between binary and decimal may seem challenging at first, but with practice it should become easier over time.

Refer to
Interactive Graphic
in online course

7.1.1.8   Activity – Decimal to Binary Conversion Utility

Refer to
Interactive Graphic
in online course

7.1.1.9   Activity – Binary Game

Refer to
Online Course
for Illustration

7.1.2   IPv4 Address Structure

7.1.2.1   Network and Host Portions

Understanding binary notation is important when determining if two hosts are in the same network. Recall that an IPv4 address is a hierarchical address that is made up of a network portion and a host portion. When determining the network portion versus the host portion, it is necessary to look at the 32-bit stream. Within the 32-bit stream, a portion of the bits identify the network, and a portion of the bits identify the host as shown in the figure.

The bits within the network portion of the address must be identical for all devices that reside in the same network. The bits within the host portion of the address must be unique to identify a specific host within a network. If two hosts have the same bit-pattern in the specified network portion of the 32-bit stream, those two hosts will reside in the same network.

But how do hosts know which portion of the 32-bits identifies the network and which identifies the host? That is the job of the *subnet mask*.

Refer to
Online Course
for Illustration

7.1.2.2   The Subnet Mask

As shown in Figure 1, three dotted decimal IPv4 addresses must be configured when assigning an IPv4 configuration to host:

■ **IPv4 address** – Unique IPv4 address of the host

■ **Subnet mask** – Used to identify the network/host portion of the IPv4 address

■ **Default gateway** – Identifies the local gateway (i.e. local router interface IPv4 address) to reach remote networks

When an IPv4 address is assigned to a device, the subnet mask is used to determine the network address where the device belongs. The network address represents all the devices on the same network.

Figure 2 displays the dotted decimal address and the 32-bit subnet mask. Notice how the subnet mask is essentially a sequence of 1 bits followed by a sequence of 0 bits.

To identify the network and host portions of an IPv4 address, the subnet mask is compared to the IPv4 address bit for bit, from left to right as shown in Figure 3. The 1s in the subnet mask identify the network portion while the 0s identify the host portion. Note that the subnet mask does not actually contain the network or host portion of an IPv4 address, it just tells the computer where to look for these portions in a given IPv4 address.

The actual process used to identify the network portion and host portion is called ANDing.

Refer to
Online Course
for Illustration

7.1.2.3   ANDing

ANDing is one of three basic binary operations used in digital logic. The other two are OR and NOT. While all three are used in data networks, only AND is used in determining the network address. Therefore, our discussion here will be limited to the logical AND operation.

Logical AND is the comparison of two bits that produce the results shown in Figure 1. Note how only a 1 AND 1 produces a 1.

To identify the network address of an IPv4 host, the IPv4 address is logically ANDed, bit by bit, with the subnet mask. ANDing between the address and the subnet mask yields the network address.

To illustrate how AND is used to discover a network address, consider a host with IPv4 address 192.168.10.10 and subnet mask of 255.255.255.0. Figure 2 displays the host IPv4 address and converted binary address. The host subnet mask binary address is added in Figure 3.

The yellow highlighted sections in Figure 4 identify the AND bits that produced a binary 1 in the AND Results row. All other bit comparison produced binary 0s. Notice how the last octet no longer has any binary 1 bits.

Finally, Figure 5 displays the resulting network address 192.168.10.0 255.255.255.0. Therefore, host 192.168.10.10 is on network 192.168.10.0 255.255.255.0

Refer to
Interactive Graphic
in online course

7.1.2.4   Activity – ANDing to Determine the Network Address

Refer to
Online Course
for Illustration

7.1.2.5   The Prefix Length

Expressing network addresses and host addresses with the dotted decimal subnet mask address can become cumbersome. Fortunately, there is an alternate shorthand method of identifying a subnet mask called the prefix length.

Specifically, the prefix length is the number of bits set to 1 in the subnet mask. It is written in "slash notation", which is a "/" followed by the number of bits set to 1. Therefore, count the number of bits in the subnet mask and prepend it with a slash.

For example, refer to the table in the figure. The first column lists various subnet masks that can be used with a host address. The second column displays the converted 32-bit binary address. The last column displays the resulting prefix length.

Using various types of prefix lengths will be discussed later. For now, the focus will be on the /24 (i.e. 255.255.255.0) subnet mask.

Refer to
Online Course
for Illustration

7.1.2.6   Network, Host, and Broadcast Addresses

Each network address contains (or identifies) host addresses and a broadcast address as described in Figure 1.

- Figure 2 lists and describes the specific addresses within network 192.168.10.0 /24.

- For another example, refer to Figures 3 through 7. In these figures, notice how the network portion of the addresses remains the same while the host portion changes.

- Figure 3 displays the network address 10.1.1.0 /24. Host bits are all 0s.

- Figure 4 displays the IPv4 address of host 10.1.1.10. Host bits are a mix of 0s and 1s.

- Figure 5 displays the first host IPv4 address 10.1.1.1. Host bits are all 0s with a 1. Notice that it is assigned to the router interface, and therefore, would become the default gateway for all of the hosts on that network.

- Figure 6 displays the last host IPv4 address 10.1.1.254. Host bits are all 1s and a 0.

- Figure 7 displays the broadcast address 10.1.1.255. Host bits are all 1s.

The concepts discussed in this topic form the basis for understanding IPv4 addressing. Make sure you understand how a network address identifies a network portion and host portion using the subnet mask or prefix length and the ANDing operation. Also make note of the various types of network addresses within a network.

Refer to **Video**
in online course

7.1.2.7   Video Demonstration - Network, Host, and Broadcast Addresses

Click Play to view a demonstration of how the network, host, and broadcast addresses are determined for a given IPv4 address and subnet mask.

Click here to read the transcript of this video.

Refer to
Lab Activity
for this chapter

7.1.2.8   Lab – Using the Windows Calculator with Network Addresses

In this lab, you will complete the following objectives:

- Part 1: Access the Windows Calculator

- Part 2: Convert between Numbering Systems

- Part 3: Convert Host IPv4 Addresses and Subnet Masks into Binary

- Part 4: Determine the Number of Hosts in a Network Using Powers of 2

- Part 5: Convert MAC Addresses and IPv6 Addresses to Binary

Refer to
Lab Activity
for this chapter

7.1.2.9   Lab – Converting IPv4 Addresses to Binary

In this lab, you will complete the following objectives:

- Part 1: Convert IPv4 Addresses from Dotted Decimal to Binary

- Part 2: Use Bitwise ANDing Operation to Determine Network Addresses

- Part 3: Apply Network Address Calculations

Refer to
Online Course
for Illustration

7.1.3   IPv4 Unicast, Broadcast, and Multicast

7.1.3.1   Static IPv4 Address Assignment to a Host

Devices can be assigned an IP address either statically or dynamically.

In networks, some devices require a fixed IP address. For instance, printers, servers, and networking devices need an IP address that does not change. For this reason, these devices are typically assigned static IP addresses.

A host can also be configured with a static IPv4 address such as shown in the figure. Assigning hosts static IP addresses is acceptable in small networks. However, it would be time-consuming to enter static addresses on each host in a large network. It is important to maintain an accurate list of static IP addresses assigned to each device.

Refer to
Online Course
for Illustration

7.1.3.2   Dynamic IPv4 Address Assignment to a Host

In most data networks, the largest population of hosts includes PCs, tablets, smartphones, printers, and IP phones. It is also often the case that the user population and their devices change frequently. It would be impractical to statically assign IPv4 addresses for each device. Therefore, these devices are assigned IPv4 addresses dynamically using the Dynamic Host Configuration Protocol (DHCP).

As shown in the figure, a host can obtain IP addressing information automatically. The host is a DHCP client and requests IP address information from a DHCP server. The DHCP server provides an IP address, subnet mask, default gateway, and other configuration information.

DHCP is generally the preferred method of assigning IPv4 addresses to hosts on large networks. An additional benefit of DHCP is the address is not permanently assigned to a host but is only "leased" for a period of time. If the host is powered down or taken off the network, the address is returned to the pool for reuse. This feature is especially helpful for mobile users that come and go on a network.

Refer to
Online Course
for Illustration

7.1.3.3   IPv4 Communication

A host successfully connected to a network can communicate with other devices in one of three ways:

- **Unicast** – The process of sending a packet from one host to an individual host as shown in Figure 1.

- **Broadcast** – The process of sending a packet from one host to all hosts in the network as shown in Figure 2.

- **Multicast** – The process of sending a packet from one host to a selected group of hosts, possibly in different networks, as shown in Figure 3.

These three types of communication are used for different purposes in data networks. In all three cases, the IPv4 address of the originating host is placed in the packet header as the source address.

Refer to
Online Course
for Illustration

7.1.3.4   Unicast Transmission

Unicast communication is used for normal host-to-host communication in both a client/ server and a peer-to-peer network. Unicast packets use the address of the destination device as the destination address and can be routed through an internetwork.

Play the animation to see an example of unicast transmission.

In an IPv4 network, the unicast address applied to an end device is referred to as the host address. For unicast communication, the addresses assigned to the two end devices are used as the source and destination IPv4 addresses. During the encapsulation process, the source host uses its IPv4 address as the source address and the IPv4 address of the destination host as the destination address. Regardless of whether the destination specified a packet as a unicast, broadcast or multicast; the source address of any packet is always the unicast address of the originating host.

Note   In this course, all communication between devices is unicast unless otherwise noted.

IPv4 unicast host addresses are in the address range of 0.0.0.0 to 223.255.255.255. However, within this range are many addresses that are reserved for special purposes. These special purpose addresses will be discussed later in this chapter.

Refer to
Online Course
for Illustration

7.1.3.5   Broadcast Transmission

Broadcast traffic is used to send packets to all hosts in the network using the broadcast address for the network. With a broadcast, the packet contains a destination IPv4 address with all ones (1s) in the host portion. This means that all hosts on that local network (broadcast domain) will receive and look at the packet. Many network protocols, such as DHCP, use broadcasts. When a host receives a packet sent to the network broadcast address, the host processes the packet as it would a packet addressed to its unicast address.

Broadcast may be directed or limited. A directed broadcast is sent to all hosts on a specific network. For example, a host on the 172.16.4.0/24 network sends a packet to 172.16.4.255. A limited broadcast is sent to 255.255.255.255. By default, routers do not forward broadcasts.

As an example, a host within the 172.16.4.0/24 network would broadcast to all hosts in its network using a packet with a destination address of 255.255.255.255.

Play the animation to see an example of a limited broadcast transmission.

When a packet is broadcast, it uses resources on the network and causes every receiving host on the network to process the packet. Therefore, broadcast traffic should be limited so that it does not adversely affect the performance of the network or devices. Because routers separate broadcast domains, subdividing networks can improve network performance by eliminating excessive broadcast traffic.

Refer to
Online Course
for Illustration

7.1.3.6   Multicast Transmission

Multicast transmission reduces traffic by allowing a host to send a single packet to a selected set of hosts that subscribe to a multicast group.

IPv4 has reserved the 224.0.0.0 to 239.255.255.255 addresses as a multicast range. The IPv4 multicast addresses 224.0.0.0 to 224.0.0.255 are reserved for multicasting on the local network only. These addresses are to be used for multicast groups on a local network. A router connected to the local network recognizes that these packets are addressed to a local network multicast group and never forwards them further. A typical use of reserved local network multicast address is in routing protocols using multicast transmission to exchange routing information. For instance, 224.0.0.9 is the multicast address used by Routing Information Protocol (RIP) version 2 to communicate with other RIPv2 routers.

Hosts that receive particular multicast data are called multicast clients. The multicast clients use services requested by a client program to subscribe to the multicast group.

Each multicast group is represented by a single IPv4 multicast destination address. When an IPv4 host subscribes to a multicast group, the host processes packets addressed to this multicast address, and packets addressed to its uniquely allocated unicast address.

The animation demonstrates clients accepting multicast packets.

Refer to **Interactive Graphic** in online course

7.1.3.7   Activity – Unicast, Broadcast, or Multicast

Refer to **Packet Tracer Activity** for this chapter

7.1.3.8   Packet Tracer – Investigate Unicast, Broadcast, and Multicast Traffic

This activity will examine unicast, broadcast, and multicast behavior. Most traffic in a network is unicast. When a PC sends an ICMP echo request to a remote router, the source address in the IPv4 packet header is the IPv4 address of the sending PC. The destination address in the IPv4 packet header is the IPv4 address of the interface on the remote router. The packet is sent only to the intended destination.

Using the ping command or the Add Complex PDU feature of Packet Tracer, you can directly ping broadcast addresses to view broadcast traffic.

For multicast traffic, you will view EIGRP traffic. EIGRP is used by Cisco routers to exchange routing information between routers. Routers using EIGRP send packets to the multicast address 224.0.0.10, which represents the group of EIGRP routers. Although these packets are received by other devices, they are dropped at Layer 3 by all devices except EIGRP routers, with no other processing required.

Refer to **Online Course** for Illustration

7.1.4   Types of IPv4 Addressses

7.1.4.1   Public and Private IPv4 Addresses

Public IPv4 addresses are addresses which are globally routed between ISP (Internet Service Provider) routers. However, not all available IPv4 addresses can be used on the Internet. There are blocks of addresses called *private addresses* that are used by most organizations to assign IPv4 addresses to internal hosts.

In the mid-1990s private IPv4 addresses were introduced because of the depletion of IPv4 address space. Private IPv4 addresses are not unique and can be used by an internal network.

Specifically, the private address blocks are:

- **10.0.0.0 /8** or **10.0.0.0** to **10.255.255.255**

- **172.16.0.0 /12** or **172.16.0.0** to **172.31.255.255**

- **192.168.0.0 /16** or **192.168.0.0** to **192.168.255.255**

It is important to know that addresses within these address blocks are not allowed on the Internet and must be filtered (discarded) by Internet routers. For example, in the figure, users in networks 1, 2, or 3 are sending packets to remote destinations. The Internet Service Provider (ISP) routers would see that the source IPv4 addresses in the packets are from private addresses and would, therefore, discard the packets.

Note   Private addresses are defined in RFC 1918.

Most organizations use private IPv4 addresses for their internal hosts. However, these RFC 1918 address are not routable in the Internet and must be translated to a public IPv4 address. Network Address Translation (NAT) is used to translate between private IPv4 and public IPv4 addresses. This is usually done on the router that connects the internal network to the ISP's network.

Home routers provide the same capability. For instance, most home routers assign IPv4 addresses to their wired and wireless hosts from the private address of 192.168.1.0 /24. The home router interface that connects to the Internet service provider (ISP) network is assigned a public IPv4 address to use on the Internet.

Refer to
Interactive Graphic
in online course

7.1.4.2   Activity – Pass or Block IPv4 Addresses

Refer to
Online Course
for Illustration

7.1.4.3   Special User IPv4 Addresses

There are certain addresses such as the network address and broadcast address that cannot be assigned to hosts. There are also special addresses that can be assigned to hosts, but with restrictions on how those hosts can interact within the network.

- **Loopback addresses (127.0.0.0 /8** or **127.0.0.1 to 127.255.255.254)** – More commonly identified as only 127.0.0.1, these are special addresses used by a host to direct traffic to itself. For example, it can be used on a host to test if the TCP/IP configuration is operational, such as shown in the figure. Notice how the 127.0.0.1 loopback address replies to the ping command. Also note how any address within this block will loop back to the local host, such as shown with the second ping in the figure.

- **Link-Local addresses (169.254.0.0 /16** or **169.254.0.1 to 169.254.255.254)** – More commonly known as the Automatic Private IP Addressing (APIPA) addresses, they are used by a Windows DCHP client to self-configure in the event that there are no DHCP servers available.Useful in a peer-to-peer connection.

- **TEST-NET addresses (192.0.2.0/24** or **192.0.2.0 to 192.0.2.255)** – These addresses are set aside for teaching and learning purposes and can be used in documentation and network examples.

Note   There are also Experimental Addresses in the block 240.0.0.0 to 255.255.255.254 that are reserved for future use (RFC 3330).

Refer to **Online Course** for Illustration

7.1.4.4   Legacy Classful Addressing

In 1981, Internet IPv4 addresses were assigned using *classful addressing* as defined in RFC 790, Assigned Numbers. The RFC divided the unicast ranges into specific classes called:

- **Class A (0.0.0.0/8 to 127.0.0.0/8)** – Designed to support extremely large networks with more than 16 million host addresses. It used a fixed /8 prefix with the first octet to indicate the network address and the remaining three octets for host addresses. All class A addresses required that the most significant bit of the high-order octet be a zero creating a total of 128 possible class A networks. Figure 1 summarizes the class A.

- **Class B (128.0.0.0 /16 – 191.255.0.0 /16)** – Designed to support the needs of moderate to large size networks with up to approximately 65,000 host addresses. It used a fixed /16 prefix with the two high-order octets to indicate the network address and the remaining two octets for host addresses. The most significant two bits of the high-order octet must be 10 creating over 16,000 networks. Figure 2 summarizes the class B.

- **Class C (192.0.0.0 /24 – 223.255.255.0 /24)** – Designed to support small networks with a maximum of 254 hosts. It used a fixed /24 prefix with the first three octets to indicate the network and the remaining octet for the host addresses. The most significant three bits of the high-order octet must be 110 creating over 2 million possible networks. Figure 3 summarizes the class C.

Note   There is also a Class D multicast block consisting of 224.0.0.0 to 239.0.0.0 and a Class E experimental address block consisting of 240.0.0.0 – 255.0.0.0.

Refer to **Video** in online course

7.1.4.5   Video Demonstration - Classful IPv4 Addressing

Click Play in the figure to view a discussion about classful IPv4 addressing.

Click here to read the transcript of this video.

Refer to **Online Course** for Illustration

7.1.4.6   Classless Addressing

As shown in the figure, the classful system allocated 50% of the available IPv4 addresses to 128 Class A networks, 25% of the addresses to Class B and then Class C shared the remaining 25% with Class D and E. The problem is that this wasted a great deal of addresses and exhausted the availability of IPv4 addresses. Not all organizations' requirements fit well into one of these three classes. For example, a company that had a network with 260 hosts would need to be given a class B address with more than 65,000 addresses wasting 64,740 addresses.

Classful addressing was abandoned in the late 1990s for the newer and current classless addressing system. However, there are still classful remnants in networks today. For example, when you assign an IPv4 address to a computer, the operating system examines the address being assigned to determine if this address is a class A, class B, or class C. The operating system then assumes the prefix used by that class and makes the default subnet mask assignment.

The system in use today is referred to as *classless addressing*. The formal name is Classless Inter-Domain Routing (CIDR, pronounced "cider"). In 1993, the IETF created a new set of standards that allowed service providers to allocate IPv4 addresses on any address bit boundary (prefix length) instead of only by a class A, B, or C address. This was to help delay the depletion and eventual exhaustion of IPv4 addresses.

The IETF knew that CIDR was only a temporary solution and that a new IP protocol would have to be developed to accommodate the rapid growth in the number of Internet users. In 1994, the IETF began its work to find a successor to IPv4, which eventually became IPv6.

So who manages and assigns these IP addresses?

7.1.4.7   Assignment of IP Addresses

Refer to
Online Course
for Illustration

For a company or organization to support network hosts, such as web servers accessible from the Internet, that organization must have a block of public addresses assigned. Remember that public addresses must be unique, and use of these public addresses is regulated and allocated to each organization separately. This is true for IPv4 and IPv6 addresses.

Both IPv4 and IPv6 addresses are managed by the Internet Assigned Numbers Authority (IANA) (http://www.iana.org). The IANA manages and allocates blocks of IP addresses to the Regional Internet Registries (RIRs). Click each of the RIRs in the figure to view more information.

RIRs are responsible for allocating IP addresses to ISPs who in turn provide IPv4 address blocks to organizations and smaller ISPs. Organizations can get their addresses directly from an RIR subject to the policies of that RIR.

Refer to the Chapter Appendix for more information about ISPs.

Refer to
Interactive Graphic
in online course

7.1.4.8   Activity – Public or Private IPv4 Addresses

Refer to
Lab Activity
for this chapter

7.1.4.9   Lab – Identifying IPv4 Addresses

In this lab, you will complete the following objectives:

- Part 1: Identify IPv4 Addresses
- Part 2: Classify IPv4 Addresses

Refer to
Online Course
for Illustration

7.2   IPv6 Network Addresses

7.2.1   IPv4 Issues

7.2.1.1   The Need for IPv6

IPv6 is designed to be the successor to IPv4. IPv6 has a larger 128-bit address space, providing for 340 undecillion addresses. (That is the number 340, followed by 36 zeroes.) However, IPv6 is more than just larger addresses. When the IETF began its development of a successor to IPv4, it used this opportunity to fix the limitations of IPv4 and include additional enhancements. One example is Internet Control Message Protocol version 6 (ICMPv6), which includes address resolution and address auto-configuration not found in ICMP for IPv4 (ICMPv4). ICMPv4 and ICMPv6 will be discussed later in this chapter.

Need for IPv6

The depletion of IPv4 address space has been the motivating factor for moving to IPv6. As Africa, Asia and other areas of the world become more connected to the Internet, there are not enough IPv4 addresses to accommodate this growth. As shown in the figure, four out of the five RIRs have run out of IPv4 addresses.

IPv4 has a theoretical maximum of 4.3 billion addresses. Private addresses in combination with Network Address Translation (NAT) have been instrumental in slowing the depletion of IPv4 address space. However, NAT breaks many applications and has limitations that severely impede peer-to-peer communications.

Internet of Everything

The Internet of today is significantly different than the Internet of past decades. The Internet of today is more than email, web pages, and file transfer between computers. The evolving Internet is becoming an Internet of things. No longer will the only devices accessing the Internet be computers, tablets, and smartphones. The sensor-equipped, Internet-ready devices of tomorrow will include everything from automobiles and biomedical devices, to household appliances and natural ecosystems.

With an increasing Internet population, a limited IPv4 address space, issues with NAT and an Internet of Everything, the time has come to begin the transition to IPv6.

Refer to
Online Course
for Illustration

7.2.1.2   IPv4 and IPv6 Coexistence

There is not a single date to move to IPv6. For the foreseeable future, both IPv4 and IPv6 will coexist. The transition is expected to take years. The IETF has created various protocols and tools to help network administrators migrate their networks to IPv6. The migration techniques can be divided into three categories:

- **Dual Stack** – As shown in Figure 1, dual stack allows IPv4 and IPv6 to coexist on the same network segment. Dual stack devices run both IPv4 and IPv6 protocol stacks simultaneously.

- **Tunneling** – As shown in Figure 2, tunneling is a method of transporting an IPv6 packet over an IPv4 network. The IPv6 packet is encapsulated inside an IPv4 packet, similar to other types of data.

■ **Translation** – As shown in Figure 3, Network Address Translation 64 (NAT64) allows IPv6-enabled devices to communicate with IPv4-enabled devices using a translation technique similar to NAT for IPv4. An IPv6 packet is translated to an IPv4 packet and vice versa.

Note   Tunneling and translation are only used where needed. The goal should be native IPv6 communications from source to destination.

Refer to
Interactive Graphic
in online course

7.2.1.3   Activity – IPv4 Issues and Solutions

Refer to
Online Course
for Illustration

7.2.2   IPv6 Addressing

7.2.2.1   IPv6 Address Representation

IPv6 addresses are 128 bits in length and written as a string of hexadecimal values. Every 4 bits is represented by a single hexadecimal digit; for a total of 32 hexadecimal values, as shown in Figure 1. IPv6 addresses are not case-sensitive and can be written in either lowercase or uppercase.

Preferred Format

As shown in Figure 1, the preferred format for writing an IPv6 address is x:x:x:x:x:x:x:x, with each "x" consisting of four hexadecimal values. When referring to 8 bits of an IPv4 address we use the term octet. In IPv6, a hextet is the unofficial term used to refer to a segment of 16 bits or four hexadecimal values. Each "x" is a single hextet, 16 bits or four hexadecimal digits.

Preferred format means the IPv6 address is written using all 32 hexadecimal digits. It does not necessarily mean it is the ideal method for representing the IPv6 address. In the following pages, we will see two rules to help reduce the number of digits needed to represent an IPv6 address.

Figure 2 is a review of the relationship between decimal, binary and hexadecimal. Figure 3 has examples of IPv6 addresses in the preferred format.

Refer to
Online Course
for Illustration

7.2.2.2   Rule 1 – Omit Leading 0s

The first rule to help reduce the notation of IPv6 addresses is to omit any leading 0s (zeros) in any 16-bit section or hextet. For example:

■ 01AB can be represented as 1AB

■ 09F0 can be represented as 9F0

■ 0A00 can be represented as A00

■ 00AB can be represented as AB

This rule only applies to leading 0s, NOT to trailing 0s, otherwise the address would be ambiguous. For example, the hextet "ABC" could be either "0ABC" or "ABC0", but these do not represent the same value.

The Figures 1 to 8 show several examples of how omitting leading 0s can be used to reduce the size of an IPv6 address. For each example, the preferred format is shown. Notice how omitting the leading 0s in most examples results in a smaller address representation.

Refer to
Online Course
for Illustration

7.2.2.3   Rule 2 – Omit All 0 Segments

The second rule to help reduce the notation of IPv6 addresses is that a double colon (::) can replace any single, contiguous string of one or more 16-bit segments (hextets) consisting of all 0s.

The double colon (::) can only be used once within an address, otherwise there would be more than one possible resulting address. When used with the omitting leading 0s technique, the notation of IPv6 address can often be greatly reduced. This is commonly known as the compressed format.

Incorrect address:

■ 2001:0DB8::ABCD::1234

Possible expansions of ambiguous compressed addresses:

■ 2001:0DB8::ABCD:0000:0000:1234

■ 2001:0DB8::ABCD:0000:0000:0000:1234

■ 2001:0DB8:0000:ABCD::1234

■ 2001:0DB8:0000:0000:ABCD::1234

The Figures 1 to 7 show several examples of how using the double colon (::) and omitting leading 0s can reduce the size of an IPv6 address.

Refer to
Interactive Graphic
in online course

7.2.2.4   Activity – Practicing IPv6 Address Representations

Refer to
Online Course
for Illustration

7.2.3   Types of IPv6 Addresses

7.2.3.1   IPv6 Address Types

There are three types of IPv6 addresses:

■ **Unicast** – An IPv6 unicast address uniquely identifies an interface on an IPv6-enabled device. As shown in the figure, a source IPv6 address must be a unicast address.

■ **Multicast** – An IPv6 multicast address is used to send a single IPv6 packet to multiple destinations.

■ **Anycast** – An IPv6 anycast address is any IPv6 unicast address that can be assigned to multiple devices. A packet sent to an anycast address is routed to the nearest device having that address. Anycast addresses are beyond the scope of this course.

Unlike IPv4, IPv6 does not have a broadcast address. However, there is an IPv6 all-nodes multicast address that essentially gives the same result.

Refer to **Online Course** for Illustration

7.2.3.2   IPv6 Prefix Length

Recall that the prefix, or network portion, of an IPv4 address, can be identified by a dotted-decimal subnet mask or prefix length (slash notation). For example, an IPv4 address of 192.168.1.10 with dotted-decimal subnet mask 255.255.255.0 is equivalent to 192.168.1.10/24.

IPv6 uses the prefix length to represent the prefix portion of the address. IPv6 does not use the dotted-decimal subnet mask notation. The prefix length is used to indicate the network portion of an IPv6 address using the IPv6 address/prefix length.

The prefix length can range from 0 to 128. A typical IPv6 prefix length for LANs and most other types of networks is /64. This means the prefix or network portion of the address is 64 bits in length, leaving another 64 bits for the interface ID (host portion) of the address.

Refer to **Online Course** for Illustration

7.2.3.3   IPv6 Unicast Addresses

An IPv6 unicast address uniquely identifies an interface on an IPv6-enabled device. A packet sent to a unicast address is received by the interface that is assigned that address. Similar to IPv4, a source IPv6 address must be a unicast address. The destination IPv6 address can be either a unicast or a multicast address.

The most common types of IPv6 unicast addresses are global unicast addresses (GUA) and link-local unicast addresses.

Global unicast

A global unicast address is similar to a public IPv4 address. These are globally unique, Internet routable addresses. Global unicast addresses can be configured statically or assigned dynamically.

Link-local

Link-local addresses are used to communicate with other devices on the same local link. With IPv6, the term link refers to a subnet. Link-local addresses are confined to a single link. Their uniqueness must only be confirmed on that link because they are not routable beyond the link. In other words, routers will not forward packets with a link-local source or destination address.

Unique local

Another type of unicast address is the unique local unicast address. IPv6 unique local addresses have some similarity to RFC 1918 private addresses for IPv4, but there are significant differences. Unique local addresses are used for local addressing within a site or between a limited number of sites. These addresses should not be routable in the global IPv6 and should not be translated to a global IPv6 address. Unique local addresses are in the range of FC00::/7 to FDFF::/7.

With IPv4, private addresses are combined with NAT/PAT to provide a many-to-one translation of private-to-public addresses. This is done because of the limited availability of IPv4 address space. Many sites also use the private nature of RFC 1918 addresses to help secure or hide their network from potential security risks. However, this was never the intended use of these technologies, and the IETF has always recommended that sites take the proper security precautions on their Internet-facing router. Unique local addresses can be used for devices that will never need or have access from another network.

Refer to the Chapter Appendix for more information on other types of IPv6 unicast addresses including loopback, unspecified and embedded IPv4.

Refer to
Online Course
for Illustration

7.2.3.4   IPv6 Link-Local Unicast Addresses

An IPv6 link-local address enables a device to communicate with other IPv6-enabled devices on the same link and only on that link (subnet). Packets with a source or destination link-local address cannot be routed beyond the link from which the packet originated.

The global unicast address is not a requirement. However, every IPv6-enabled network interface is required to have a link-local address.

If a link-local address is not configured manually on an interface, the device will automatically create its own without communicating with a DHCP server. IPv6-enabled hosts create an IPv6 link-local address even if the device has not been assigned a global unicast IPv6 address. This allows IPv6-enabled devices to communicate with other IPv6-enabled devices on the same subnet. This includes communication with the default gateway (router).

IPv6 link-local addresses are in the FE80::/10 range. The /10 indicates that the first 10 bits are 1111 1110 10xx xxxx. The first hextet has a range of 1111 1110 10**00 0000** (FE80) to 1111 1110 10**11 1111** (FEBF).

Figure 1 shows an example of communication using IPv6 link-local addresses.

Figure 2 shows some of the uses for IPv6 link-local addresses.

Note   Typically, it is the link-local address of the router and not the global unicast address, that is used as the default gateway for other devices on the link.

Refer to
Interactive Graphic
in online course

7.2.3.5   Activity – Identify Types of IPv6 Addresses

Refer to
Online Course
for Illustration

7.2.4   IPv6 Unicast Addresses

7.2.4.1   Structure of an IPv6 Global Unicast Address

IPv6 global unicast addresses are globally unique and routable on the IPv6 Internet. These addresses are equivalent to public IPv4 addresses. The Internet Committee for Assigned Names and Numbers (ICANN), the operator for IANA, allocates IPv6 address blocks to the five RIRs. Currently, only global unicast addresses with the first three bits of 001 or 2000::/3 are being assigned. This is only 1/8th of the total available IPv6 address space, excluding only a very small portion for other types of unicast and multicast addresses.

Note   The 2001:0DB8::/32 address has been reserved for documentation purposes, including use in examples.

Figure 1 shows the structure and range of a global unicast address.

A global unicast address has three parts:

- Global routing prefix
- Subnet ID
- Interface ID

Global Routing Prefix

The global routing prefix is the prefix, or network, portion of the address that is assigned by the provider, such as an ISP, to a customer or site. Typically, RIRs assign a /48 global routing prefix to customers. This can include everyone from enterprise business networks to individual households.

Figure 2 shows the structure of a global unicast address using a /48 global routing prefix. /48 prefixes are the most common global routing prefixes assigned and will be used in most of the examples throughout this course.

For example, the IPv6 address 2001:0DB8:ACAD::/48 has a prefix that indicates that the first 48 bits (3 hextets) (2001:0DB8:ACAD) is the prefix or network portion of the address. The double colon (::) prior to the /48 prefix length means the rest of the address contains all 0s.

The size of the global routing prefix determines the size of the subnet ID.

Subnet ID

The Subnet ID is used by an organization to identify subnets within its site. The larger the subnet ID, the more subnets available.

Interface ID

The IPv6 Interface ID is equivalent to the host portion of an IPv4 address. The term Interface ID is used because a single host may have multiple interfaces, each having one or more IPv6 addresses. It is highly recommended that in most cases /64 subnets should be used. In other words a 64-bit interface ID as shown in Figure 2.

Note   Unlike IPv4, in IPv6, the all-0s and all-1s host addresses can be assigned to a device. The all-1s address can be used due to the fact that broadcast addresses are not used within IPv6. The all-0s address can also be used, but is reserved as a Subnet-Router anycast address, and should be assigned only to routers.

An easy way to read most IPv6 addresses is to count the number of hextets. As shown in Figure 3, in a /64 global unicast address the first four hextets are for the network portion of the address, with the fourth hextet indicating the Subnet ID. The remaining four hextets are for the Interface ID.

7.2.4.2   Static Configuration of a Global Unicast Address

Refer to **Online Course** for Illustration

Router Configuration

Most IPv6 configuration and verification commands in the Cisco IOS are similar to their IPv4 counterparts. In many cases, the only difference is the use of **ipv6** in place of **ip** within the commands.

The command to configure an IPv6 global unicast address on an interface is **ipv6 address** *ipv6-address/prefix-length*.

Notice that there is not a space between *ipv6-address* and *prefix-length*.

The example configuration uses the topology shown in Figure 1 and these IPv6 subnets:

- 2001:0DB8:ACAD:0001:/64 (*or* 2001:DB8:ACAD:1::/64)

- 2001:0DB8:ACAD:0002:/64 (*or* 2001:DB8:ACAD:2::/64)

- 2001:0DB8:ACAD:0003:/64 (*or* 2001:DB8:ACAD:3::/64)

Figure 1 also shows the commands required to configure the IPv6 global unicast address on the GigabitEthernet 0/0, GigabitEthernet 0/1, and Serial 0/0/0 interface of R1.

Host Configuration

Manually configuring the IPv6 address on a host is similar to configuring an IPv4 address.

As shown in Figure 2, the default gateway address configured for PC1 is 2001:DB8:ACAD:1::1. This is the global unicast address of the R1 GigabitEthernet interface on the same network. Alternatively, the default gateway address can be configured to match the link-local address of the GigabitEthernet interface. Either configuration will work.

Use the Syntax Checker in Figure 3 to configure the IPv6 global unicast address.

Just as with IPv4, configuring static addresses on clients does not scale to larger environments. For this reason, most network administrators in an IPv6 network will enable dynamic assignment of IPv6 addresses.

There are two ways in which a device can obtain an IPv6 global unicast address automatically:

- Stateless Address Autoconfiguration (SLAAC)

- DHCPv6

Note When DHCPv6 or SLAAC is used, the local router's link-local address will automatically be specified as the default gateway address.

Refer to
Online Course
for Illustration

7.2.4.3 Dynamic Configuration - SLAAC

Stateless Address Autoconfiguration (SLAAC) is a method that allows a device to obtain its prefix, prefix length, default gateway address, and other information from an *IPv6 router* without the use of a DHCPv6 server. Using SLAAC, devices rely on the local router's ICMPv6 Router Advertisement (RA) messages to obtain the necessary information.

IPv6 routers periodically send out ICMPv6 RA messages, every 200 seconds, to all IPv6-enabled devices on the network. An RA message will also be sent in response to a host sending an ICMPv6 Router Solicitation (RS) message.

IPv6 routing is not enabled by default. To enable a router as an IPv6 router, the **ipv6 unicast-routing** global configuration command must be used.

Note IPv6 addresses can be configured on a router without it being an IPv6 router.

The ICMPv6 RA message is a suggestion to a device on how to obtain an IPv6 global unicast address. The ultimate decision is up to the device's operating system. The ICMPv6 RA message includes:

- **Network prefix and prefix length** – Tells the device which network it belongs to.

- **Default gateway address** – This is an IPv6 link-local address, the source IPv6 address of the RA message.

- **DNS addresses and domain name** – Addresses of DNS servers and a domain name.

As shown in Figure 1, there are three options for RA messages:

- Option 1: SLAAC

- Option 2: SLAAC with a stateless DHCPv6 server

- Option 3: Stateful DHCPv6 (no SLAAC)

RA Option 1: SLAAC

By default, the RA message suggests that the receiving device use the information in the RA message to create its own IPv6 global unicast address and for all other information. The services of a DHCPv6 server are not required.

SLAAC is stateless, which means there is no central server (for example, a stateful DHCPv6 server) allocating global unicast addresses and keeping a list of devices and their addresses. With SLAAC, the client device uses the information in the RA message to create its own global unicast address. As shown in Figure 2, the two parts of the address are created as follows:

- **Prefix** – Received in the RA message

- **Interface ID** – Uses the EUI-64 process or by generating a random 64-bit number

Refer to
Online Course
for Illustration

7.2.4.4   Dynamic Configuration – DHCPv6

By default, the RA message is option 1, SLAAC only. The router's interface can be configured to send a router advertisement using SLAAC and stateless DHCPv6, or stateful DHCPv6 only.

RA Option 2: SLAAC and Stateless DHCPv6

With this option, the RA message suggests devices use:

- SLAAC to create its own IPv6 global unicast address

- The router's link-local address, the RA's source IPv6 address for the default gateway address.

- A stateless DHCPv6 server to obtain other information such as a DNS server address and a domain name.

A stateless DHCPv6 server distributes DNS server addresses and domain names. It does not allocate global unicast addresses.

RA Option 3: Stateful DHCPv6

Stateful DHCPv6 is similar to DHCP for IPv4. A device can automatically receive its addressing information including a global unicast address, prefix length, and the addresses of DNS servers using the services of a stateful DHCPv6 server.

With this option the RA message suggests devices use:

- The router's link-local address, the RA's source IPv6 address for the default gateway address.

- A stateful DHCPv6 server to obtain a global unicast address, DNS server address, domain name and all other information.

A stateful DHCPv6 server allocates and maintains a list of which device receives which IPv6 address. DHCP for IPv4 is stateful.

Note   The default gateway address can only be obtained dynamically from the RA message. The stateless or stateful DHCPv6 server does not provide the default gateway address.

Refer to **Online Course** for Illustration

7.2.4.5   EUI-64 Process and Randomly Generated

When the RA message is either SLAAC or SLAAC with stateless DHCPv6, the client must generate its own Interface ID. The client knows the prefix portion of the address from the RA message but must create its own Interface ID. The Interface ID can be created using the EUI-64 process or a randomly generated 64-bit number, as shown in Figure 1.

EUI-64 Process

IEEE defined the Extended Unique Identifier (EUI) or modified EUI-64 process. This process uses a client's 48-bit Ethernet MAC address, and inserts another 16 bits in the middle of the 48-bit MAC address to create a 64-bit Interface ID.

Ethernet MAC addresses are usually represented in hexadecimal and are made up of two parts:

- **Organizationally Unique Identifier (OUI)** – The OUI is a 24-bit (6 hexadecimal digits) vendor code assigned by IEEE.

- **Device Identifier** – The device identifier is a unique 24-bit (6 hexadecimal digits) value within a common OUI.

An EUI-64 Interface ID is represented in binary and is made up of three parts:

- 24-bit OUI from the client MAC address, but the 7th bit (the Universally/Locally (U/L) bit) is reversed. This means that if the 7th bit is a 0, it becomes a 1, and vice versa.

- The inserted 16-bit value FFFE (in hexadecimal)

- 24-bit Device Identifier from the client MAC address

The EUI-64 process is illustrated in Figure 2, using R1's GigabitEthernet MAC address of FC99:4775:CEE0.

Step 1.   Divide the MAC address between the OUI and device identifier.

Step 2.   Insert the hexadecimal value FFFE, which in binary is: 1111 1111 1111 1110.

Step 3.   Convert the first 2 hexadecimal values of the OUI to binary and flip the U/L bit (bit 7). In this example, the 0 in bit 7 is changed to a 1.

The result is an EUI-64 generated Interface ID of FE99:47FF:FE75:CEE0.

Note   The use of the U/L bit, and the reasons for reversing its value, are discussed in RFC 5342.

Figure 3 shows PCA's IPv6 global unicast address dynamically created using SLAAC and the EUI-64 process. An easy way to identify that an address was more than likely created using EUI-64 is the FFFE located in the middle of the Interface ID, as shown in Figure 3.

The advantage of EUI-64 is the Ethernet MAC address can be used to determine the Interface ID. It also allows network administrators to easily track an IPv6 address to an end-device using the unique MAC address. However, this has caused privacy concerns among many users. They are concerned that their packets can be traced to the actual physical computer. Due to these concerns, a randomly generated Interface ID may be used instead.

Randomly Generated Interface IDs

Depending upon the operating system, a device may use a randomly generated Interface ID instead of using the MAC address and the EUI-64 process. For example, beginning with Windows Vista, Windows uses a randomly generated Interface ID instead of one created with EUI-64. Windows XP and previous Windows operating systems used EUI-64.

After the Interface ID is established, either through the EUI-64 process or through random generation, it can be combined with an IPv6 prefix in the RA message to create a global unicast address, as shown in Figure 4.

Note   To ensure the uniqueness of any IPv6 unicast address, the client may use a process known as Duplicate Address Detection (DAD). This is similar to an ARP request for its own address. If there isn't a reply, then the address is unique.

Refer to
Online Course
for Illustration

7.2.4.6   Dynamic Link-Local Addresses

All IPv6 devices must have an IPv6 link-local address. A link-local address can be established dynamically or configured manually as a static link-local address.

Figure 1 shows the link-local address is dynamically created using the FE80::/10 prefix and the Interface ID using the EUI-64 process or a randomly generated 64-bit number. Operating systems will typically use the same method for both a SLAAC created global unicast address and a dynamically assigned link-local address, as shown in Figure 2.

Cisco routers automatically create an IPv6 link-local address whenever a global unicast address is assigned to the interface. By default, Cisco IOS routers use EUI-64 to generate the Interface ID for all link-local address on IPv6 interfaces. For serial interfaces, the router will use the MAC address of an Ethernet interface. Recall that a link-local address must be unique only on that link or network. However, a drawback to using the dynamically assigned link-local address is its length, which makes it challenging to identify and remember assigned addresses. Figure 3 displays the MAC address on router R1's GigabitEthernet 0/0 interface. This address is used to dynamically create the link-local address on the same interface.

To make it easier to recognize and remember these addresses on routers, it is common to statically configure IPv6 link-local addresses on routers.

Refer to
Online Course
for Illustration

7.2.4.7   Static Link-Local Addresses

Configuring the link-local address manually provides the ability to create an address that is recognizable and easier to remember.

Link-local addresses can be configured manually using the same interface command used to create IPv6 global unicast addresses but with the additional **link-local** parameter. When an address begins with this hextet within the range of FE80 to FEBF, the link-local parameter must follow the address.

The figure shows the configuration of a link-local address using the **ipv6 address** interface command. The link-local address FE80::1 is used to make it easily recognizable as belonging to router R1. The same IPv6 link-local address is configured on all of R1's interfaces. FE80::1 can be configured on each link because it only has to be unique on that link.

Similar to R1, router R2 would be configured with FE80::2 as the IPv6 link-local address on all of its interfaces.

Refer to
Online Course
for Illustration

7.2.4.8   Verifying IPv6 Address Configuration

As shown in Figure 1, the command to verify the IPv6 interface configuration is similar to the command used for IPv4.

The **show interface** command displays the MAC address of the Ethernet interfaces. EUI-64 uses this MAC address to generate the Interface ID for the link-local address. Additionally, the **show ipv6 interface brief** command displays abbreviated output for each of the interfaces. The **[up/up]** output on the same line as the interface indicates the Layer 1/Layer 2 interface state. This is the same as the **Status** and **Protocol** columns in the equivalent IPv4 command.

Notice that each interface has two IPv6 addresses. The second address for each interface is the global unicast address that was configured. The first address, the one that begins with FE80, is the link-local unicast address for the interface. Recall that the link-local address is automatically added to the interface when a global unicast address is assigned.

Also, notice that R1's Serial 0/0/0 link-local address is the same as its GigabitEthernet 0/0 interface. Serial interfaces do not have Ethernet MAC addresses, so Cisco IOS uses the MAC address of the first available Ethernet interface. This is possible because link-local interfaces only have to be unique on that link.

The link-local address of the router interface is typically the default gateway address for devices on that link or network.

As shown in Figure 2, the **show ipv6 route** command can be used to verify that IPv6 networks and specific IPv6 interface addresses have been installed in the IPv6 routing table. The **show ipv6 route** command will only display IPv6 networks, not IPv4 networks.

Within the route table, a **C** next to a route indicates that this is a directly connected network. When the router interface is configured with a global unicast address and is in the "up/up" state, the IPv6 prefix and prefix length is added to the IPv6 routing table as a connected route.

The IPv6 global unicast address configured on the interface is also installed in the routing table as a local route. The local route has a /128 prefix. Local routes are used by the routing table to efficiently process packets with a destination address of the router's interface address.

The **ping** command for IPv6 is identical to the command used with IPv4, except that an IPv6 address is used. As shown in Figure 3, the command is used to verify Layer 3 connectivity between R1 and PC1. When pinging a link-local address from a router, Cisco IOS will prompt the user for the exit interface. Because the destination link-local address can be on one or more of its links or networks, the router needs to know which interface to send the ping to.

Use the Syntax Checker in Figure 4 to verify IPv6 address configuration.

Refer to **Packet Tracer Activity** for this chapter

7.2.4.9   Packet Tracer – Configuring IPv6 Addressing

In this activity, you will practice configuring IPv6 addresses on a router, servers, and clients. You will also practice verifying your IPv6 addressing implementation.

Refer to **Online Course** for Illustration

7.2.5   IPv6 Multicast Addresses

7.2.5.1   Assigned IPv6 Multicast Addresses

IPv6 multicast addresses are similar to IPv4 multicast addresses. Recall that a multicast address is used to send a single packet to one or more destinations (multicast group). IPv6 multicast addresses have the prefix FF00::/8.

Note   Multicast addresses can only be destination addresses and not source addresses.

There are two types of IPv6 multicast addresses:

■ Assigned multicast

■ Solicited node multicast

Assigned Multicast

Assigned multicast addresses are reserved multicast addresses for predefined groups of devices. An assigned multicast address is a single address used to reach a group of devices running a common protocol or service. Assigned multicast addresses are used in context with specific protocols such as DHCPv6.

Two common IPv6 assigned multicast groups include:

- **FF02::1 All-nodes multicast group** – This is a multicast group that all IPv6-enabled devices join. A packet sent to this group is received and processed by all IPv6 interfaces on the link or network. This has the same effect as a broadcast address in IPv4. The figure shows an example of communication using the all-nodes multicast address. An IPv6 router sends Internet Control Message Protocol version 6 (ICMPv6) RA messages to the all-node multicast group. The RA message informs all IPv6-enabled devices on the network about addressing information, such as the prefix, prefix length, and default gateway.

- **FF02::2 All-routers multicast group** – This is a multicast group that all IPv6 routers join. A router becomes a member of this group when it is enabled as an IPv6 router with the **ipv6 unicast-routing** global configuration command. A packet sent to this group is received and processed by all IPv6 routers on the link or network.

IPv6-enabled devices send ICMPv6 Router Solicitation (RS) messages to the all-routers multicast address. The RS message requests an RA message from the IPv6 router to assist the device in its address configuration.

Refer to
Online Course
for Illustration

7.2.5.2   Solicited-Node IPv6 Multicast Addresses

A solicited-node multicast address is similar to the all-nodes multicast address. The advantage of a solicited-node multicast address is that it is mapped to a special Ethernet multicast address. This allows the Ethernet NIC to filter the frame by examining the destination MAC address without sending it to the IPv6 process to see if the device is the intended target of the IPv6 packet.

Refer to the Chapter Appendix for more information on the solicited-node multicast address.

Refer to
Lab Activity
for this chapter

7.2.5.3   Lab – Identifying IPv6 Addresses

In this lab, you will complete the following objectives:

- Part 1: Identify the Different Types of IPv6 Addresses
- Part 2: Examine a Host IPv6 Network Interface and Address
- Part 3: Practice IPv6 Address Abbreviation

Refer to
Lab Activity
for this chapter

7.2.5.4   Lab – Configuring IPv6 Addresses on Network Devices

In this lab, you will complete the following objectives:

- Part 1: Set Up Topology and Configure Basic Router and Switch Settings
- Part 2: Configure IPv6 Addresses Manually
- Part 3: Verify End-to-End Connectivity

Refer to
Online Course
for Illustration

7.3 Connectivity Verification

7.3.1 ICMP

7.3.1.1 ICMPv4 and ICMPv6

Although IP is not a reliable protocol, the TCP/IP suite does provide for messages to be sent in the event of certain errors. These messages are sent using the services of ICMP. The purpose of these messages is to provide feedback about issues related to the processing of IP packets under certain conditions, not to make IP reliable. ICMP messages are not required and are often not allowed within a network for security reasons.

ICMP is available for both IPv4 and IPv6. ICMPv4 is the messaging protocol for IPv4. ICMPv6 provides these same services for IPv6 but includes additional functionality. In this course, the term ICMP will be used when referring to both ICMPv4 and ICMPv6.

The types of ICMP messages and the reasons why they are sent, are extensive. We will discuss some of the more common messages.

ICMP messages common to both ICMPv4 and ICMPv6 include:

- Host confirmation
- Destination or Service Unreachable
- Time exceeded
- Route redirection

Host Confirmation

An ICMP Echo Message can be used to determine if a host is operational. The local host sends an ICMP Echo Request to a host. If the host is available, the destination host responds with an Echo Reply. In the figure, click the Play button to see an animation of the ICMP Echo Request/Echo Reply. This use of the ICMP Echo messages is the basis of the ping utility.

Destination or Service Unreachable

When a host or gateway receives a packet that it cannot deliver, it can use an ICMP Destination Unreachable message to notify the source that the destination or service is unreachable. The message will include a code that indicates why the packet could not be delivered.

Some of the Destination Unreachable codes for ICMPv4 are:

- 0 - Net unreachable
- 1 - Host unreachable
- 2 - Protocol unreachable
- 3 - Port unreachable

Note ICMPv6 has similar but slightly different codes for Destination Unreachable messages.

Time Exceeded

An ICMPv4 Time Exceeded message is used by a router to indicate that a packet cannot be forwarded because the Time to Live (TTL) field of the packet was decremented to 0. If a router receives a packet and decrements the TTL field in the IPv4 packet to zero, it discards the packet and sends a Time Exceeded message to the source host.

ICMPv6 also sends a Time Exceeded message if the router cannot forward an IPv6 packet because the packet has expired. IPv6 does not have a TTL field; it uses the hop limit field to determine if the packet has expired.

Refer to
Online Course
for Illustration

7.3.1.2   ICMPv6 Router Solicitation and Router Advertisement Messages

The informational and error messages found in ICMPv6 are very similar to the control and error messages implemented by ICMPv4. However, ICMPv6 has new features and improved functionality not found in ICMPv4. ICMPv6 messages are encapsulated in IPv6.

ICMPv6 includes four new protocols as part of the Neighbor Discovery Protocol (ND or NDP).

Messaging between an IPv6 router and an IPv6 device:

- Router Solicitation (RS) message
- Router Advertisement (RA) message

Messaging between IPv6 devices:

- Neighbor Solicitation message
- Neighbor Advertisement message

Figure 1 shows an example of a PC and router exchanging Solicitation and Router Advertisement messages. Click each message for more information.

Neighbor Solicitation and Neighbor Advertisement messages are used for Address resolution and Duplicate Address Detection (DAD).

Address Resolution

Address resolution is used when a device on the LAN knows the IPv6 unicast address of a destination but does not know its Ethernet MAC address. To determine the MAC address for the destination, the device will send an NS message to the solicited node address. The message will include the known (targeted) IPv6 address. The device that has the targeted IPv6 address will respond with an NA message containing its Ethernet MAC address. Figure 2 shows two PCs exchanging NS and NA messages. Click each message for more information.

Duplicate Address Detection

When a device is assigned a global unicast or link-local unicast address, it is recommended that DAD is performed on the address to ensure that it is unique. To check the uniqueness of an address, the device will send an NS message with its own IPv6 address as the targeted IPv6 address, shown in Figure 3. If another device on the network has this address, it will respond with an NA message. This NA message will notify the sending device that the address is in use. If a corresponding NA message is not returned within a certain period of time, the unicast address is unique and acceptable for use.

Note DAD is not required, but RFC 4861 recommends that DAD is performed on unicast addresses.

Refer to **Online Course** for Illustration

7.3.2 Testing and Verification

7.3.2.1 Ping - Testing the Local Stack

Ping is a testing utility that uses ICMP echo request and echo reply messages to test connectivity between hosts. Ping works with both IPv4 and IPv6 hosts.

To test connectivity to another host on a network, an echo request is sent to the host address using the ping command. If the host at the specified address receives the echo request, it responds with an echo reply. As each echo reply is received, ping provides feedback on the time between when the request was sent and when the reply was received. This can be a measure of network performance.

Ping has a timeout value for the reply. If a reply is not received within the timeout, ping provides a message indicating that a response was not received. This usually indicates that there is a problem, but could also indicate that security features blocking ping messages have been enabled on the network.

After all the requests are sent, the ping utility provides a summary that includes the success rate and average round-trip time to the destination.

Pinging the Local Loopback

There are some special testing and verification cases for which we can use ping. One case is for testing the internal configuration of IPv4 or IPv6 on the local host. To perform this test, we ping the local loopback address of 127.0.0.1 for IPv4 (::1 for IPv6). Testing the IPv4 loopback is shown in the figure.

A response from 127.0.0.1 for IPv4, or ::1 for IPv6, indicates that IP is properly installed on the host. This response comes from the network layer. This response is not, however, an indication that the addresses, masks, or gateways are properly configured. Nor does it indicate anything about the status of the lower layer of the network stack. This simply tests IP down through the network layer of IP. An error message indicates that TCP/IP is not operational on the host.

Refer to **Online Course** for Illustration

7.3.2.2 Ping – Testing Connectivity to the Local LAN

You can also use ping to test the ability of a host to communicate on the local network. This is generally done by pinging the IP address of the gateway of the host. A ping to the gateway indicates that the host and the router interface serving as the gateway are both operational on the local network.

For this test, the gateway address is most often used because the router is normally always operational. If the gateway address does not respond, a ping can be sent to the IP address of another host on the local network that is known to be operational.

If either the gateway or another host responds, then the local host can successfully communicate over the local network. If the gateway does not respond but another host does, this could indicate a problem with the router interface serving as the gateway.

One possibility is that the wrong gateway address has been configured on the host. Another possibility is that the router interface may be fully operational but have security applied to it that prevents it from processing or responding to ping requests.

Refer to **Online Course** for Illustration

7.3.2.3   Ping – Testing Connectivity to Remote

Ping can also be used to test the ability of a local host to communicate across an internetwork. The local host can ping an operational IPv4 host of a remote network, as shown in the figure.

If this ping is successful, the operation of a large piece of the internetwork can be verified. A successful ping across the internetwork confirms communication on the local network, the operation of the router serving as the gateway, and the operation of all other routers that might be in the path between the local network and the network of the remote host.

Additionally, the functionality of the remote host can be verified. If the remote host could not communicate outside of its local network, it would not have responded.

Note   Many network administrators limit or prohibit the entry of ICMP messages into the corporate network; therefore, the lack of a ping response could be due to security restrictions.

Refer to **Online Course** for Illustration

7.3.2.4   Traceroute – Testing the Path

Ping is used to test connectivity between two hosts but does not provide information about the details of devices between the hosts. Traceroute (tracert) is a utility that generates a list of hops that were successfully reached along the path. This list can provide important verification and troubleshooting information. If the data reaches the destination, then the trace lists the interface of every router in the path between the hosts. If the data fails at some hop along the way, the address of the last router that responded to the trace can provide an indication of where the problem or security restrictions are found.

Round Trip Time (RTT)

Using traceroute provides round trip time for each hop along the path and indicates if a hop fails to respond. The round trip time is the time a packet takes to reach the remote host and for the response from the host to return. An asterisk (*) is used to indicate a lost or unreplied packet.

This information can be used to locate a problematic router in the path. If the display shows high response times or data losses from a particular hop, this is an indication that the resources of the router or its connections may be stressed.

IPv4 TTL and IPv6 Hop Limit

Traceroute makes use of a function of the TTL field in IPv4 and the Hop Limit field in IPv6 in the Layer 3 headers, along with the ICMP time exceeded message.

Play the animation in the figure to see how Traceroute takes advantage of TTL.

The first sequence of messages sent from traceroute will have a TTL field value of 1. This causes the TTL to time out the IPv4 packet at the first router. This router then responds with an ICMPv4 message. Traceroute now has the address of the first hop.

Traceroute then progressively increments the TTL field (2, 3, 4...) for each sequence of messages. This provides the trace with the address of each hop as the packets timeout further down the path. The TTL field continues to be increased until the destination is reached, or it is incremented to a predefined maximum.

After the final destination is reached, the host responds with either an ICMP port unreachable message or an ICMP echo reply message instead of the ICMP time exceeded message.

Refer to Packet Tracer Activity for this chapter

7.3.2.5   Packet Tracer – Verifying IPv4 and IPv6 Addressing

IPv4 and IPv6 can coexist on the same network. From the command prompt of a PC, there are some differences in the way commands are issued and in the way output is displayed.

Refer to Packet Tracer Activity for this chapter

7.3.2.6   Packet Tracer – Pinging and Tracing to Test the Path

There are connectivity issues in this activity. In addition to gathering and documenting information about the network, you will locate the problems and implement acceptable solutions to restore connectivity.

Refer to Lab Activity for this chapter

7.3.2.7   Lab – Testing Network Connectivity with Ping and Traceroute

In this lab, you will complete the following objectives:

■ Part 1: Build and Configure the Network

■ Part 2: Use Ping Command for Basic Network Testing

■ Part 3: Use Tracert and Traceroute Commands for Basic Network Testing

■ Part 4: Troubleshoot the Topology

Refer to Lab Activity for this chapter

7.3.2.8   Lab – Mapping the Internet

In this lab, you will complete the following objectives:

■ Part 1: Test Network Connectivity Using Ping

■ Part 2: Trace a Route to a Remote Server Using Windows Tracert

■ Part 3: Trace a Route to a Remote Server Using Web-Based and Software Tools

■ Part 4: Compare Traceroute Results

Refer to Packet Tracer Activity for this chapter

7.3.2.9   Packet Tracer – Troubleshooting IPv4 and IPv6 Addressing

You are a network technician working for a company that has decided to migrate from IPv4 to IPv6. In the interim, they must support both protocols (dual stack). Three co-workers have called the help desk with problems and have received limited assistance. The help desk has escalated the matter to you, a Level 2 support technician.

7.4   Summary

7.4.1   Conclusion

Refer to **Lab Activity** for this chapter

7.4.1.1   Class Activity – The Internet of Everything...Naturally!

In this chapter, you learned about how small to medium-sized businesses are connected to networks in groups. The Internet of Everything was also introduced in the beginning modeling activity.

For this activity, choose one of the following:

- Online banking
- World news
- Weather forecasting/climate
- Traffic conditions

Devise an IPv6 addressing scheme for the area you chose. Include in your addressing scheme how you would plan for:

- Subnetting
- Unicasts
- Multicasts
- Broadcasts

Keep a copy of your scheme to share with the class or learning community. Be prepared to explain:

- How subnetting, unicasts, multicasts and broadcasts would be incorporated.
- Where your addressing scheme could be used.
- How small to medium-size businesses would be impacted by using your plan.

Refer to **Packet Tracer Activity** for this chapter

7.4.1.2   Packet Tracer – Skills Integration Challenge

Your company has won a contract to set up a small network for a restaurant owner. There are two restaurants near each other, and they all share one connection. The equipment and cabling is installed, and the network administrator has designed the implementation plan. Your job is to implement the rest of the addressing scheme according to the abbreviated Addressing Table and verify connectivity.

Refer to **Online Course** for Illustration

7.4.1.3   IP Addressing

IP addresses are hierarchical with network, subnetwork, and host portions. An IP address can represent a complete network, a specific host, or the broadcast address of the network.

Understanding binary notation is important when determining if two hosts are in the same network. The bits within the network portion of the IP address must be identical for all devices that reside in the same network. The subnet mask or prefix is used to determine the network portion of an IP address. IP addresses can be assigned either statically or dynamically. DHCP enables the automatic assignment of addressing information such as IP address, subnet mask, default gateway, and other configuration information.

IPv4 hosts can communicate one of three different ways: unicast, broadcast, or multicast. Also, blocks of addresses that are used in networks that require limited or no Internet access are called private addresses. The private IPv4 address blocks are: 10.0.0.0/8, 172.16.0.0/12 and 192.168.0.0/16.

The depletion of IPv4 address space is the motivating factor for moving to IPv6. Each IPv6 address has 128 bits versus the 32 bits in an IPv4 address. IPv6 does not use the dotted-decimal subnet mask notation. The prefix length is used to indicate the network portion of an IPv6 address using the following format: IPv6 address/prefix length.

There are three types of IPv6 addresses: unicast, multicast, and anycast. An IPv6 link-local address enables a device to communicate with other IPv6-enabled devices on the same link and only on that link (subnet). Packets with a source or destination link-local address cannot be routed beyond the link from which the packet originated. IPv6 link-local addresses are in the FE80::/10 range.

ICMP is available for both IPv4 and IPv6. ICMPv4 is the messaging protocol for IPv4. ICMPv6 provides the same services for IPv6 but includes additional functionality.

After it is implemented, an IP network needs to be tested to verify its connectivity and operational performance.

Go to the online course to take the quiz and exam.

Chapter 7 Quiz

This quiz is designed to provide an additional opportunity to practice the skills and knowledge presented in the chapter and to prepare for the chapter exam. You will be allowed multiple attempts and the grade does not appear in the gradebook.

Chapter 7 Exam

The chapter exam assesses your knowledge of the chapter content.

Your Chapter Notes

Subnetting IP Networks

8.0 Introduction

8.0.1.1 Subnetting IP Networks

Designing, implementing and managing an effective IP addressing plan ensures that networks can operate effectively and efficiently. This is especially true as the number of host connections to a network increases. Understanding the hierarchical structure of the IP address and how to modify that hierarchy in order to more efficiently meet routing requirements is an important part of planning an IP addressing scheme.

In the original IPv4 address, there are two levels of hierarchy: a network and a host. These two levels of addressing allow for basic network groupings that facilitate in routing packets to a destination network. A router forwards packets based on the network portion of an IP address. When the network is located, the host portion of the address allows for identification of the destination device.

However, as networks grow, with many organizations adding hundreds, and even thousands of hosts to their network, the two-level hierarchy is insufficient.

Subdividing a network adds a level to the network hierarchy, creating, in essence, three levels: a network, a subnetwork, and a host. Introducing an additional level to the hierarchy creates additional sub-groups within an IP network that facilitates faster packet delivery and added filtration, by helping to minimize 'local' traffic.

This chapter examines, in detail, the creation and assignment of IP network and subnetwork addresses through the use of the subnet mask.

Refer to **Lab Activity** for this chapter

8.0.1.2 Class Activity – Call Me!

In this chapter, you will be learning how devices can be grouped into subnets, or smaller network groups, from a large network.

In this modeling activity, you are asked to think about a number you probably use every day, a number such as your telephone number. As you complete the activity, think about how your telephone number compares to strategies that network administrators might use to identify hosts for efficient data communication.

Complete the two questions listed below and record your answers. Save the two sections in either hard- or soft-copy format to use later for class discussion purposes.

- Explain how your smartphone or landline telephone number is divided into identifying groups of numbers. Does your telephone number use an area code? An ISP identifier? A city, state, or country code?

- In what ways does separating your telephone number into managed parts assist in contacting or communicating with others?

Refer to
Online Course
for Illustration

8.1   Subnetting an IPv4 Network

8.1.1   Network Segmentation

8.1.1.1   Broadcast Domains

In an Ethernet LAN, devices use broadcasts to locate:

- **Other devices** – A device uses Address Resolution Protocol (ARP) which sends Layer 2 broadcasts to a known IPv4 address on the local network to discover the associated MAC address.

- **Services** – A host typically acquires its IP address configuration using the Dynamic Host Configuration Protocol (DHCP) which sends broadcasts on the local network to locate a DHCP server.

Switches propagate broadcasts out all interfaces except the interface on which it was received. For example, if a switch in the figure were to receive a broadcast, it would forward it to the other switches and other users connected in the network.

Routers do not propagate broadcasts. When a router receives a broadcast, it does not forward it out other interfaces. For instance, when R1 receives a broadcast on its Gigabit Ethernet 0/0 interface, it does not forward out another interface.

Therefore, each router interface connects a *broadcast domain* and broadcasts are only propagated within its specific broadcast domain.

Refer to
Online Course
for Illustration

8.1.1.2   Problems with Large Broadcast Domains

A large broadcast domain is a network that connects many hosts. A problem with a large broadcast domain is that these hosts can generate excessive broadcasts and negatively affect the network. In Figure 1, LAN 1 connects 400 users that could generate broadcast traffic resulting in:

- Slow network operations due to the significant amount of traffic it can cause

- Slow device operations because a device must accept and process each broadcast packet

The solution is to reduce the size of the network to create smaller broadcast domains in a process called *subnetting*. These smaller network spaces are called *subnets*.

In Figure 2 for example, the 400 users in LAN 1 with network address 172.16.0.0 /16 have been divided into two subnets of 200 users each; 172.16.0.0 /24 and 172.16.1.0 /24. Broadcasts are only propagated within the smaller broadcast domains. Therefore a broadcast in LAN 1 would not propagate to LAN 2.

Notice how the prefix length has changed from a /16 to a /24. This is the basis of subnetting; using host bits to create additional subnets.

Note   The terms *subnet* and *network* are often used interchangeably. Most networks are a subnet of some larger address block.

Refer to
Online Course
for Illustration

8.1.1.3   Reasons for Subnetting

Subnetting reduces overall network traffic and improves network performance. It also enables an administrator to implement security policies such as which subnets are allowed or not allowed to communicate together.

There are various ways of using subnets to help manage network devices. Network administrators can group devices and services into subnets that are determined by:

■ Location, such as floors in a building (Figure 1)

■ Organizational unit (Figure 2)

■ Device type (Figure 3)

■ Any other division that makes sense for the network.

Notice in each figure, the subnets use longer prefix lengths to identify networks.

This chapter describes how subnetting is performed. Understanding how to subnet networks is a fundamental skill that all network administrators must develop. Various methods have been developed to help understand this process. This chapter will focus on looking at the binary method. Although a little overwhelming at first, focus and pay close attention to the detail and with practice, subnetting should become easier.

Refer to
Online Course
for Illustration

8.1.2   Subnetting an IPv4 Network

8.1.2.1   Octet Boundaries

Every interface on a router is connected to a network. The IP address and subnet mask configured on the router interface are used to identify the specific broadcast domain. Recall that the prefix length and the subnet mask are different ways of identifying the network portion of an address.

IPv4 subnets are created by using one or more of the host bits as network bits. This is done by extending the subnet mask to borrow some of the bits from the host portion of the address to create additional network bits. The more host bits that are borrowed, the more subnets that can be defined.

Networks are most easily subnetted at the octet boundary of /8, /16, and /24. The table in the figure identifies these prefix lengths, equivalent subnet masks, the network and host bits, and the number of hosts each subnet can connect. Notice that using longer prefix lengths decreases the number of hosts per subnet.

Refer to
Online Course
for Illustration

8.1.2.2   Subnetting on the Octet Boundary

To understand how subnetting on the octet boundary can be useful, consider the following example. Assume an enterprise has chosen the private address 10.0.0.0/8 as its internal network address. That network address can connect 16,777,214 hosts in one broadcast domain. Obviously, this is not ideal.

The enterprise could further subnet the 10.0.0.0/8 address at the octet boundary of /16 as shown in Figure 1. This would provide the enterprise the ability to define up to 256 subnets (i.e., 10.0.0.0/16 – 10.255.0.0/16) with each subnet capable of connecting 65,534 hosts. Notice how the first two octets identify the network portion of the address while the last two octets are for host IP addresses.

Alternatively, the enterprise could choose to subnet at the /24 octet boundary as shown in Figure 2. This would enable the enterprise to define 65,536 subnets each capable of connecting 254 hosts. The /24 boundary is very popular in subnetting because it accommodates a reasonable number of hosts and conveniently subnets at the octet boundary.

Refer to **Online Course** for Illustration

8.1.2.3   Classless Subnetting

The examples seen so far borrowed host bits from the common /8, /16, and /24 network prefixes. However, subnets can borrow bits from *any* host bit position to create other masks.

For instance, a /24 network address is commonly subnetted using longer prefix lengths by borrowing bits from the fourth octet. This provides the administrator with additional flexibility when assigning network addresses to a smaller number of end devices.

As shown in the figure:

- /25 row - Borrowing 1 bit from the fourth octet creates 2 subnets supporting 126 hosts each.

- /26 row - Borrowing 2 bits creates 4 subnets supporting 62 hosts each.

- /27 row – Borrowing 3 bits creates 8 subnets supporting 30 hosts each.

- /28 row – Borrowing 4 bits creates 16 subnets supporting 14 hosts each.

- /29 row – Borrowing 5 bits creates 32 subnets supporting 6 hosts each.

- /30 row – Borrowing 6 bits creates 64 subnets supporting 2 hosts each.

For each bit borrowed in the fourth octet, the number of subnetworks available is doubled while reducing the number of host addresses per subnet.

Refer to **Video** in online course

8.1.2.4   Video Demonstration – The Subnet Mask

Click Play to view an explanation of the subnet mask.

Click here to read the transcript of this video.

Refer to **Video** in online course

8.1.2.5   Video Demonstration – Subnetting with the Magic Number

Click Play to view an explanation of the magic number.

Click here to read the transcript of this video.

Refer to **Online Course** for Illustration

8.1.2.6   Classless Subnetting Example

To understand how subnetting at a classless level can be useful, consider the following examples.

Consider the private network address 192.168.1.0/24 shown in Figure 1. The first three octets are displayed in decimal, while the last octet is displayed in binary. The reason for this is because we will be borrowing bits from the last octet to create subnets of the 192.168.1.0/24 network.

The subnet mask is 255.255.255.0 as indicated by the /24 prefix length. This identifies the first three octets as the network portion and the remaining 8 bits in the last octet as the host portion. Without subnetting, this network supports a single LAN interface providing

254 host IP addresses. If an additional LAN is needed, the network would need to be sub-netted.

In Figure 2, 1 bit is borrowed from the most significant bit (leftmost bit) in the host por-tion, thus extending the network portion to 25 bits or /25. This enables the creation of two subnets.

Figure 3 displays the two subnets: 192.168.1.0/25 and 192.168.1.128/25. The two subnets are derived from changing the value of the bit borrowed to either 0 or 1. Because the bit borrowed is the 128 bit, the decimal value of the fourth octet for the 2nd subnet is 128.

Figure 4 displays the resulting subnet mask for both networks. Notice how it uses a 1 in the borrowed bit position to indicate that this bit is now part of the network portion.

Figure 5 displays the dotted decimal representation of the two subnet addresses and their common subnet mask. Because one bit has been borrowed, the subnet mask for each sub-net is 255.255.255.128 or /25.

Refer to
Online Course
for Illustration

8.1.2.7   Creating 2 Subnets

To see how a /25 subnet is applied in a network; consider the topology in Figure 1. R1 has two LAN segments attached to its GigabitEthernet interfaces. Each LAN is assigned one of the subnets.

Figure 2 displays the important addresses of the first subnet, 192.168.1.0/25. Notice how the:

- **Network address** is 192.168.1.0 and contains all 0 bits in the host portion of the address.

- **First host address** is 192.168.1.1 and contains all 0 bits plus a right-most 1 bit in the host portion of the address.

- **Last host address** is 192.168.1.126 and contains all 1 bits plus a right-most 0 bit in the host portion of the address.

- **Broadcast address** is 192.168.1.127 and contains all 1 bits in the host portion of the address.

Figure 3 displays the important addresses of the second subnet, 192.168.1.128/25.

Router interfaces must be assigned an IP address within the valid host range for the assigned subnet. This is the address that hosts on that network will use as their default gateway. A very common practice is to use the first or last available address in a network range for the router interface address. Figure 4 shows the configuration for R1's interfaces with the first IP address for their respective subnets using the **ip address** interface configu-ration command.

Hosts on each subnet must be configured with an IP address and default gateway. Figure 5 displays the IP configuration for PC2 host on the 192.168.1.128/25 network. Notice that the default gateway IP address is the address configured on the G0/1 interface of R1, 192.168.1.129, and the subnet mask is 255.255.255.128.

Refer to **Video**
in online course

8.1.2.8   Video Demonstration – Creating Two Equal-Sized Subnets

Click Play to view a demonstration of creating two equal-sized subnets.

Click here to read the transcript of this video.

Refer to
Online Course
for Illustration

8.1.2.9   Subnetting Formulas

To calculate the number of subnets that can be created from the bits borrowed, use the formula displayed in Figure 1. Figure 2 displays the possible number of subnets that can be created when borrowing 1, 2, 3, 4, 5, or 6 bits.

Note   The last two bits cannot be borrowed from the last octet because there would be no host addresses available. Therefore, the longest prefix length possible when subnetting is /30 or 255.255.255.252.

To calculate the number of hosts that can be supported, use the formula displayed in Figure 3. There are two subnet addresses that cannot be assigned to a host, the network address and the broadcast address, so we must subtract 2.

As shown in Figure 4, there are 7 host bits remaining, so the calculation is $2^7 = 128\text{-}2 = 126$. This means that each of the subnets has 126 valid host addresses.

Therefore, borrowing 1 host bit toward the network results in creating 2 subnets, and each subnet can have a total of 126 hosts assigned.

Refer to
Online Course
for Illustration

8.1.2.10   Creating 4 Subnets

Now consider the network topology shown in Figure 1. The enterprise is using the private network address 192.168.1.0/24 range and requires three subnets. Borrowing a single bit only provided 2 subnets; therefore, another host bit must be borrowed as shown in Figure 2. Using the **2^n** formula for two borrowed bits results in **$2^2 = 4$** subnets. The specifics of the four subnets are shown in Figure 3. The resulting subnet mask of /26 or 255.255.255.192 is used by all four subnets.

To calculate the number of hosts, examine the last octet as shown in Figure 4. After borrowing 2 bits for the subnet, there are 6 host bits remaining. Apply the host calculation formula **$2^n - 2$** as shown to reveal that each subnet can support 62 host addresses. The significant addresses of the first subnet (i.e., Net 0) are displayed in Figure 5.

Only the first three subnets are required because there are only three interfaces. Figure 6 displays the specifics of the first three subnets that will be used to satisfy the topology in Figure 1.

Finally, Figure 7 applies the first valid host address from each subnet to the respective R1 LAN interface.

Refer to **Video**
in online course

8.1.2.11   Video Demonstration – Creating Four Equal-Sized Subnets

Click Play to view a demonstration of creating four equal-sized subnets.

Click here to read the transcript of this video.

Refer to **Video** in online course

8.1.2.12   Video Demonstration – Creating Eight Equal-Sized Subnets

Click Play to view a demonstration of creating eight equal-sized subnets.

Click here to read the transcript of this video.

Refer to **Online Course** for Illustration

8.1.3   Subnetting a /16 and /8 Prefix

8.1.3.1   Creating Subnets with a /16 prefix

In a situation requiring a larger number of subnets, an IP network is required that has more hosts bits to borrow from. For example, the network address 172.16.0.0 has a default mask of 255.255.0.0, or /16. This address has 16 bits in the network portion and 16 bits in the host portion. The 16 bits in the host portion are available to borrow for creating subnets. The table in the figure highlights all the possible scenarios for subnetting a /16 prefix.

Although a complete memorization of the table is not required, it is suggested that you gain a good understanding of how each value in the table is generated. Do not let the size of the table intimidate you. The reason it is big is because it has 8 additional bits that can be borrowed, and, therefore, the number of subnets and hosts are simply larger.

Refer to **Online Course** for Illustration

8.1.3.2   Creating 100 Subnets with a /16 Network

Consider a large enterprise that requires at least 100 subnets and has chosen the private address 172.16.0.0/16 as its internal network address.

When borrowing bits from a /16 address, start borrowing bits in the third octet, going from left to right. Borrow a single bit at a time until the number of bits necessary to create 100 subnets is reached.

Figure 1 displays the number of subnets that can be created when borrowing bits from the third octet and the fourth octet. Notice there is now up to 14 host bits that can be borrowed.

To satisfy the requirements of the enterprise, 7 bits (i.e., $2^7 = 128$ subnets) would need to be borrowed, as shown in Figure 2.

Recall that the subnet mask must change to reflect the borrowed bits. In this example, when 7 bits are borrowed, the mask is extended 7 bits into the third octet. In decimal, the mask is represented as 255.255.254.0, or a /23 prefix, because the third octet is 11111110 in binary and the fourth octet is 00000000 in binary.

Figure 3 displays the resulting subnets from 172.16.0.0 /23 up to 172.16.254.0 /23.

Refer to **Online Course** for Illustration

8.1.3.3   Calculating the Hosts

To calculate the number of hosts each subnet can support, examine the third and fourth octet. After borrowing 7 bits for the subnet, there is one host bit remaining in the third octet and 8 host bits remaining in the fourth octet for a total of 9 bits that were not borrowed.

Apply the host calculation formula as shown in Figure 1. There are only 510 host addresses that are available for each /23 subnet.

As shown in Figure 2, the first host address for the first subnet is 172.16.0.1, and the last host address is 172.16.1.254.

Refer to **Video**
in online course

8.1.3.4   Video Demonstration – Creating One Hundred Equal-Sized Subnets

Click Play to view a demonstration of creating 100 equal-sized subnets.

Click here to read the transcript of this video.

Refer to
Online Course
for Illustration

8.1.3.5   Creating 1000 Subnets with a /8 Network

Some organizations, such as small service providers or large enterprises, may need even more subnets. Take, for example, a small ISP that requires 1000 subnets for its clients. Each client will need plenty of space in the host portion to create their own subnets.

The network address 10.0.0.0 has a default subnet mask of 255.0.0.0 or /8. This means there are 8 bits in the network portion and 24 host bits available to borrow toward subnetting. Therefore, the small ISP will subnet the 10.0.0.0/8 network.

As always, in order to create subnets we must borrow bits from the host portion of the IP address of the existing internetwork. Starting from the left to the right with the first available host bit, we will borrow a single bit at a time until we reach the number of bits necessary to create 1000 subnets. As shown in Figure 1, we need to borrow 10 bits to create 1024 subnets. Specifically, we need to borrow the 8 bits in the second octet and 2 additional bits from the third octet.

Figure 2 displays the network address and the resulting subnet mask which converts to 255.255.192.0 or a /18 prefix.

Figure 3 displays the resulting subnets of borrowing 10 bits creating subnets from 10.0.0.0 /18 to 10.255.255.128.0 /18.

Figure 4 displays that 14 host bits were not borrowed, therefore, $2^{14} - 2 = 16382$. This indicates that each of the 1000 subnets can support up to 16,382 hosts.

Figure 5 displays the specifics of the first subnet.

Refer to **Video**
in online course

8.1.3.6   Video Demonstration – Subnetting Across Multiple Octets

Click Play to view an explanation of using the magic number across classful bit boundaries.

Click here to read the transcript of this video.

Refer to
Online Course
for Illustration

8.1.4   Subnetting to Meet Requirements

8.1.4.1   Subnetting Based on Host Requirements

There are two considerations when planning subnets:

- the number of host addresses required for each network
- the number of individual subnets needed

The table in the figure displays the specifics for subnetting a /24 network. Notice how there is an inverse relationship between the number of subnets and the number of hosts. The more bits borrowed to create subnets, the fewer host bits available. If more host addresses are needed, more host bits are required, resulting in fewer subnets.

The number of host addresses required in the largest subnet will determine how many bits must be left in the host portion. Recall that two of the addresses cannot be used, so the usable number of addresses can be calculated as 2^n-2.

Refer to
Online Course
for Illustration

8.1.4.2   Subnetting Based on Network Requirements

Sometimes a certain number of subnets is required, with less emphasis on the number of host addresses per subnet. This may be the case if an organization chooses to separate their network traffic based on internal structure or department setup, as shown in the figure. For example, an organization may choose to put all host devices used by employees in the Engineering department in one network, and all host devices used by management in a separate network. In this case, the number of subnets is most important in determining how many bits to borrow.

Recall the number of subnets created when bits are borrowed can be calculated using the formula 2^n (where n is the number of bits borrowed). The key is to balance the number of subnets needed and the number of hosts required for the largest subnet. The more bits borrowed to create additional subnets means fewer hosts available per subnet.

Refer to
Online Course
for Illustration

8.1.4.3   Network Requirement Example

Network administrators must devise the network addressing scheme to accommodate the maximum number of hosts for each network and the number of subnets. The addressing scheme should allow for growth in the both the number of host addresses per subnet and the total number of subnets.

In this example, corporate headquarters has allocated a private network address of 172.16.0.0/22 (10 host bits) to a branch location. As shown in Figure 1, this will provide 1,022 host addresses.

The topology for the branch locations, shown in Figure 2, consists of 5 LAN segments and 4 internetwork connections between routers. Therefore, 9 subnets are required. The largest subnet requires 40 hosts.

The 172.16.0.0/22 network address has 10 host bits as shown in Figure 3. Because the largest subnet requires 40 hosts, a minimum of 6 host bits are needed to provide addressing for 40 hosts. This is determined by using this formula: 2^6 − 2 = 62 hosts.

Using the formula for determining subnets, results in 16 subnets: 2^4 = 16. Because the example internetwork requires 9 subnets this will meet the requirement and allow for some additional growth.

Therefore, the first 4 host bits can be used to allocate subnets, as shown in Figure 4. When 4 bits are borrowed, the new prefix length is /26 with a subnet mask of 255.255.255.192.

As shown in Figure 5, the subnets can be assigned to the LAN segments and router-to-router connections.

This topic concludes with four activities to practice subnetting. The Chapter Appendix includes additional practice activities.

Refer to
Interactive Graphic
in online course

8.1.4.4   Activity – Calculate the Subnet Mask

Refer to
Interactive Graphic
in online course

8.1.4.5   Activity – Determining the Number of Bits to Borrow

Refer to
Lab Activity
for this chapter

8.1.4.6   Lab - Calculating IPv4 Subnets

In this lab, you will complete the following objectives:

- Part 1: Determine IPv4 Address Subnetting
- Part 2: Calculate IPv4 Address Subnetting

Refer to **Packet
Tracer Activity**
for this chapter

8.1.4.7   Packet Tracer - Subnetting Scenario 1

In this activity, you are given the network address of 192.168.100.0/24 to subnet and provide the IP addressing for the network shown in the topology. Each LAN in the network requires enough space for, at least, 25 addresses for end devices, the switch and the router. The connection between R1 to R2 will require an IP address for each end of the link.

Note   Refer to the Chapter Appendix for Subnetting Scenario 2.

Refer to
Lab Activity
for this chapter

8.1.4.8   Lab – Designing and Implementing a Subnetted IPv4 Addressing Scheme

In this lab, you will complete the following objectives:

- Part 1: Design a Network Subnetting Scheme
- Part 2: Configure the Devices
- Part 3: Test and Troubleshoot the Network

Refer to
Online Course
for Illustration

8.1.5   Benefits of Variable Length Subnet Masking

8.1.5.1   Traditional Subnetting Wastes Addresses

Using traditional subnetting, the same number of addresses is allocated for each subnet. If all the subnets have the same requirements for the number of hosts, these fixed size address blocks would be efficient. However, most often that is not the case.

For example, the topology shown in Figure 1 requires seven subnets, one for each of the four LANs, and one for each of the three WAN connections between routers. Using traditional subnetting with the given address of 192.168.20.0/24, 3 bits can be borrowed from the host portion in the last octet to meet the subnet requirement of seven subnets. As shown in Figure 2, borrowing 3 bits creates 8 subnets and leaves 5 host bits with 30 usable hosts per subnet. This scheme creates the needed subnets and meets the host requirement of the largest LAN.

Although this traditional subnetting meets the needs of the largest LAN and divides the address space into an adequate number of subnets, it results in significant waste of unused addresses.

For example, only two addresses are needed in each subnet for the three WAN links. Because each subnet has 30 usable addresses, there are 28 unused addresses in each of these subnets. As shown in Figure 3, this results in 84 unused addresses (28x3).

Further, this limits future growth by reducing the total number of subnets available. This inefficient use of addresses is characteristic of traditional subnetting. Applying a traditional subnetting scheme to this scenario is not very efficient and is wasteful.

Subnetting a subnet, or using Variable Length Subnet Mask (VLSM), was designed to avoid wasting addresses.

Refer to
Online Course
for Illustration

8.1.5.2 Variable Length Subnet Masks

In all of the previous examples of subnetting, notice that the same subnet mask was applied for all the subnets. This means that each subnet has the same number of available host addresses.

As illustrated in Figure 1, traditional subnetting creates subnets of equal size. Each subnet in a traditional scheme uses the same subnet mask. As shown in Figure 2, VLSM allows a network space to be divided into unequal parts. With VLSM, the subnet mask will vary depending on how many bits have been borrowed for a particular subnet, thus the "variable" part of the VLSM.

VLSM subnetting is similar to traditional subnetting in that bits are borrowed to create subnets. The formulas to calculate the number of hosts per subnet and the number of subnets created still apply.

The difference is that subnetting is not a single pass activity. With VLSM, the network is first subnetted, and then the subnets are subnetted again. This process can be repeated multiple times to create subnets of various sizes.

Note   When using VLSM, always begin by satisfying the host requirements of the largest subnet. Continue subnetting until the host requirements of the smallest subnet are satisfied.

Refer to
Online Course
for Illustration

8.1.5.3   Basic VLSM

To better understand the VLSM process, go back to the previous example, shown in Figure 1. The network 192.168.20.0/24 was subnetted into eight equal-sized subnets. Seven of the eight subnets were allocated. Four subnets were used for the LANs and three subnets for the WAN connections between the routers. Recall that the wasted address space was in the subnets used for the WAN connections, because those subnets required only two usable addresses: one for each router interface. To avoid this waste, VLSM can be used to create smaller subnets for the WAN connections.

To create smaller subnets for the WAN links, one of the subnets will be divided. In this example, the last subnet, 192.168.20.224/27, will be further subnetted.

Recall that when the number of needed host addresses is known, the formula 2^n-2 (where n equals the number of host bits remaining) can be used. To provide two usable addresses, 2 host bits must be left in the host portion.

Because there are 5 host bits in the subnetted 192.168.20.224/27 address space, 3 more bits can be borrowed, leaving 2 bits in the host portion, as shown in Figure 2. The calculations at this point are exactly the same as those used for traditional subnetting. The bits are borrowed, and the subnet ranges are determined.

This VLSM subnetting scheme reduces the number of addresses per subnet to a size appropriate for the WANs. Subnetting subnet 7 for WANs, allows subnets 4, 5, and 6 to be available for future networks, as well as 5 additional subnets available for WANs.

Refer to **Video** in online course

8.1.5.4   Video Demonstration – Basic VLSM

Click Play to view a demonstration of basic VLSM techniques.

Click here to read the transcript of this video.

Refer to **Online Course** for Illustration

8.1.5.5   VLSM in Practice

Using the VLSM subnets, the LAN and WAN segments can be addressed without unnecessary waste.

As shown in Figure 1, the hosts in each of the LANs will be assigned a valid host address with the range for that subnet and /27 mask. Each of the four routers will have a LAN interface with a /27 subnet and a one or more serial interfaces with a /30 subnet.

Using a common addressing scheme, the first host IPv4 address for each subnet is assigned to the LAN interface of the router. The WAN interfaces of the routers are assigned the IP addresses and mask for the /30 subnets.

Figures 2 - 5 show the interface configuration for each of the routers.

Hosts on each subnet will have a host IPv4 address from the range of host addresses for that subnet and an appropriate mask. Hosts will use the address of the attached router LAN interface as the default gateway address.

- Default gateway for Building A hosts (192.168.20.0/27) will be 192.168.20.1.
- Default gateway for Building B hosts (192.168.20.32/27) will be 192.168.20.33.
- Default gateway for Building C hosts (192.168.20.64/27) will be 192.168.20.65.
- Default gateway for Building D hosts (192.168.20.96/27) will be 192.168.20.97.

Refer to **Online Course** for Illustration

8.1.5.6   VLSM Chart

An addressing chart can be used to identify which blocks of addresses are available for use and which ones are already assigned, as shown in Figure 1. This method helps to prevent assigning addresses that have already been allocated.

In order to use the address space more efficiently, /30 subnets are created for WAN links, as shown in the VLSM chart in Figure 2. To keep the unused blocks of addresses together in a block of contiguous address space, the last /27 subnet was further subnetted to create the /30 subnets. The first 3 subnets were assigned to WAN links.

Designing the addressing scheme in this way leaves 3 unused, contiguous /27 subnets and 5 unused contiguous /30 subnets.

Refer to **Video** in online course

8.1.5.7   Video Demonstration – VLSM Example

Click Play to view a demonstration of VLSM subnetting.

Click here to read the transcript of this video.

Refer to **Interactive Graphic** in online course

8.1.5.8   Activity – Practicing VLSM

Refer to **Online Course** for Illustration

8.2   Addressing Schemes

8.2.1   Structured Design

8.2.1.1   Network Address Planning

As shown in the figure, the allocation of network layer address space within the corporate network needs to be well designed. Address assignment should not be random.

Planning network subnets requires examination of both the needs of an organization's network usage, and how the subnets will be structured. Performing a network requirement study is the starting point. This means looking at the entire network and determining the main sections of the network and how they will be segmented. The address plan includes determining the needs of each subnet in terms of size, how many hosts per subnet, how host addresses will be assigned, which hosts will require static IP addresses, and which hosts can use DHCP for obtaining their addressing information.

The size of the subnet involves planning the number of hosts that will require IP host addresses in each subnet of the subdivided private network. For example, in a campus network design, you might consider how many hosts are needed in the Administrative LAN, how many in the Faculty LAN, and how many in the Student LAN. In a home network, a consideration might be done by the number of hosts in the Main House LAN and the number of hosts in the Home Office LAN.

As discussed earlier, the private IP address range used on a LAN is the choice of the network administrator and needs careful consideration to be sure that enough host addresses will be available for the currently known hosts and for future expansion. Remember the private IP address ranges are:

- 10.0.0.0 - 10.255.255.255 with a subnet mask of 255.0.0.0 or /8

- 172.16.0.0 – 172.31.255.255 with a subnet mask of 255.240.0.0 or /12

- 192.168.0.0 – 192.168.255.255 with a subnet mask of 255.255.0.0 or /16

Knowing your IP address requirements will determine the range or ranges of host addresses you implement. Subnetting the selected private IP address space will provide the host addresses to cover your network needs.

Public addresses used to connect to the Internet are typically allocated from a service provider. So, while the same principles for subnetting would apply, this is not generally the responsibility of the organization's network administrator.

Refer to
Online Course
for Illustration

8.2.1.2   Planning to Address the Network

Three primary considerations for planning address allocation are displayed in the figure.

Preventing the duplication of addresses refers to the fact that each host in an internetwork must have a unique address. Without the proper planning and documentation, an address could be assigned to more than one host, resulting in access issues for both hosts.

Providing and controlling access refers to the fact that some hosts, such as servers, provide resources to internal hosts as well as to external hosts. The Layer 3 address assigned to a server can be used to control access to that server. If, however, the address is randomly assigned and not well documented, controlling access is more difficult.

Monitoring security and performance of hosts means network traffic is examined for source IP addresses that are generating or receiving excessive packets. If there is proper planning and documentation of the network addressing, problematic network devices should easily be found.

Refer to
Online Course
for Illustration

8.2.1.3   Assigning Addresses to Devices

Within a network, there are different types of devices that require addresses, including:

- **End user clients** – Most networks allocate addresses dynamically using Dynamic Host Configuration Protocol (DHCP). This reduces the burden on network support staff and virtually eliminates entry errors. As well, addresses are only leased for a period of time. Changing the subnetting scheme means that the DHCP server needs to be reconfigured, and the clients must renew their IP addresses.

- **Servers and peripherals** – These should have a predictable static IP address. Use a consistent numbering system for these devices.

- **Servers that are accessible from the Internet** – In many networks, servers must be made available to the remote users. In most cases, these servers are assigned private addresses internally, and the router or firewall at the perimeter of the network must be configured to translate the internal address into a public address.

- **Intermediary devices** – These devices are assigned addresses for network management, monitoring, and security. Because we must know how to communicate with intermediary devices, they should have predictable, statically assigned addresses.

- **Gateway** – Routers and firewall devices have an IP address assigned to each interface which serves as the gateway for the hosts in that network. Typically, the router interface uses either the lowest or highest address in the network.

The table in the figure provides a sample of address allocation for a small network.

When developing an IP addressing scheme, it is generally recommended to have a set pattern of how addresses are allocated to each type of device. This benefits administrators when adding and removing devices, filtering traffic based on IP, as well as simplifying documentation.

Refer to **Packet Tracer Activity** for this chapter

8.2.1.4   Packet Tracer – Designing and Implementing a VLSM Addressing Scheme

In this activity, you are given a /24 network address to use to design a VLSM addressing scheme. Based on a set of requirements, you will assign subnets and addressing, configure devices and verify connectivity.

Refer to **Lab Activity** for this chapter

8.2.1.5   Lab – Designing and Implementing a VLSM Addressing Scheme

In this lab, you will complete the following objectives:

- Part 1: Examine Network Requirements
- Part 2: Design the VLSM Address Scheme
- Part 3: Cable and Configure the IPv4 Network

Refer to **Online Course** for Illustration

8.3   Design Considerations for IPv6

8.3.1   Subnetting an IPv6 Network

8.3.1.1   The IPv6 Global Unicast Address

IPv6 subnetting requires a different approach than IPv4 subnetting. The primary reason is that with IPv6 there are so many addresses, that the reason for subnetting is completely different. Refer to the figure for a quick review of the structure of an IPv6 global unicast address.

IPv4 subnetting is not only about limiting broadcast domains but is also about managing address scarcity. Determining the subnet mask and the use of VLSM is done to help conserve IPv4 addresses. IPv6 subnetting is not concerned with conserving address space. The subnet ID includes more than enough subnets. IPv6 subnetting is about building an addressing hierarchy based on the number of subnetworks needed.

Recall that there are two types of assignable IPv6 addresses. An IPv6 link-local address is never subnetted because it exists only on the local link. However, an IPv6 global unicast address can be subnetted.

The IPv6 global unicast address normally consists of a /48 global routing prefix, a 16 bit subnet ID, and a 64 bit interface ID.

Refer to **Online Course** for Illustration

8.3.1.2   Subnetting Using the Subnet ID

The 16 bit subnet ID section of the IPv6 global unicast address can be used by an organization to create internal subnets.

The subnet ID provides more than enough subnets and host support than will ever be needed in one subnet. For instance, the 16 bit section can:

- Create up to 65,536 /64 subnets. This does not include the possibility of borrowing any bits from the interface ID of the address.
- Support up to 18 quintillion host IPv6 addresses per subnet (i.e., 18,000,000,000,000,000,000).

Note   Subnetting into the 64 bit Interface ID (or host portion) is also possible but it is rarely required.

IPv6 subnetting is also easier to implement than IPv4, because there is no conversion to binary required. To determine the next available subnet, just count up in hexadecimal.

For example, assume an organization has been assigned the 2001:0DB8:ACAD::/48 global routing prefix with a 16 bit subnet ID. This would allow the organization to create /64 subnets, as shown in the figure. Notice how the global routing prefix is the same for all subnets. Only the subnet ID hextet is incremented in hexadecimal for each subnet.

Refer to
Online Course
for Illustration

8.3.1.3   IPv6 Subnet Allocation

With over 65,000 subnets to choose from, the task of the network administrator becomes one of designing a logical scheme to address the network.

As shown in Figure 1, the example topology will require subnets for each LAN as well as for the WAN link between R1 and R2. Unlike the example for IPv4, with IPv6 the WAN link subnet will not be subnetted further. Although this may "waste" addresses, that is not a concern when using IPv6.

As shown in Figure 2, the allocation of five IPv6 subnets, with the subnet ID field 0001 through 0005 will be used for this example. Each /64 subnet will provide more addresses than will ever be needed.

As shown in Figure 3, each LAN segment and the WAN link is assigned a /64 subnet.

Similar to configuring IPv4, Figure 4 shows that each of the router interfaces has been configured to be on a different IPv6 subnet.

Refer the Chapter Appendix for more information subnetting IPv6 into the interface ID.

Refer to **Packet Tracer Activity** for this chapter

8.3.1.4   Packet Tracer – Implementing a Subnetted IPv6 Addressing Scheme

Your network administrator wants you to assign five /64 IPv6 subnets to the network shown in the topology. Your job is to determine the IPv6 subnets, assign IPv6 addresses to the routers and set the PCs to automatically receive IPv6 addressing. Your final step is to verify connectivity between IPv6 hosts.

8.4   Summary

8.4.1   Conclusion

Refer to
Lab Activity
for this chapter

8.4.1.1   Class Activity – Can you call me now?

Note   This activity may be completed individually or in small/large groups using Packet Tracer software.

You are setting up a dedicated, computer addressing scheme for patient rooms in a hospital. The switch will be centrally located in the nurses' station, as each of the five rooms will be wired so that patients can just connect to a RJ-45 port built into the wall of their room. Devise a physical and logical topology for only one of the six floors using the following addressing scheme requirements:

- There are six floors, with five patient rooms on each floor, for a total of thirty connections. Each room needs a network connection.

- Subnetting must be incorporated into your scheme.

- Use one router, one switch, and five host stations for addressing purposes.

- Validate that all PCs can connect to the hospital's in-house services.

Keep a copy of your scheme to share later with the class or learning community. Be prepared to explain how subnetting, unicasts, multicasts, and broadcasts would be incorporated, and where your addressing scheme could be used.

Refer to **Packet Tracer Activity** for this chapter

8.4.1.2   Packet Tracer – Skills Integration Challenge

As a network technician familiar with IPv4 and IPv6 addressing implementations, you are now ready to take an existing network infrastructure and apply your knowledge and skills to finalize the configuration. The network administrator has already configured some commands on the routers. **Do not erase or modify those configurations**. Your task is to complete the IPv4 and IPv6 addressing scheme, implement IPv4 and IPv6 addressing, and verify connectivity.

Refer to **Online Course** for Illustration

8.4.1.3   Subnetting IP Networks

The process of segmenting a network by dividing it into to multiple smaller network spaces is called subnetting.

Every network address has a valid range of host addresses. All devices attached to the same network will have an IPv4 host address for that network and a common subnet mask or network prefix. Traffic can be forwarded between hosts directly if they are on the same subnet. Traffic cannot be forwarded between subnets without the use of a router. To determine if traffic is local or remote, the router uses the subnet mask. The prefix and the subnet mask are different ways of representing the same thing - the network portion of an address.

IPv4 subnets are created by using one or more of the host bits as network bits. Two very important factors that will lead to the determination of the IP address block with the subnet mask are the number of subnets required, and the maximum number of hosts needed per subnet. There is an inverse relationship between the number of subnets and the number of hosts. The more bits that are borrowed to create subnets, the fewer host bits that are available; therefore, there are fewer hosts per subnet.

The formula 2^n (where n is the number of host bits remaining) is used to calculate how many addresses will be available on each subnet. However, the network address and broadcast address within a range are not useable. Therefore, to calculate the useable number of addresses, the calculation 2^n-2 is required.

Subnetting a subnet, or using Variable Length Subnet Mask (VLSM), was designed to avoid wasting addresses.

IPv6 subnetting requires a different approach than IPv4 subnetting. An IPv6 address space is not subnetted to conserve addresses; rather it is subnetted to support a hierarchical, logical design of the network. So, while IPv4 subnetting is about managing address scarcity, IPv6 subnetting is about building an addressing hierarchy based on the number of routers and the networks they support.

Careful planning is required to make best use of the available address space. Size, location, use, and access requirements are all considerations in the address planning process.

After it is implemented, an IP network needs to be tested to verify its connectivity and operational performance.

Go to the online course to take the quiz and exam.

Chapter 8 Quiz

This quiz is designed to provide an additional opportunity to practice the skills and knowledge presented in the chapter and to prepare for the chapter exam. You will be allowed multiple attempts and the grade does not appear in the gradebook.

Chapter 8 Exam

The chapter exam assesses your knowledge of the chapter content.

Your Chapter Notes

Transport Layer

9.0 Introduction

9.0.1.1 Transport Layer

Data networks and the Internet support the human network by supplying reliable communication between people. On a single device, people can use multiple applications and services such as email, the web, and instant messaging to send messages or retrieve information. Data from each of these applications is packaged, transported and delivered to the appropriate application on the destination device.

The processes described in the OSI transport layer accept data from the application layer and prepare it for addressing at the network layer. A source computer communicates with a receiving computer to decide how to break up data into segments, how to make sure none of the segments get lost, and how to verify all the segments arrived. When thinking about the transport layer, think of a shipping department preparing a single order of multiple packages for delivery.

Refer to
Lab Activity
for this chapter

9.0.1.2 Class Activity - We Need to Talk - Game

Note This activity works best with medium-sized groups of 6 to 8 students per group.

The instructor will whisper a complex message to the first student in a group. An example of the message might be "Our final exam will be given next Tuesday, February 5th, at 2 p.m. in Room 1151."

That student whispers the message to the next student in the group. Each group follows this process until all members of each group have heard the whispered message. Here are the rules you are to follow:

- You can whisper the message only once to your neighbor.

- The message must keep moving from one person to the other with no skipping of participants.

- The instructor should ask a student to track how long it takes for the message to travel from the first person to the last. The first or last person is most likely the best to keep the time.

- The last student will say aloud exactly what he or she heard.

The instructor will then restate the original message so that the group can compare it to the message that was delivered by the last student in the group.

Refer to **Online Course** for Illustration

9.1 Transport Layer Protocols

9.1.1 Transportation of Data

9.1.1.1 Role of the Transport Layer

The transport layer is responsible for establishing a temporary communication session between two applications and delivering data between them. An application generates data that is sent from an application on a source host to an application on a destination host. This is without regard to the destination host type, the type of media over which the data must travel, the path taken by the data, the congestion on a link, or the size of the network. As shown in the figure, the transport layer is the link between the application layer and the lower layers that are responsible for network transmission.

Refer to **Online Course** for Illustration

9.1.1.2 Transport Layer Responsibilities

Tracking Individual Conversations

At the transport layer, each set of data flowing between a source application and a destination application is known as a conversation (Figure 1). A host may have multiple applications that are communicating across the network simultaneously. Each of these applications communicates with one or more applications on one or more remote hosts. It is the responsibility of the transport layer to maintain and track these multiple conversations.

Segmenting Data and Reassembling Segments

Data must be prepared to be sent across the media in manageable pieces. Most networks have a limitation on the amount of data that can be included in a single packet. Transport layer protocols have services that segment the application data into blocks that are an appropriate size (Figure 2). This service includes the encapsulation required on each piece of data. A header, used for reassembly, is added to each block of data. This header is used to track the data stream.

At the destination, the transport layer must be able to reconstruct the pieces of data into a complete data stream that is useful to the application layer. The protocols at the transport layer describe how the transport layer header information is used to reassemble the data pieces into streams to be passed to the application layer.

Identifying the Applications

To pass data streams to the proper applications, the transport layer must identify the target application (Figure 3). To accomplish this, the transport layer assigns each application an identifier called a port number. Each software process that needs to access the network is assigned a port number unique to that host.

Refer to **Online Course** for Illustration

9.1.1.3 Conversation Multiplexing

Sending some types of data (for example, a streaming video) across a network, as one complete communication stream, can consume all of the available bandwidth. This will then prevent other communications from occurring at the same time. It would also make error recovery and retransmission of damaged data difficult.

The figure shows that segmenting the data into smaller chunks enables many different communications, from many different users, to be interleaved (multiplexed) on the same network.

To identify each segment of data, the transport layer adds a header containing binary data organized into several fields. It is the values in these fields that enable various transport layer protocols to perform different functions in managing data communication.

Refer to **Online Course** for Illustration

9.1.1.4 Transport Layer Reliability

The transport layer is also responsible for managing reliability requirements of a conversation. Different applications have different transport reliability requirements.

IP is concerned only with the structure, addressing, and routing of packets. IP does not specify how the delivery or transportation of the packets takes place. Transport protocols specify how to transfer messages between hosts. TCP/IP provides two transport layer protocols, Transmission Control Protocol (TCP) and User Datagram Protocol (UDP), as shown in the figure. IP uses these transport protocols to enable hosts to communicate and transfer data.

TCP is considered a reliable, full-featured transport layer protocol, which ensures that all of the data arrives at the destination. In contrast, UDP is a very simple transport layer protocol that does not provide for any reliability.

Refer to **Online Course** for Illustration

9.1.1.5 TCP

TCP transport is analogous to sending packages that are tracked from source to destination. If a shipping order is broken up into several packages, a customer can check online to see the order of the delivery.

With TCP, there are three basic operations of reliability:

- Numbering and tracking data segments transmitted to a specific host from a specific application
- Acknowledging received data
- Retransmitting any unacknowledged data after a certain period of time

Click Play in the figure to see how TCP segments and acknowledgments are transmitted between sender and receiver.

Refer to **Online Course** for Illustration

9.1.1.6 UDP

While the TCP reliability functions provide more robust communication between applications, they also incur additional overhead and possible delays in transmission. There is a trade-off between the value of reliability and the burden it places on network resources. Adding overhead to ensure reliability for some applications could reduce the usefulness of the application and can even be detrimental. In such cases, UDP is a better transport protocol.

UDP provides the basic functions for delivering data segments between the appropriate applications, with very little overhead and data checking. UDP is known as a best-effort delivery protocol. In the context of networking, best-effort delivery is referred to as unreliable because there is no acknowledgment that the data is received at the destination. With UDP, there are no transport layer processes that inform the sender of a successful delivery.

UDP is similar to placing a regular, non-registered, letter in the mail. The sender of the letter is not aware of the availability of the receiver to receive the letter. Nor is the post office responsible for tracking the letter or informing the sender if the letter does not arrive at the final destination.

Click Play in the figure to see an animation of UDP segments being transmitted from sender to receiver.

Refer to
Online Course
for Illustration

9.1.1.7   The Right Transport Layer Protocol for the Right Application

For some applications, segments must arrive in a very specific sequence to be processed successfully. With other applications, all data must be fully received before any is considered useful. In both of these instances, TCP is used as the transport protocol. Application developers must choose which transport protocol type is appropriate based on the requirements of the applications.

For example, applications such as databases, web browsers, and email clients, require that all data that is sent arrives at the destination in its original condition. Any missing data could cause a corrupt communication that is either incomplete or unreadable. These applications are designed to use TCP.

In other cases, an application can tolerate some data loss during transmission over the network, but delays in transmission are unacceptable. UDP is the better choice for these applications because less network overhead is required. UDP is preferable for applications such as streaming live audio, live video, and Voice over IP (VoIP). Acknowledgments and retransmission would slow down delivery.

For example, if one or two segments of a live video stream fail to arrive, it creates a momentary disruption in the stream. This may appear as distortion in the image or sound, but may not be noticeable to the user. If the destination device had to account for lost data, the stream could be delayed while waiting for retransmissions, therefore causing the image or sound to be greatly degraded. In this case, it is better to render the best media possible with the segments received, and forego reliability.

Note   Applications that stream stored audio and video use TCP. For example, if your network suddenly cannot support the bandwidth needed to watch an on-demand movie, the application pauses the playback. During the pause, you might see a "buffering..." message while TCP works to re-establish the stream. Once all the segments are in order and a minimum level of bandwidth is restored, your TCP session resumes and the movie begins playing.

Refer to
Online Course
for Illustration

9.1.2   TCP and UDP Overview

9.1.2.1   TCP Features

To understand the differences between TCP and UDP, it is important to understand how each protocol implements specific reliability features and how they track conversations. In addition to supporting the basic functions of data segmentation and reassembly, TCP, as shown in the figure, also provides other services.

Establishing a Session

TCP is a connection-oriented protocol. A connection-oriented protocol is one that negotiates and establishes a permanent connection (or session) between source and destination devices prior to forwarding any traffic. Through session establishment, the devices negotiate the amount of traffic that can be forwarded at a given time, and the communication data between the two can be closely managed.

Reliable Delivery

In networking terms, reliability means ensuring that each segment that the source sends arrives at the destination. For many reasons, it is possible for a segment to become corrupted or lost completely, as it is transmitted over the network.

Same-Order Delivery

Because networks may provide multiple routes that can have different transmission rates, data can arrive in the wrong order. By numbering and sequencing the segments, TCP can ensure that these segments are reassembled into the proper order.

Flow Control

Network hosts have limited resources, such as memory and processing power. When TCP is aware that these resources are overtaxed, it can request that the sending application reduce the rate of data flow. This is done by TCP regulating the amount of data the source transmits. Flow control can prevent the need for retransmission of the data when the receiving host's resourses are overwhelmed.

For more information on TCP, read the RFC.

Refer to
Online Course
for Illustration

9.1.2.2   TCP Header

TCP is a stateful protocol. A stateful protocol is a protocol that keeps track of the state of the communication session. To track the state of a session, TCP records which information it has sent and which information has been acknowledged. The stateful session begins with the session establishment and ends when closed with the session termination.

As shown in the figure, each TCP segment has 20 bytes of overhead in the header encapsulating the application layer data:

- **Source Port (16 bits) and Destination Port (16 bits)** – Used to identify the application.

- **Sequence number (32 bits)** – Used for data reassembly purposes.

- **Acknowledgment number (32 bits)** – Indicates the data that has been received.

- **Header length (4 bits)** – Known as "data offset". Indicates the length of the TCP segment header.

- **Reserved (6 bits)** – This field is reserved for the future.

- **Control bits (6 bits)** – Includes bit codes, or flags, which indicate the purpose and function of the TCP segment.

- **Window size (16 bits)** – Indicates the number of bytes that can be accepted at one time.

- **Checksum (16 bits)** – Used for error checking of the segment header and data.

- **Urgent (16 bits)** – Indicates if data is urgent.

Refer to
Online Course
for Illustration

9.1.2.3   UDP Features

User Datagram Protocol (UDP) is considered a best-effort transport protocol. UDP is a lightweight transport protocol that offers the same data segmentation and reassembly as TCP, but without TCP reliability and flow control. UDP is such a simple protocol that it is usually described in terms of what it does not do compared to TCP.

The features of UDP are described in the figure.

For more information on UDP, read the RFC.

Refer to
Online Course
for Illustration

9.1.2.4   UDP Header

UDP is a stateless protocol, meaning neither the client, nor the server, is obligated to keep track of the state of the communication session. If reliability is required when using UDP as the transport protocol, it must be handled by the application.

One of the most important requirements for delivering live video and voice over the network is that the data continues to flow quickly. Live video and voice applications can tolerate some data loss with minimal or no noticeable effect, and are perfectly suited to UDP.

The pieces of communication in UDP are called datagrams, as shown in the figure. These datagrams are sent as best-effort by the transport layer protocol. UDP has a low overhead of 8 bytes.

Refer to
Online Course
for Illustration

9.1.2.5   Multiple Separate Conversations

The transport layer must be able to separate and manage multiple communications with different transport requirement needs. Users expect to be able to simultaneously receive and send email and instant messages, view websites, and conduct a VoIP phone call. Each of these applications is sending and receiving data over the network at the same time, despite different reliability requirements. Additionally, data from the phone call is not directed to the web browser, and text from an instant message does not appear in an email.

TCP and UDP manage these multiple simultaneous conversations by using header fields that can uniquely identify these applications. These unique identifiers are the port numbers.

Refer to
Online Course
for Illustration

9.1.2.6   Port Numbers

The source port number is associated with the originating application on the local host. The destination port number is associated with the destination application on the remote host.

Source Port

The source port number is dynamically generated by the sending device to identify a conversation between two devices. This process allows multiple conversations to occur simultaneously. It is common for a device to send multiple HTTP service requests to a web server at the same time. Each separate HTTP conversation is tracked based on the source ports.

Destination Port

The client places a destination port number in the segment to tell the destination server what service is being requested, as shown in the figure. For example, when a client specifies port 80 in the destination port, the server that receives the message knows that web services are being requested. A server can offer more than one service simultaneously such as web services on port 80 at the same time that it offers File Transfer Protocol (FTP) connection establishment on port 21.

Refer to **Online Course** for Illustration

9.1.2.7 Socket Pairs

The source and destination ports are placed within the segment. The segments are then encapsulated within an IP packet. The IP packet contains the IP address of the source and destination. The combination of the source IP address and source port number, or the destination IP address and destination port number is known as a socket. The socket is used to identify the server and service being requested by the client. A client socket might look like this, with 1099 representing the source port number: 192.168.1.5:1099

The socket on a web server might be: 192.168.1.7:80

Together, these two sockets combine to form a socket pair: 192.168.1.5:1099, 192.168.1.7:80

Sockets enable multiple processes, running on a client, to distinguish themselves from each other, and multiple connections to a server process to be distinguished from each other.

The source port number acts as a return address for the requesting application. The transport layer keeps track of this port and the application that initiated the request so that when a response is returned, it can be forwarded to the correct application.

Refer to **Online Course** for Illustration

9.1.2.8 Port Number Groups

The Internet Assigned Numbers Authority (IANA) is the standards body responsible for assigning various addressing standards, including port numbers. There are different types of port numbers, as shown in Figure 1:

- **Well-known Ports (Numbers 0 to 1023)** – These numbers are reserved for services and applications. They are commonly used for applications such as web browsers, email clients, and remote access clients. By defining these well-known ports for server applications, client applications can be programmed to request a connection to that specific port and its associated service.

- **Registered Ports (Numbers 1024 to 49151)** – These port numbers are assigned by IANA to a requesting entity to use with specific processes or applications. These processes are primarily individual applications that a user has chosen to install, rather than common applications that would receive a well-known port number. For example, Cisco has registered port 1985 for its Hot Standby Routing Protocol (HSRP) process.

- **Dynamic or Private Ports (Numbers 49152 to 65535)** – Also known as ephemeral ports, these are usually assigned dynamically by the client's OS when a connection to a service is initiated. The dynamic port is then used to identify the client application during communication.

Note Some client operating systems may use registered port numbers instead of dynamic port numbers for assigning source ports.

Figure 2 displays some common well-known port numbers and their associated applications. Some applications may use both TCP and UDP. For example, DNS uses UDP when clients send requests to a DNS server. However, communication between two DNS servers always uses TCP.

Click here to view the full list of port numbers and associated applications at IANA's website.

Refer to
Online Course
for Illustration

9.1.2.9   The netstat Command

Unexplained TCP connections can pose a major security threat. They can indicate that something or someone is connected to the local host. Sometimes it is necessary to know which active TCP connections are open and running on a networked host. Netstat is an important network utility that can be used to verify those connections. As shown in the figure, enter the command **netstat** to list the protocols in use, the local address and port numbers, the foreign address and port numbers, and the connection state.

By default, the **netstat** command will attempt to resolve IP addresses to domain names and port numbers to well-known applications. The **-n** option can be used to display IP addresses and port numbers in their numerical form.

Refer to
Interactive Graphic
in online course

9.1.2.10   Activity - Compare TCP and UDP Characteristics

Refer to
Online Course
for Illustration

9.2   TCP and UDP

9.2.1   TCP Communication Process

9.2.1.1   TCP Server Processes

Each application process running on the server is configured to use a port number, either by default or manually, by a system administrator. An individual server cannot have two services assigned to the same port number within the same transport layer services.

For example, a host running a web server application and a file transfer application cannot have both configured to use the same port (for example, TCP port 80). An active server application assigned to a specific port is considered to be open, which means that the transport layer accepts and processes segments addressed to that port. Any incoming client request addressed to the correct socket is accepted, and the data is passed to the server application. There can be many ports open simultaneously on a server, one for each active server application.

Refer to Figures 1 through 5 to see the typical allocation of source and destination ports in TCP client/server operations.

Refer to
Online Course
for Illustration

9.2.1.2   TCP Connection Establishment

In some cultures, when two persons meet, they often greet each other by shaking hands. The act of shaking hands is understood by both parties as a signal for a friendly greeting. Connections on the network are similar. In TCP connections, the host client establishes the connection with the server.

A TCP connection is established in three steps:

Step 1.   The initiating client requests a client-to-server communication session with the server.

Step 2.   The server acknowledges the client-to-server communication session and requests a server-to-client communication session.

Step 3.   The initiating client acknowledges the server-to-client communication session.

In the figure, click buttons 1 through 3 to see the TCP connection establishment.

Refer to
Online Course
for Illustration

9.2.1.3   TCP Session Termination

To close a connection, the Finish (FIN) control flag must be set in the segment header. To end each one-way TCP session, a two-way handshake, consisting of a FIN segment and an Acknowledgment (ACK) segment, is used. Therefore, to terminate a single conversation supported by TCP, four exchanges are needed to end both sessions.

In the figure, click buttons 1 through 4 to see the TCP connection termination.

Note   In this explanation, the terms client and server are used as a reference for simplicity, but the termination process can be initiated by any two hosts that have an open session:

Step 1.   When the client has no more data to send in the stream, it sends a segment with the FIN flag set.

Step 2.   The server sends an ACK to acknowledge the receipt of the FIN to terminate the session from client to server.

Step 3.   The server sends a FIN to the client to terminate the server-to-client session.

Step 4.   The client responds with an ACK to acknowledge the FIN from the server.

When all segments have been acknowledged, the session is closed.

Refer to
Online Course
for Illustration

9.2.1.4   TCP Three-way Handshake Analysis

Hosts track each data segment within a session and exchange information about what data is received using the information in the TCP header. TCP is a full-duplex protocol, where each connection represents two one-way communication streams or sessions. To establish the connection, the hosts perform a three-way handshake. Control bits in the TCP header indicate the progress and status of the connection.

The three-way handshake:

- Establishes that the destination device is present on the network

- Verifies that the destination device has an active service and is accepting requests on the destination port number that the initiating client intends to use

- Informs the destination device that the source client intends to establish a communication session on that port number

After the communication is completed, the sessions are closed, and the connection is terminated. The connection and session mechanisms enable TCP's reliability function.

The six bits in the Control Bits field of the TCP segment header are also known as flags. A flag is a bit that is either set to on or off. Click the Control Bits field in the figure to see all six flags. We have discussed SYN, ACK, and FIN. The RST flag is used to reset a connection when an error or timeout occurs. Click here to learn more about the PSH and URG flags.

Refer to **Video** in online course

9.2.1.5   Video Demonstration – TCP 3-Way Handshake

Click Play in the figure to see a video demonstration, using Wireshark, of the TCP 3-Way handshake.

Click here to download video support documentation.

Click here to read the transcript of this video.

Refer to **Lab Activity** for this chapter

9.2.1.6   Lab - Using Wireshark to Observe the TCP 3-Way Handshake

In this lab, you will complete the following objectives:

- Part 1: Prepare Wireshark to Capture Packets
- Part 2: Capture, Locate, and Examine Packets

Refer to **Interactive Graphic** in online course

9.2.1.7   Activity - TCP Connection and Termination Process

9.2.2   Reliability and Flow Control

Refer to **Online Course** for Illustration

9.2.2.1   TCP Reliability - Ordered Delivery

TCP segments may arrive at their destination out of order. For the original message to be understood by the recipient, the data in these segments is reassembled into the original order. Sequence numbers are assigned in the header of each packet to achieve this goal. The sequence number represents the first data byte of the TCP segment.

During session setup, an initial sequence number (ISN) is set. This ISN represents the starting value of the bytes for this session that is transmitted to the receiving application. As data is transmitted during the session, the sequence number is incremented by the number of bytes that have been transmitted. This data byte tracking enables each segment to be uniquely identified and acknowledged. Missing segments can then be identified.

Note   The ISN does not begin at one but is effectively a random number. This is to prevent certain types of malicious attacks. For simplicity, we will use an ISN of 1 for the examples in this chapter.

Segment sequence numbers indicate how to reassemble and reorder received segments, as shown in the figure.

The receiving TCP process places the data from a segment into a receiving buffer. Segments are placed in the proper sequence order and passed to the application layer when reassembled. Any segments that arrive with sequence numbers that are out of order are held for later processing. Then, when the segments with the missing bytes arrive, these segments are processed in order.

Refer to **Video** in online course

9.2.2.2   Video Demonstration - Sequence Numbers and Acknowledgments

One of the functions of TCP is ensuring that each segment reaches its destination. The TCP services on the destination host acknowledge the data that it has received by the source application.

Click Play in the figure to view a lesson on TCP sequence numbers and acknowledgments.

Click here to download the video support documentation.

Click here to read the transcript of this video.

Refer to **Video** in online course

9.2.2.3   Video Demonstration - Data Loss and Retransmission

No matter how well designed a network is, data loss occasionally occurs; therefore, TCP provides methods of managing these segment losses. Among these is a mechanism to retransmit segments for unacknowledged data.

In the figure, play the video and click the link to download the PDF file. The video and PDF file examine TCP data loss and retransmission.

Click Play in the figure to view a lesson on TCP retransmission.

Click here to download video support documentation.

Click here to read the transcript of this video.

Note   Hosts today may also employ an optional feature called selective acknowledgment (SACK). If both hosts support SACK, it is possible for the destination to acknowledge bytes in discontinuous segments and the host would only need to retransmit the missing data. To learn more about SACK, refer to the Chapter Appendix.

Refer to **Online Course** for Illustration

9.2.2.4   TCP Flow Control - Window Size and Acknowledgments

TCP also provides mechanisms for flow control, the amount of data that the destination can receive and process reliably. Flow control helps maintain the reliability of TCP transmission by adjusting the rate of data flow between source and destination for a given session. To accomplish this, the TCP header includes a 16-bit field called the window size.

The figure shows an example of window size and acknowledgments. The window size is the number of bytes that the destination device of a TCP session can accept and process at one time. In this example, PC B's initial window size for the TCP session is 10,000 bytes. Starting with the first byte, byte number 1, the last byte PC A can send without receiving an acknowledgment is byte 10,000. This is known as PC A's send window. The window size is included in every TCP segment so the destination can modify the window size at any time depending on buffer availability.

Note   In the figure, the source is transmitting 1,460 bytes of data within each TCP segment. This is known as the MSS (Maximum Segment Size). Refer to the Chapter Appendix for more information on MSS.

The initial window size is agreed upon when the TCP session is established during the three-way handshake. The source device must limit the number of bytes sent to the destination device based on the destination's window size. Only after the source device receives an acknowledgment that the bytes have been received, can it continue sending more data for the session. Typically, the destination will not wait for all the bytes for its window size to be received before replying with an acknowledgment. As the bytes are received and processed, the destination will send acknowledgments to inform the source that it can continue to send additional bytes.

Typically, PC B will not wait until all 10,000 bytes have been received before sending an acknowledgment. This means PC A can adjust its send window as it receives acknowledgments from PC B. As shown in the figure, when PC A receives an acknowledgment with the acknowledgment number 2,921, PC A's send window will increment another 10,000 bytes (the size of PC B's current window size) to 12,920. PC A can now continue to send up to another 10,000 bytes to PC B as long as it does not send past its new send window at 12,920.

The process of the destination sending acknowledgments as it processes bytes received and the continual adjustment of the source's send window is known as sliding windows.

If the availability of the destination's buffer space decreases, it may reduce its window size to inform the source to reduce the number of bytes it should send without receiving an acknowledgment.

Refer to
Online Course
for Illustration

9.2.2.5   TCP Flow Control - Congestion Avoidance

When congestion occurs on a network, it results in packets being discarded by the overloaded router. When packets containing TCP segments don't reach their destination, they are left unacknowledged. By determining the rate at which TCP segments are sent but not acknowledged, the source can assume a certain level of network congestion.

Whenever there is congestion, retransmission of lost TCP segments from the source will occur. If the retransmission is not properly controlled, the additional retransmission of the TCP segments can make the congestion even worse. Not only are new packets with TCP segments introduced into the network, but the feedback effect of the retransmitted TCP segments that were lost will also add to the congestion. To avoid and control congestion, TCP employs several congestion handling mechanisms, timers, and algorithms.

If the source determines that the TCP segments are either not being acknowledged or not acknowledged in a timely manner, then it can reduce the number of bytes it sends before receiving an acknowledgment. Notice that it is the source that is reducing the number of unacknowledged bytes it sends and not the window size determined by the destination.

Note   Explanation of actual congestion handling mechanisms, timers, and algorithms are beyond the scope of this course.

Refer to
Online Course
for Illustration

9.2.3   UDP Communication

9.2.3.1   UDP Low Overhead versus Reliability

UDP is a simple protocol that provides the basic transport layer functions. It has much lower overhead than TCP because it is not connection-oriented and does not offer the sophisticated retransmission, sequencing, and flow control mechanisms that provide reliability.

This does not mean that applications that use UDP are always unreliable, nor does it mean that UDP is an inferior protocol. It simply means that these functions are not provided by the transport layer protocol and must be implemented elsewhere if required.

The low overhead of UDP makes it very desirable for protocols that make simple request and reply transactions. For example, using TCP for DHCP would introduce unnecessary network traffic. If there is a problem with a request or a reply, the device simply sends the request again if no response is received.

9.2.3.2   UDP Datagram Reassembly

Refer to Online Course for Illustration

Like segments with TCP, when UDP datagrams are sent to a destination, they often take different paths and arrive in the wrong order. UDP does not track sequence numbers the way TCP does. UDP has no way to reorder the datagrams into their transmission order, as shown in the figure.

Therefore, UDP simply reassembles the data in the order that it was received and forwards it to the application. If the data sequence is important to the application, the application must identify the proper sequence and determine how the data should be processed.

9.2.3.3   UDP Server Processes and Requests

Refer to Online Course for Illustration

Like TCP-based applications, UDP-based server applications are assigned well-known or registered port numbers, as shown in the figure. When these applications or processes are running on a server, they accept the data matched with the assigned port number. When UDP receives a datagram destined for one of these ports, it forwards the application data to the appropriate application based on its port number.

Note   The Remote Authentication Dial-in User Service (RADIUS) server shown in the figure provides authentication, authorization, and accounting services to manage user access. The operation of RADIUS is beyond scope for this course.

9.2.3.4   UDP Client Processes

Refer to Online Course for Illustration

As with TCP, client-server communication is initiated by a client application that requests data from a server process. The UDP client process dynamically selects a port number from the range of port numbers and uses this as the source port for the conversation. The destination port is usually the well-known or registered port number assigned to the server process.

After a client has selected the source and destination ports, the same pair of ports is used in the header of all datagrams used in the transaction. For the data returning to the client from the server, the source and destination port numbers in the datagram header are reversed.

Click through Figures 1 through 5 to see details of the UDP client processes.

Refer to
Lab Activity
for this chapter

9.2.3.5   Lab - Using Wireshark to Examine a UDP DNS Capture

In this lab, you will complete the following objectives:

- Part 1: Record a PC's IP Configuration Information
- Part 2: Use Wireshark to Capture DNS Queries and Responses
- Part 3: Analyze Captured DNS or UDP Packets

Refer to
Online Course
for Illustration

9.2.4   TCP or UDP

9.2.4.1   Applications that use TCP

TCP is a great example of how the different layers of the TCP/IP protocol suite have specific roles. TCP handles all tasks associated with dividing the data stream into segments, providing reliability, controlling data flow, and the reordering of segments. TCP frees the application from having to manage any of these tasks. Applications, like those shown in the figure, can simply send the data stream to the transport layer and use the services of TCP.

Refer to
Online Course
for Illustration

9.2.4.2   Applications that use UDP

There are three types of applications that are best suited for UDP:

- **Live video and multimedia applications** – Can tolerate some data loss, but require little or no delay. Examples include VoIP and live streaming video.

- **Simple request and reply applications** – Applications with simple transactions where a host sends a request and may or may not receive a reply. Examples include DNS and DHCP.

- **Applications that handle reliability themselves** – Unidirectional communications where flow control, error detection, acknowledgments, and error recovery is not required or can be handled by the application. Examples include SNMP and TFTP.

Although DNS and SNMP use UDP by default, both can also use TCP. DNS will use TCP if the DNS request or DNS response is more than 512 bytes, such as when a DNS response includes a large number of name resolutions. Similarly, under some situations the network administrator may want to configure SNMP to use TCP.

Refer to
Lab Activity
for this chapter

9.2.4.3   Lab - Using Wireshark to Examine FTP and TFTP Captures

In this lab, you will complete the following objectives:

- Part 1: Identify TCP Header Fields and Operation Using a Wireshark FTP Session Capture

- Part 2: Identify UDP Header Fields and Operation Using a Wireshark TFTP Session Capture

Refer to
Interactive Graphic
in online course

9.2.4.4   Activity - TCP, UDP, or Both

9.3   Summary

9.3.1   Conclusion

Refer to **Lab Activity** for this chapter

9.3.1.1   Class Activity - We Need to Talk, Again - Game
We Need to Talk, Again

Note   It is important that the students have completed the Introductory Modeling Activity for this chapter. This activity works best in medium-sized groups of 6 to 8 students.

The instructor will whisper a complex message to the first student in a group. An example of the message might be "We are expecting a blizzard tomorrow. It should be arriving in the morning, and school will be delayed two hours, so bring your homework."

That student whispers the message to the next student in the group. The last student of each group whispers the message to a student in the following group. Each group follows this process until all members of each group have heard the whispered message.

Here are the rules you are to follow:

- You can whisper the message in short parts to your neighbor AND you can repeat the message parts after verifying your neighbor heard the correct message.

- Small parts of the message may be checked and repeated (clockwise OR counter-clockwise to ensure accuracy of the message parts) by whispering. A student will be assigned to time the entire activity.

- When the message has reached the end of the group, the last student will say aloud what she or he heard. Small parts of the message may be repeated (i.e., re-sent), and the process can be restarted to ensure that ALL parts of the message are fully delivered and correct.

- The Instructor will restate the original message to check for quality delivery.

Refer to **Packet Tracer Activity** for this chapter

9.3.1.2   Packet Tracer - TCP and UDP Communications

This simulation activity is intended to provide a foundation for understanding the TCP and UDP in detail. Simulation mode provides the ability to view the functionality of the different protocols.

As data moves through the network, it is broken down into smaller pieces and identified in some fashion so that the pieces can be put back together. Each of these pieces is assigned a specific name (PDU) and associated with a specific layer. Packet Tracer Simulation mode enables the user to view each of the protocols and the associated PDU.

This activity provides an opportunity to explore the functionality of the TCP and UDP protocols, multiplexing and the function of port numbers in determining which local application requested the data or is sending the data.

Refer to
Online Course
for Illustration

9.3.1.3 Transport Layer

The transport layer provides transport-related services by:

- Dividing data received from an application into segments
- Adding a header to identify and manage each segment
- Using the header information to reassemble the segments back into application data
- Passing the assembled data to the correct application

UDP and TCP are common transport layer protocols.

UDP datagrams and TCP segments have headers added in front of the data that include a source port number and destination port number. These port numbers enable data to be directed to the correct application running on the destination computer.

TCP does not pass any data to the network until it knows that the destination is ready to receive it. TCP then manages the flow of the data and resends any data segments that are not acknowledged as being received at the destination. TCP uses mechanisms of handshaking, timers, acknowledgment messages, and dynamic windowing to achieve reliability. The reliability process, however, imposes overhead on the network in terms of much larger segment headers and more network traffic between the source and destination.

If the application data needs to be delivered across the network quickly, or if network bandwidth cannot support the overhead of control messages being exchanged between the source and the destination systems, UDP would be the developer's preferred transport layer protocol. UDP provides none of the TCP reliability features. However, this does not necessarily mean that the communication itself is unreliable; there may be mechanisms in the application layer protocols and services that process lost or delayed datagrams if the application has these requirements.

The application developer decides the transport layer protocol that best meets the requirements for the application. It is important to remember that the other layers all play a part in data network communications and influences its performance.

Go to the online course to take the quiz and exam.

Chapter 9 Quiz

This quiz is designed to provide an additional opportunity to practice the skills and knowledge presented in the chapter and to prepare for the chapter exam. You will be allowed multiple attempts and the grade does not appear in the gradebook.

Chapter 9 Exam

The chapter exam assesses your knowledge of the chapter content.

Your Chapter Notes

Application Layer

10.0 Introduction

10.0.1.1 Chapter 10: Application Layer

Applications, such as web browsers, online gaming, chatting with and emailing friends, enable us to send and receive data with relative ease. Typically we can access and use these applications without knowing how they work. However, for network professionals, it is important to know how an application is able to format, transmit and interpret messages that are sent and received across the network.

Visualizing the mechanisms that enable communication across the network is made easier if we use the layered framework of the OSI model.

In this chapter, we will explore the role of the application layer and how the applications, services, and protocols within the application layer make robust communication across data networks possible.

Refer to Lab Activity for this chapter

10.0.1.2 Class Activity – Application Investigation

In this activity, you will envision what it would be like not to have network applications available to use in the workplace. You may also estimate what it would cost to not use networked applications for a short period of time.

Refer to Online Course for Illustration

10.1 Application Layer Protocols

10.1.1 Application, Presentation, and Session

10.1.1.1 Application Layer

The Application Layer

The application layer is closest to the end user. As shown in the figure, it is the layer that provides the interface between the applications used to communicate and the underlying network over which messages are transmitted. Application layer protocols are used to exchange data between programs running on the source and destination hosts.

The upper three layers of the OSI model (application, presentation, and session) define functions of the single TCP/IP application layer.

There are many application layer protocols, and new protocols are always being developed. Some of the most widely known application layer protocols include Hypertext Transfer

Protocol (HTTP), File Transfer Protocol (FTP), Trivial File Transfer Protocol (TFTP), Internet Message Access Protocol (IMAP), and Domain Name System (DNS) protocol.

10.1.1.2   Presentation and Session Layer

The Presentation Layer

The presentation layer has three primary functions:

- Formatting, or presenting, data at the source device into a compatible form for receipt by the destination device

- Compressing data in a way that can be decompressed by the destination device

- Encrypting data for transmission and decrypting data upon receipt

As shown in the figure, the presentation layer formats data for the application layer, and it sets standards for file formats. Some well-known standards for video include QuickTime and Motion Picture Experts Group (MPEG). Some well-known graphic image formats that are used on networks are Graphics Interchange Format (GIF), Joint Photographic Experts Group (JPEG), and Portable Network Graphics (PNG) format.

The Session Layer

As the name implies, functions at the session layer create and maintain dialogs between source and destination applications. The session layer handles the exchange of information to initiate dialogs, keep them active, and to restart sessions that are disrupted or idle for a long period of time.

10.1.1.3   TCP/IP Application Layer Protocols

The TCP/IP application protocols specify the format and control information necessary for many common Internet communication functions. Click each application protocol in the figure to learn more about them.

Application layer protocols are used by both the source and destination devices during a communication session. For the communications to be successful the application layer protocols implemented on the source and destination host must be compatible.

10.1.1.4   Activity – Application and Presentation (Protocols and Standards)

10.1.2   How Application Protocols Interact with End-User Applications

10.1.2.1   Client-Server Model

In the client-server model, the device requesting the information is called a client and the device responding to the request is called a server. Client and server processes are considered to be in the application layer. The client begins the exchange by requesting data from the server, which responds by sending one or more streams of data to the client. Application layer protocols describe the format of the requests and responses between clients and servers. In addition to the actual data transfer, this exchange may also require user authentication and the identification of a data file to be transferred.

One example of a client-server network is using an ISP's email service to send, receive and store email. The email client on a home computer issues a request to the ISP's email server for any unread mail. The server responds by sending the requested email to the client. As shown in the figure, data transfer from a client to a server is referred to as an upload and data from a server to a client as a download.

Refer to
Online Course
for Illustration

10.1.2.2   Peer-to-Peer Networks

In the peer-to-peer (P2P) networking model, the data is accessed from a peer device without the use of a dedicated server.

The P2P network model involves two parts: P2P networks and P2P applications. Both parts have similar features, but in practice work quite differently.

In a P2P network, two or more computers are connected via a network and can share resources (such as printers and files) without having a dedicated server. Every connected end device (known as a peer) can function as both a server and a client. One computer might assume the role of server for one transaction while simultaneously serving as a client for another. The roles of client and server are set on a per request basis.

A simple example of P2P networking is shown in the figure. In addition to sharing files, a network such as this one would allow users to enable networked games, or share an Internet connection.

Refer to
Online Course
for Illustration

10.1.2.3   Peer-to-Peer Applications

A P2P application allows a device to act as both a client and a server within the same communication, as shown in the figure. In this model, every client is a server and every server a client. P2P applications require that each end device provide a user interface and run a background service.

Some P2P applications use a hybrid system where resource sharing is decentralized, but the indexes that point to resource locations are stored in a centralized directory. In a hybrid system, each peer accesses an index server to get the location of a resource stored on another peer.

Refer to
Online Course
for Illustration

10.1.2.4   Common P2P Applications

With P2P applications, each computer in the network running the application can act as a client or a server for the other computers in the network running the application. Common P2P networks include:

- eDonkey
- G2
- BitTorrent
- Bitcoin

Some P2P applications are based on the Gnutella protocol, where each user shares whole files with other users. As shown in the figure, Gnutella-compatible client software allows users to connect to Gnutella services over the Internet and to locate and access resources shared by other Gnutella peers. Many Gnutella client applications are available, including gtk-gnutella, WireShare, Shareaza, and Bearshare.

Many P2P applications allow users to share pieces of many files with each other at the same time. Clients use a small file called a torrent file to locate other users who have pieces that they need so that they can connect directly to them. This file also contains information about tracker computers that keep track of which users have what files. Clients ask for pieces from multiple users at the same time, known as a swarm. This technology is called BitTorrent. There are many BitTorrent clients including BitTorrent, uTorrent, Frostwire, and qBittorrent.

Note   Any type of file can be shared between users. Many of these files are copyrighted, meaning that only the creator has the right to use and distribute them. It is against the law to download or distribute copyrighted files without permission from the copyright holder. Copyright violation can result in criminal charges and civil lawsuits. Complete the lab on the following page to find out more about these legal issues.

Refer to
Lab Activity
for this chapter

10.1.2.5   Lab – Researching Peer-to-Peer File Sharing

In this lab, you will complete the following objectives:

■ Part 1: Identify P2P Networks, File Sharing Protocols, and Applications

■ Part 2: Research P2P File Sharing Issues

■ Part 3: Research P2P Copyright Litigations

Refer to
Online Course
for Illustration

10.2   Well-Known Application Layer Protocols and Services

10.2.1   Web and Email Protocols

10.2.1.1   Hypertext Transfer Protocol and Hypertext Markup Language

When a web address or uniform resource locator (URL) is typed into a web browser, the web browser establishes a connection to the web service running on the server using the HTTP protocol. URLs and Uniform Resource Identifier (URIs) are the names most people associate with web addresses.

To better understand how the web browser and web server interact, we can examine how a web page is opened in a browser. For this example, use the http://www.cisco.com/index.html URL.

First, as shown in Figure 1, the browser interprets the three parts of the URL:

1. **http** (the protocol or scheme)

2. **www.cisco.com** (the server name)

3. **index.html** (the specific filename requested)

As shown in Figure 2, the browser then checks with a name server to convert www.cisco.com into a numeric address, which it uses to connect to the server. Using HTTP requirements, the browser sends a GET request to the server and asks for the **index.html** file.

The server, as shown in Figure 3, sends the HTML code for this web page to the browser. Finally, as shown in Figure 4, the browser deciphers the HTML code and formats the page for the browser window.

Refer to
Online Course
for Illustration

10.2.1.2   HTTP and HTTPS

HTTP is a request/response protocol. When a client, typically a web browser, sends a request to a web server, HTTP specifies the message types used for that communication. The three common message types are GET, POST, and PUT (see the figure):

■ **GET** – A client request for data. A client (web browser) sends the GET message to the web server to request HTML pages.

■ **POST** – Uploads data files to the web server such as form data.

■ **PUT** – Uploads resources or content to the web server such as an image.

Although HTTP is remarkably flexible, it is not a secure protocol. The request messages send information to the server in plain text that can be intercepted and read. The server responses, typically HTML pages, are also unencrypted.

For secure communication across the Internet, the HTTP Secure (HTTPS) protocol is used. HTTPS uses authentication and encryption to secure data as it travels between the client and server. HTTPS uses the same client request-server response process as HTTP, but the data stream is encrypted with Secure Socket Layer (SSL) before being transported across the network.

Refer to
Online Course
for Illustration

10.2.1.3   Email Protocols

One of the primary services offered by an ISP is email hosting. To run on a computer or other end device, email requires several applications and services, as shown in the figure. Email is a store-and-forward method of sending, storing, and retrieving electronic messages across a network. Email messages are stored in databases on mail servers.

Email clients communicate with mail servers to send and receive email. Mail servers communicate with other mail servers to transport messages from one domain to another. An email client does not communicate directly with another email client when sending email. Instead, both clients rely on the mail server to transport messages.

Email supports three separate protocols for operation: Simple Mail Transfer Protocol (SMTP), Post Office Protocol (POP), and IMAP. The application layer process that sends mail uses SMTP. A client retrieves email, however, using one of the two application layer protocols: POP or IMAP.

Refer to
Online Course
for Illustration

10.2.1.4   SMTP Operation

SMTP message formats require a message header and a message body. While the message body can contain any amount of text, the message header must have a properly formatted recipient email address and a sender address.

When a client sends email, the client SMTP process connects with a server SMTP process on well-known port 25. After the connection is made, the client attempts to send the email to the server across the connection. When the server receives the message, it either places the message in a local account, if the recipient is local, or forwards the message to another mail server for delivery, as shown in the figure.

The destination email server may not be online or may be busy when email messages are sent. Therefore, SMTP spools messages to be sent at a later time. Periodically, the server checks the queue for messages and attempts to send them again. If the message is still not delivered after a predetermined expiration time, it is returned to the sender as undeliverable.

Refer to **Online Course** for Illustration

10.2.1.5   POP Operation

POP is used by an application to retrieve mail from a mail server. With POP, mail is downloaded from the server to the client and then deleted on the server. This is how POP operates, by default.

The server starts the POP service by passively listening on TCP port 110 for client connection requests. When a client wants to make use of the service, it sends a request to establish a TCP connection with the server. When the connection is established, the POP server sends a greeting. The client and POP server then exchange commands and responses until the connection is closed or aborted.

With POP, email messages are downloaded to the client and removed from the server, so there is no centralized location where email messages are kept. Because POP does not store messages, it is undesirable for a small business that needs a centralized backup solution.

Refer to **Online Course** for Illustration

10.2.1.6   IMAP Operation

IMAP is another protocol that describes a method to retrieve email messages. Unlike POP, when the user connects to an IMAP-capable server, copies of the messages are downloaded to the client application. The original messages are kept on the server until manually deleted. Users view copies of the messages in their email client software.

Users can create a file hierarchy on the server to organize and store mail. That file structure is duplicated on the email client as well. When a user decides to delete a message, the server synchronizes that action and deletes the message from the server.

Click here to learn more about email protocols.

Refer to **Packet Tracer Activity** for this chapter

10.2.1.7   Packet Tracer – Web and Email

In this activity, you will configure HTTP and email services using the simulated server in Packet Tracer. You will then configure clients to access the HTTP and email services.

Refer to **Online Course** for Illustration

10.2.2   IP Addressing Services

10.2.2.1   Domain Name Service

In data networks, devices are labeled with numeric IP addresses to send and receive data over networks. Domain names were created to convert the numeric address into a simple, recognizable name.

On the Internet, these domain names, such as http://www.cisco.com, are much easier for people to remember than 198.133.219.25, which is the actual numeric address for this server. If Cisco decides to change the numeric address of www.cisco.com, it is transparent to the user because the domain name remains the same. The new address is simply linked to the existing domain name and connectivity is maintained.

The DNS protocol defines an automated service that matches resource names with the required numeric network address. It includes the format for queries, responses, and data. The DNS protocol communications use a single format called a message. This message format is used for all types of client queries and server responses, error messages, and the transfer of resource record information between servers.

Figures 1 through 5 display the steps involved in DNS resolution.

Refer to
Online Course
for Illustration

10.2.2.2 DNS Message Format

The DNS server stores different types of resource records used to resolve names. These records contain the name, address, and type of record. Some of these record types are:

- **A** – An end device IPv4 address

- **NS** – An authoritative name server

- **AAAA** – An end device IPv6 address (pronounced quad-A)

- **MX** – A mail exchange record

When a client makes a query, the server's DNS process first looks at its own records to resolve the name. If it is unable to resolve the name using its stored records, it contacts other servers to resolve the name. After a match is found and returned to the original requesting server, the server temporarily stores the numbered address in the event that the same name is requested again.

The DNS Client service on Windows PCs also stores previously resolved names in memory. The **ipconfig /displaydns** command displays all of the cached DNS entries.

Refer to
Online Course
for Illustration

10.2.2.3 DNS Hierarchy

The DNS protocol uses a hierarchical system to create a database to provide name resolution. The hierarchy looks like an inverted tree with the root at the top and branches below (see the figure). DNS uses domain names to form the hierarchy.

The naming structure is broken down into small, manageable zones. Each DNS server maintains a specific database file and is only responsible for managing name-to-IP mappings for that small portion of the entire DNS structure. When a DNS server receives a request for a name translation that is not within its DNS zone, the DNS server forwards the request to another DNS server within the proper zone for translation.

Note DNS is scalable because hostname resolution is spread across multiple servers.

The different top-level domains represent either the type of organization or the country of origin. Examples of top-level domains are:

- **.com** – a business or industry

- **.org** – a non-profit organization

- **.au** – Australia

- **.co** – Colombia

Refer to
Online Course
for Illustration

10.2.2.4   The nslookup Command

When configuring a network device, one or more DNS Server addresses are provided that the DNS client can use for name resolution. Usually the Internet service provider (ISP) provides the addresses to use for the DNS servers. When a user's application requests to connect to a remote device by name, the requesting DNS client queries the name server to resolve the name to a numeric address.

Computer operating systems also have a utility called nslookup that allows the user to manually query the name servers to resolve a given host name. This utility can also be used to troubleshoot name resolution issues and to verify the current status of the name servers.

In Figure 1, when the nslookup command is issued, the default DNS server configured for your host is displayed. The name of a host or domain can be entered at the **nslookup** prompt. The nslookup utility has many options available for extensive testing and verification of the DNS process.

In Figure 2, use the Syntax Checker activity to practice entering the **nslookup** command in both Windows and Linux.

Refer to
Online Course
for Illustration

10.2.2.5   Dynamic Host Configuration Protocol

The Dynamic Host Configuration Protocol (DHCP) for IPv4 service automates the assignment of IPv4 addresses, subnet masks, gateways, and other IPv4 networking parameters. This is referred to as dynamic addressing. The alternative to dynamic addressing is static addressing. When using static addressing, the network administrator manually enters IP address information on hosts.

When a host connects to the network, the DHCP server is contacted, and an address is requested. The DHCP server chooses an address from a configured range of addresses called a pool and assigns (leases) it to the host.

On larger networks, or where the user population changes frequently, DHCP is preferred for address assignment. New users may arrive and need connections; others may have new computers that must be connected. Rather than use static addressing for each connection, it is more efficient to have IP addresses assigned automatically using DHCP.

DHCP-distributed addresses are leased for a set period of time. When the lease is expired, the address is returned to the pool for reuse if the host has been powered down or taken off the network. Users can freely move from location to location and easily re-establish network connections through DHCP.

As the figure shows, various types of devices can be DHCP servers. The DHCP server in most medium-to-large networks is usually a local, dedicated PC-based server. With home networks, the DHCP server is usually located on the local router that connects the home network to the ISP.

Many networks use both DHCP and static addressing. DHCP is used for general purpose hosts, such as end user devices. Static addressing is used for network devices, such as gateways, switches, servers, and printers.

DHCPv6 (DHCP for IPv6) provides similar services for IPv6 clients. One important difference is that DHCPv6 does not provide a default gateway address. This can only be obtained dynamically from the router's Router Advertisement message.

Refer to
Online Course
for Illustration

10.2.2.6 DHCP Operation

As shown in the figure, when an IPv4, DHCP-configured device boots up or connects to the network, the client broadcasts a DHCP discover (DHCPDISCOVER) message to identify any available DHCP servers on the network. A DHCP server replies with a DHCP offer (DHCPOFFER) message, which offers a lease to the client. The offer message contains the IPv4 address and subnet mask to be assigned, the IPv4 address of the DNS server, and the IPv4 address of the default gateway. The lease offer also includes the duration of the lease.

The client may receive multiple DHCPOFFER messages if there is more than one DHCP server on the local network. Therefore, it must choose between them, and sends a DHCP request (DHCPREQUEST) message that identifies the explicit server and lease offer that the client is accepting. A client may also choose to request an address that it had previously been allocated by the server.

Assuming that the IPv4 address requested by the client, or offered by the server, is still available, the server returns a DHCP acknowledgment (DHCPACK) message that acknowledges to the client that the lease has been finalized. If the offer is no longer valid, then the selected server responds with a DHCP negative acknowledgment (DHCPNAK) message. If a DHCPNAK message is returned, then the selection process must begin again with a new DHCPDISCOVER message being transmitted. After the client has the lease, it must be renewed prior to the lease expiration through another DHCPREQUEST message.

The DHCP server ensures that all IP addresses are unique (the same IP address cannot be assigned to two different network devices simultaneously). Most Internet providers use DHCP to allocate addresses to their customers.

DHCPv6 has similar set of messages to those shown in the figure for DHCP for IPv4. The DHCPv6 messages are SOLICIT, ADVERTISE, INFORMATION REQUEST, and REPLY

Refer to **Packet Tracer Activity** for this chapter

10.2.2.7 Packet Tracer – DHCP and DNS Servers

In this activity, you will configure and verify static IP addressing and DHCP addressing. You will then configure a DNS server to map IP addresses to the web site names.

Refer to **Lab Activity** for this chapter

10.2.2.8 Lab – Observing DNS Servers

In this lab, you will complete the following objectives:

■ Part 1: Observe the DNS Conversion of a URL to an IP Address

■ Part 2: Observe DNS Lookup Using the nslookup Command on a Web Site

■ Part 3: Observe DNS Lookup Using the nslookup Command on Mail Servers

Refer to
Online Course
for Illustration

10.2.3 File Sharing Services

10.2.3.1 File Transfer Protocol

FTP is another commonly used application layer protocol. FTP was developed to allow for data transfers between a client and a server. An FTP client is an application that runs on a computer that is used to push and pull data from a server running an FTP daemon (FTPd).

As the figure illustrates, to successfully transfer data, FTP requires two connections between the client and the server, one for commands and replies, the other for the actual file transfer:

■ The client establishes the first connection to the server for control traffic using TCP port 21, consisting of client commands and server replies.

■ The client establishes the second connection to the server for the actual data transfer using TCP port 20. This connection is created every time there is data to be transferred.

The data transfer can happen in either direction. The client can download (pull) data from the server, or the client can upload (push) data to the server.

Refer to
Online Course
for Illustration

10.2.3.2   Server Message Block

The Server Message Block (SMB) is a client/server file sharing protocol that describes the structure of shared network resources, such as directories, files, printers, and serial ports. It is a request-response protocol. All SMB messages share a common format. This format uses a fixed-sized header, followed by a variable-sized parameter and data component.

SMB messages can:

■ Start, authenticate, and terminate sessions

■ Control file and printer access

■ Allow an application to send or receive messages to or from another device

SMB file-sharing and print services have become the mainstay of Microsoft networking. With the introduction of the Windows 2000 software series, Microsoft changed the underlying structure for using SMB. In previous versions of Microsoft products, the SMB services used a non-TCP/IP protocol to implement name resolution. Beginning with Windows2000, all subsequent Microsoft products use DNS naming, which allows TCP/IP protocols to directly support SMB resource sharing, as shown in Figure 1. The SMB file exchange process between Windows PCs is shown in Figure 2.

Unlike the file sharing supported by FTP, clients establish a long-term connection to servers. After the connection is established, the user of the client can access the resources on the server as if the resource is local to the client host.

The LINUX and UNIX operating systems also provide a method of sharing resources with Microsoft networks using a version of SMB called SAMBA. The Apple Macintosh operating systems also support resource sharing using the SMB protocol.

Refer to **Packet
Tracer Activity**
for this chapter

10.2.3.3   Packet Tracer - FTP

In this activity, you will configure FTP services. You will then use the FTP services to transfer files between clients and the server.

Refer to
Lab Activity
for this chapter

10.2.3.4   Lab – Exploring FTP

In this lab, you will complete the following objectives:

■ Part 1: Use FTP from a Command Prompt

■ Part 2: Download an FTP File Using WS_FTP LE

■ Part 3: Use FTP in a Browser

10.3   Summary

10.3.1   Conclusion

Refer to
Lab Activity
for this chapter

10.3.1.1   Modeling Activity – Make it happen!

In this activity, you will apply new knowledge of application layer protocols and methods of the TCP/IP layer in streamlining data/network communication.

Refer to **Packet
Tracer Activity**
for this chapter

10.3.1.2   Packet Tracer - Explore a Network

This simulation activity is intended to help you understand the flow of traffic and the contents of data packets as they traverse a complex network. Communications will be examined at three different locations simulating typical business and home networks.

Refer to **Packet
Tracer Activity**
for this chapter

10.3.1.3   Packet Tracer - Multiuser - Tutorial

The multiuser feature in Packet Tracer allows multiple point-to-point connections between multiple instances of Packet Tracer. This first Packet Tracer Multiuser (PTMU) activity is a quick tutorial demonstrating the steps to establish and verify a multiuser connection to another instance of Packet Tracer within the same LAN. Ideally, this activity is meant for two students. However, it can also be completed as a solo activity simply by opening the two separate files to create two separate instances of Packet Tracer on your local machine.

Refer to **Packet
Tracer Activity**
for this chapter

10.3.1.4   Packet Tracer Multiuser - Implement Services

In this multiuser activity, two students (players) cooperate to implement and verify services including DHCP, HTTP, Email, DNS, and FTP. The server side player will implement and verify services on one server. The client side player will configure two clients and verify access to services.

Refer to
Online Course
for Illustration

10.3.1.5   Application Layer

The application layer is responsible for directly accessing the underlying processes that manage and deliver communication to the human network. This layer serves as the source and destination of communications across data networks. The application layer applications, services, and protocols enable users to interact with the data network in a way that is meaningful and effective.

■ Applications are computer programs with which the user interacts and which initiate the data transfer process at the user's request.

- Services are background programs that provide the connection between the application layer and the lower layers of the networking model.

- Protocols provide a structure of agreed-upon rules and processes that ensure services running on one particular device can send and receive data from a range of different network devices.

Delivery of data over the network can be requested from a server by a client, or between devices that operate in a P2P arrangement. In P2P, the client/server relationship is established according to which device is the source and destination at that time. Messages are exchanged between the application layer services at each end device in accordance with the protocol specifications to establish and use these relationships.

Protocols like HTTP, for example, support the delivery of web pages to end devices. SMTP, IMAP , and POP support sending and receiving email. SMB and FTP enable users to share files. P2P applications make it easier for consumers to seamlessly share media in a distributed fashion. DNS resolves the human-legible names, used to refer to network resources, into numeric addresses usable by the network. Clouds are remote upstream locations that store data and host applications so that users do not require as many local resources, and so that users can seamlessly access content on different devices from any location.

All of these elements work together, at the application layer. The application layer enables users to work and play over the Internet.

Go to the online course to take the quiz and exam.

Chapter 10 Quiz

This quiz is designed to provide an additional opportunity to practice the skills and knowledge presented in the chapter and to prepare for the chapter exam. You will be allowed multiple attempts and the grade does not appear in the gradebook.

Chapter 10 Exam

The chapter exam assesses your knowledge of the chapter content.

Your Chapter Notes

Build a Small Network

11.0 Introduction

11.0.1.1 Build a Small Network

Up to this point in the course, we have considered the services that a data network can provide to the human network, examined the features of each layer of the OSI model and the operations of TCP/IP protocols, and looked in detail at Ethernet, a universal LAN technology. The next step is to learn how to assemble these elements together in a functioning network that can be maintained.

Refer to
Lab Activity
for this chapter

11.0.1.2 Class Activity - Did You Notice...?

Refer to
Online Course
for Illustration

Note Students can work singularly, in pairs, or the full classroom can complete this activity together.

Take a look at the two networks in the diagram. Visually compare and contrast the two networks. Make note of the devices used in each network design. Since the devices are labeled, you already know what types of end devices and intermediate devices are on each network.

How are the two networks different? Is it just that there are more devices present on Network B than on Network A?

Select the network you would use if you owned a small to medium-sized business. Be able to justify your selected network based on cost, speed, ports, expandability, and manageability.

Refer to
Online Course
for Illustration

11.1 Network Design

11.1.1 Devices in a Small Network

11.1.1.1 Small Network Topologies

The majority of businesses are small. It is not surprising then that the majority of networks are also small. A typical small-business network is shown in the figure.

With small networks, the design of the network is usually simple. The number and type of devices included are significantly reduced compared to that of a larger network. The network topologies typically involve a single router and one or more switches. Small networks may also have wireless access points (possibly built into the router) and IP phones. As for connection to the Internet, normally a small network has a single WAN connection provided by DSL, cable, or an Ethernet connection.

Managing a small network requires many of the same skills as those required for managing a larger one. The majority of work is focused on maintenance and troubleshooting of existing equipment, as well as securing devices and information on the network. The management of a small network is either done by an employee of the company or a person contracted by the company, depending on the size and type of the business.

Refer to **Online Course** for Illustration

11.1.1.2   Device Selection for a Small Network

In order to meet user requirements, even small networks require planning and design. Planning ensures that all requirements, cost factors, and deployment options are given due consideration.

When implementing a small network, one of the first design considerations is the type of intermediate devices to use to support the network. When selecting the type of intermediate devices, there are a number of factors that need to be considered, as shown in the figure.

Cost

The cost of a switch or router is determined by its capacity and features. The device capacity includes the number and types of ports available and the backplane speed. Other factors that impact the cost are network management capabilities, embedded security technologies, and optional advanced switching technologies. The expense of cable runs required to connect every device on the network must also be considered. Another key element affecting cost considerations is the amount of redundancy to incorporate into the network.

Speed and Types of Ports/Interfaces

Choosing the number and type of ports on a router or switch is a critical decision. Newer computers have built-in 1 Gb/s NICs. 10 Gb/s ports are already included with some workstations and servers. While it is more expensive, choosing Layer 2 devices that can accommodate increased speeds allows the network to evolve without replacing central devices.

Expandability

Networking devices come in both fixed and modular physical configurations. Fixed configurations have a specific number and type of ports or interfaces. Modular devices have expansion slots that provide the flexibility to add new modules as requirements evolve. Switches are available with additional ports for high-speed uplinks. Routers can be used to connect different types of networks. Care must be taken to select the appropriate modules and interfaces for the specific media.

Operating System Features and Services

Depending on the version of the operating system, a network device can support certain features and services, such as:

- Security
- Quality of Service (QoS)
- Voice over IP (VoIP)

- Layer 3 switching

- Network Address Translation (NAT)

- Dynamic Host Configuration Protocol (DHCP)

Refer to
Online Course
for Illustration

11.1.1.3   IP Addressing for a Small Network

When implementing a small network, it is necessary to plan the IP addressing space. All hosts within an internetwork must have a unique address. The IP addressing scheme should be planned, documented and maintained based on the type of device receiving the address.

Examples of different types of devices that will factor into the IP design are:

- End devices for users

- Servers and peripherals

- Hosts that are accessible from the Internet

- Intermediary devices

Planning and documenting the IP addressing scheme helps the administrator track device types. For example, if all servers are assigned a host address between the range of 50-100, it is easy to identify server traffic by IP address. This can be very useful when troubleshooting network traffic issues using a protocol analyzer.

Additionally, administrators are better able to control access to resources on the network based on IP address when a deterministic IP addressing scheme is used. This can be especially important for hosts that provide resources to the internal network as well, as to the external network. Web servers or e-commerce servers play such a role. If the addresses for these resources are not planned and documented, the security and accessibility of the devices are not easily controlled. If a server has a random address assigned, blocking access to this address is difficult, and clients may not be able to locate this resource.

Each of these different device types should be allocated to a logical block of addresses within the address range of the network.

Click the buttons in the figure to see the method for assignment.

Refer to
Online Course
for Illustration

11.1.1.4   Redundancy in a Small Network

Another important part of network design is reliability. Even small businesses often rely heavily on their network for business operation. A failure of the network can be very costly. In order to maintain a high degree of reliability, redundancy is required in the network design. Redundancy helps to eliminate single points of failure. There are many ways to accomplish redundancy in a network. Redundancy can be accomplished by installing duplicate equipment, but it can also be accomplished by supplying duplicate network links for critical areas, as shown in the figure.

Small networks typically provide a single exit point toward the Internet via one or more default gateways. If the router fails, the entire network loses connectivity to the Internet. For this reason, it may be advisable for a small business to pay for a second service provider as backup.

Refer to
Online Course
for Illustration

11.1.1.5   Traffic Management

The network administrator should consider the various types of traffic and their treatment in the network design. The routers and switches in a small network should be configured to support real-time traffic, such as voice and video, in a distinct manner relative to other data traffic. In fact, a good network design will classify traffic carefully according to priority, as shown in the figure. In the end, the goal for a good network design, even for a small network, is to enhance the productivity of the employees and minimize network downtime.

Refer to
Online Course
for Illustration

11.1.2   Small Network Applications and Protocols

11.1.2.1   Common Applications

The network is only as useful as the applications that are on it. There are two forms of software programs or processes that provide access to the network: network applications and application layer services.

Network Applications

Applications are the software programs used to communicate over the network. Some end-user applications are network-aware, meaning that they implement application layer protocols and are able to communicate directly with the lower layers of the protocol stack. Email clients and web browsers are examples of this type of application.

Application Layer Services

Other programs may need the assistance of application layer services to use network resources like file transfer or network print spooling. Though transparent to an employee, these services are the programs that interface with the network and prepare the data for transfer. Different types of data, whether text, graphics or video, require different network services to ensure that they are properly prepared for processing by the functions occurring at the lower layers of the OSI model.

Each application or network service uses protocols, which define the standards and data formats to be used. Without protocols, the data network would not have a common way to format and direct data. In order to understand the function of various network services, it is necessary to become familiar with the underlying protocols that govern their operation.

Use the Task Manager to view the current applications, processes, and services running on a Windows PC, as shown in the figure.

Refer to
Online Course
for Illustration

11.1.2.2   Common Protocols

Most of a technician's work, in either a small or a large network, will in some way be involved with network protocols. Network protocols support the applications and services used by employees in a small network. Common network protocols are shown in the figure. Click each server for a brief description.

These network protocols comprise the fundamental toolset of a network professional. Each of these network protocols define:

- Processes on either end of a communication session

- Types of messages

- Syntax of the messages

- Meaning of informational fields

- How messages are sent and the expected response

- Interaction with the next lower layer

Many companies have established a policy of using secure versions of these protocols whenever possible. These protocols are HTTPS, SFTP, and SSH.

Refer to **Online Course** for Illustration

11.1.2.3   Voice and Video Applications

Businesses today are increasingly using IP telephony and streaming media to communicate with customers and business partners, as shown in Figure 1. The network administrator must ensure the proper equipment is installed in the network and that the network devices are configured to ensure priority delivery. Figure 2 shows elements of a small network that support real-time applications.

Infrastructure

To support the existing and proposed real-time applications, the infrastructure must accommodate the characteristics of each type of traffic. The network designer must determine whether the existing switches and cabling can support the traffic that will be added to the network.

VoIP

VoIP devices convert analog into digital IP packets. The device could be an analog telephone adapter (ATA) that is attached between a traditional analog phone and the Ethernet switch. After the signals are converted into IP packets, the router sends those packets between corresponding locations. VoIP is much less expensive than an integrated IP telephony solution, but the quality of communications does not meet the same standards. Voice and video over IP solutions for small businesses can be realized, for example, with Skype and non-enterprise versions of Cisco WebEx.

IP Telephony

In IP telephony, the IP phone itself performs voice-to-IP conversion. Voice-enabled routers are not required within a network with an integrated IP telephony solution. IP phones use a dedicated server for call control and signaling. There are now many vendors with dedicated IP telephony solutions for small networks.

Real-time Applications

To transport streaming media effectively, the network must be able to support applications that require delay-sensitive delivery. Real-Time Transport Protocol (RTP) and Real-Time Transport Control Protocol (RTCP) are two protocols that support this requirement. RTP and RTCP enable control and scalability of the network resources by allowing Quality of Service (QoS) mechanisms to be incorporated. These QoS mechanisms provide valuable tools for minimizing latency issues for real-time streaming applications.

Refer to
Online Course
for Illustration

11.1.3   Scale to Larger Networks

11.1.3.1   Small Network Growth

Growth is a natural process for many small businesses, and their networks must grow accordingly. Ideally, the network administrator has enough lead time to make intelligent decisions about growing the network in-line with the growth of the company.

To scale a network, several elements are required:

- **Network documentation** - physical and logical topology
- **Device inventory** - list of devices that use or comprise the network
- **Budget** - itemized IT budget, including fiscal year equipment purchasing budget
- **Traffic analysis** - protocols, applications, and services and their respective traffic requirements, should be documented

These elements are used to inform the decision-making that accompanies the scaling of a small network.

Refer to
Online Course
for Illustration

11.1.3.2   Protocol Analysis

When trying to determine how to manage network traffic, especially as the network grows, it is important to understand the type of traffic that is crossing the network as well as the current traffic flow. If the types of traffic are unknown, a protocol analyzer will help identify the traffic and its source.

To determine traffic flow patterns, it is important to:

- Capture traffic during peak utilization times to get a good representation of the different traffic types.
- Perform the capture on different network segments; some traffic will be local to a particular segment.

Information gathered by the protocol analyzer is evaluated based on the source and destination of the traffic, as well as the type of traffic being sent. This analysis can be used to make decisions on how to manage the traffic more efficiently. This can be done by reducing unnecessary traffic flows or changing flow patterns altogether by moving a server, for example.

Sometimes, simply relocating a server or service to another network segment improves network performance and accommodates the growing traffic needs. At other times, optimizing the network performance requires major network redesign and intervention.

Refer to
Online Course
for Illustration

11.1.3.3   Employee Network Utilization

In addition to understanding changing traffic trends, a network administrator must also be aware of how network use is changing. As shown in the figure, a small network administrator has the ability to obtain in-person IT "snapshots" of employee application utilization for a significant portion of the employee workforce over time. These snapshots typically include information such as:

- OS and OS Version

- Non-Network Applications

- Network Applications

- CPU Utilization

- Drive Utilization

- RAM Utilization

Documenting snapshots for employees in a small network over a period of time will go a long way toward informing the network administrator of evolving protocol requirements and associated traffic flows. A shift in resource utilization may require the network administrator to adjust network resource allocations accordingly.

Refer to **Online Course** for Illustration

11.2   Network Security

11.2.1   Security Threats and Vulnerabilities

11.2.1.1   Types of Threats

Whether wired or wireless, computer networks are essential to everyday activities. Individuals and organizations alike depend on their computers and networks. Intrusion by an unauthorized person can result in costly network outages and loss of work. Attacks on a network can be devastating and can result in a loss of time and money due to damage or theft of important information or assets.

Intruders can gain access to a network through software vulnerabilities, hardware attacks or through guessing someone's username and password. Intruders who gain access by modifying software or exploiting software vulnerabilities are often called hackers.

After the hacker gains access to the network, four types of threats may arise, as shown in the figure. Click each image for more information.

Refer to **Online Course** for Illustration

11.2.1.2   Physical Security

An equally important vulnerability is the physical security of devices. An attacker can deny the use of network resources if those resources can be physically compromised.

The four classes of physical threats are:

- **Hardware threats** – physical damage to servers, routers, switches, cabling plant, and workstations

- **Environmental threats** – temperature extremes (too hot or too cold) or humidity extremes (too wet or too dry)

- **Electrical threats** – voltage spikes, insufficient supply voltage (brownouts), unconditioned power (noise), and total power loss

- **Maintenance threats** – poor handling of key electrical components (electrostatic discharge), lack of critical spare parts, poor cabling, and poor labeling

These issues must be dealt with in an organizational policy, as shown in the figure.

Refer to
Online Course
for Illustration

11.2.1.3   Types of Vulnerabilities

Vulnerability is the degree of weakness which is inherent in every network and device. This includes routers, switches, desktops, servers, and even security devices. Typically, the network devices under attack are the endpoints, such as servers and desktop computers.

There are three primary vulnerabilities or weaknesses:

- Technological, as shown in Figure 1

- Configuration, as shown in Figure 2

- Security policy, as shown in Figure 3

All three of these vulnerabilities or weaknesses can lead to various attacks, including malicious code attacks and network attacks.

Refer to
Interactive Graphic
in online course

11.2.1.4   Activity - Security Threats and Vulnerabilities

11.2.2   Network Attacks

Refer to
Online Course
for Illustration

11.2.2.1   Types of Malware

Malware or malicious code (malcode) is short for malicious software. It is code or software that is specifically designed to damage, disrupt, steal, or inflict "bad" or illegitimate action on data, hosts, or networks. Viruses, worms, and Trojan horses are types of malware.

Click Play to view an animation on these three threats.

Viruses

A computer virus is a type of malware that propagates by inserting a copy of itself into, and becoming part of, another program. It spreads from one computer to another, leaving infections as it travels. Viruses can range in severity from causing mildly annoying effects to damaging data or software and causing denial-of-service (DoS) conditions. Almost all viruses are attached to an executable file, which means the virus may exist on a system but will not be active or able to spread until a user runs or opens the malicious host file or program. When the host code is executed, the viral code is executed as well. Normally, the host program keeps functioning after it is infected by the virus. However, some viruses overwrite other programs with copies of themselves, which destroys the host program altogether. Viruses spread when the software or document they are attached to is transferred from one computer to another using the network, a disk, file sharing, or infected e-mail attachments.

Worms

Computer worms are similar to viruses in that they replicate functional copies of themselves and can cause the same type of damage. In contrast to viruses, which require the spreading of an infected host file, worms are standalone software and do not require a host program or human help to propagate. A worm does not need to attach to a program to infect a host and enter a computer through a vulnerability in the system. Worms take advantage of system features to travel through the network unaided.

Trojan Horses

A Trojan horse is another type of malware named after the wooden horse the Greeks used to infiltrate Troy. It is a harmful piece of software that looks legitimate. Users are typically tricked into loading and executing it on their systems. After it is activated, it can achieve any number of attacks on the host, from irritating the user (popping up windows or changing desktops) to damaging the host (deleting files, stealing data, or activating and spreading other malware, such as viruses). Trojan horses are also known to create back doors to give malicious users access to the system.

Unlike viruses and worms, Trojan horses do not reproduce by infecting other files, nor do they self-replicate. Trojan horses must spread through user interaction such as opening an e-mail attachment or downloading and running a file from the Internet.

Refer to **Online Course** for Illustration

11.2.2.2   Reconnaissance Attacks

In addition to malicious code attacks, it is also possible for networks to fall prey to various network attacks. Network attacks can be classified into three major categories:

- **Reconnaissance attacks** – the discovery and mapping of systems, services, or vulnerabilities

- **Access attacks** – the unauthorized manipulation of data, system access, or user privileges

- **Denial of service** – the disabling or corruption of networks, systems, or services

For reconnaissance attacks, external attackers can use Internet tools, such as the **nslookup** and **whois** utilities, to easily determine the IP address space assigned to a given corporation or entity. After the IP address space is determined, an attacker can then ping the publicly available IP addresses to identify the addresses that are active. To help automate this step, an attacker may use a ping sweep tool, such as *fping* or *gping*, which systematically pings all network addresses in a given range or subnet. This is similar to going through a section of a telephone book and calling each number to see who answers.

Click each type of reconnaissance attack tool to see an animation of the attack.

Refer to **Online Course** for Illustration

11.2.2.3   Access Attacks

Access attacks exploit known vulnerabilities in authentication services, FTP services, and web services to gain entry to web accounts, confidential databases, and other sensitive information. An access attack allows an individual to gain unauthorized access to information that they have no right to view. Access attacks can be classified into four types:

- Password attacks (Figure 1)

- Trust Exploitation (Figure 2)

- Port Redirection (Figure 3)

- Man-in-the-Middle (Figure 4)

Refer to
Online Course
for Illustration

11.2.2.4 Denial of Service Attacks

Denial of Service (DoS) attacks are the most publicized form of attack and also among the most difficult to eliminate. Even within the attacker community, DoS attacks are regarded as trivial and considered bad form because they require so little effort to execute. But because of their ease of implementation and potentially significant damage, DoS attacks deserve special attention from security administrators.

DoS attacks take many forms. Ultimately, they prevent authorized people from using a service by consuming system resources.

Click the buttons in the figure to see examples of DoS and DDoS attacks.

To help prevent DoS attacks it is important to stay up to date with the latest security updates for operating systems and applications. For example, the ping of death is no longer a threat because updates to operating systems have fixed the vulnerability that it exploited.

Refer to
Interactive Graphic
in online course

11.2.2.5 Activity - Types of Attack

11.2.2.6 Lab - Researching Network Security Threats

Refer to
Lab Activity
for this chapter

In this lab, you will complete the following objectives:

- Part 1: Explore the SANS Website
- Part 2: Identify Recent Network Security Threats
- Part 3: Detail a Specific Network Security Threat

Refer to
Online Course
for Illustration

11.2.3 Network Attack Mitigation

11.2.3.1 Backup, Upgrade, Update, and Patch

Keeping up-to-date with the latest developments can lead to a more effective defense against network attacks. As new malware is released, enterprises need to keep current with the latest versions of antivirus software.

The most effective way to mitigate a worm attack is to download security updates from the operating system vendor and patch all vulnerable systems. Administering numerous systems involves the creation of a standard software image (operating system and accredited applications that are authorized for use on client systems) that is deployed on new or upgraded systems. However, security requirements change and already deployed systems may need to have updated security patches installed.

One solution to the management of critical security patches is to create a central patch server that all systems must communicate with after a set period of time, as shown in the figure. Any patches that are not applied to a host are automatically downloaded from the patch server and installed without user intervention.

Refer to
Online Course
for Illustration

11.2.3.2 Authentication, Authorization, and Accounting

Authentication, authorization, and accounting (AAA, or "triple A") network security services provide the primary framework to set up access control on a network device. AAA is a way to control who is permitted to access a network (authenticate), what they can do while they are there (authorize), and what actions they perform while accessing the network (accounting).

The concept of AAA is similar to the use of a credit card. The credit card identifies who can use it, how much that user can spend, and keeps account of what items the user spent money on, as shown in the figure. Refer to the Chapter Appendix to learn more about AAA.

Refer to
Online Course
for Illustration

11.2.3.3   Firewalls

A firewall is one of the most effective security tools available for protecting users from external threats. Network firewalls reside between two or more networks, control the traffic between them, and help prevent unauthorized access. Host-based firewalls or personal firewalls are installed on end systems. Firewall products use various techniques for determining what is permitted or denied access to a network. These techniques are:

- **Packet filtering** – Prevents or allows access based on IP or MAC addresses

- **Application filtering** – Prevents or allows access by specific application types based on port numbers

- **URL filtering** – Prevents or allows access to websites based on specific URLs or keywords

- **Stateful packet inspection (SPI)** – Incoming packets must be legitimate responses to requests from internal hosts. Unsolicited packets are blocked unless permitted specifically. SPI can also include the capability to recognize and filter out specific types of attacks, such as denial of service (DoS)

Firewall products may support one or more of these filtering capabilities. Firewall products come packaged in various forms, as shown in the figure. Click each type to see more information.

Refer to
Online Course
for Illustration

11.2.3.4   Endpoint Security

An endpoint, or host, is an individual computer system or device that acts as a network client. Common endpoints, as shown in the figure, are laptops, desktops, servers, smartphones, and tablets. Securing endpoint devices is one of the most challenging jobs of a network administrator because it involves human nature. A company must have well-documented policies in place and employees must be aware of these rules. Employees need to be trained on proper use of the network. Policies often include the use of antivirus software and host intrusion prevention. More comprehensive endpoint security solutions rely on network access control.

Refer to
Online Course
for Illustration

11.2.4   Device Security

11.2.4.1   Device Security Overview

When a new operating system is installed on a device, the security settings are set to the default values. In most cases, this level of security is inadequate. For Cisco routers, the Cisco AutoSecure feature can be used to assist securing the system, as shown in the figure. In addition, there are some simple steps that should be taken that apply to most operating systems:

- Default usernames and passwords should be changed immediately.

- Access to system resources should be restricted to only the individuals that are authorized to use those resources.

- Any unnecessary services and applications should be turned off and uninstalled when possible.

Often, devices shipped from the manufacturer have been sitting in a warehouse for a period of time and do not have the most up-to-date patches installed. It is important to update any software and install any security patches prior to implementation.

Refer to **Online Course** for Illustration

11.2.4.2   Passwords

To protect network devices, it is important to use strong passwords. Here are standard guidelines to follow:

- Use a password length of at least 8 characters, preferably 10 or more characters. A longer password is a better password.

- Make passwords complex. Include a mix of uppercase and lowercase letters, numbers, symbols, and spaces, if allowed.

- Avoid passwords based on repetition, common dictionary words, letter or number sequences, usernames, relative or pet names, biographical information, such as birth-dates, ID numbers, ancestor names, or other easily identifiable pieces of information.

- Deliberately misspell a password. For example, Smith = Smyth = 5mYth or Security = 5ecur1ty.

- Change passwords often. If a password is unknowingly compromised, the window of opportunity for the attacker to use the password is limited.

- Do not write passwords down and leave them in obvious places such as on the desk or monitor.

The figure shows examples of strong and weak passwords.

On Cisco routers, leading spaces are ignored for passwords, but spaces after the first character are not. Therefore, one method to create a strong password is to use the space bar and create a phrase made of many words. This is called a passphrase. A pass phrase is often easier to remember than a simple password. It is also longer and harder to guess.

Refer to **Online Course** for Illustration

11.2.4.3   Basic Security Practices

Additional Password Security

Strong passwords are only as useful as they are secret. There are several steps that can be taken to help ensure that passwords remain secret. Using the global configuration command **service password-encryption** prevents unauthorized individuals from viewing passwords in plain text in the configuration file, as shown in the figure. This command causes the encryption of all passwords that are unencrypted.

Additionally, to ensure that all configured passwords are a minimum of a specified length, use the **security passwords min-length** command in global configuration mode.

Another way hackers learn passwords is simply by brute-force attacks, trying multiple passwords until one works. It is possible to prevent this type of attack by blocking login attempts to the device if a set number of failures occur within a specific amount of time.

```
Router(config)# login block-for 120 attempts 3 within 60
```

This command will block login attempts for 120 seconds if there are three failed login attempts within 60 seconds.

Exec Timeout

Another recommendation is setting executive timeouts. By setting the exec timeout, you are telling the Cisco device to automatically disconnect users on a line after they have been idle for the duration of the exec timeout value. Exec timeouts can be configured on console, VTY, and aux ports using the **exec-timeout** command in line configuration mode.

```
Router(config)# line vty 0 4

Router(config-line)# exec-timeout 10
```

This command configures the device to disconnect idle users after 10 minutes.

Refer to **Online Course** for Illustration

11.2.4.4   Enable SSH

Telnet is not secure. Data contained within a Telnet packet is transmitted unencrypted. For this reason, it is highly recommended to enable SSH on devices for secure remote access. It is possible to configure a Cisco device to support SSH using four steps, as shown in the figure.

Step 1.   Ensure that the router has a unique hostname, and then configure the IP domain name of the network using the **ip domain-name** command in global configuration mode.

Step 2.   One-way secret keys must be generated for a router to encrypt SSH traffic. To generate the SSH key, use the **crypto key generate rsa general-keys** command in global configuration mode. The specific meaning of the various parts of this command are complex and out of scope for this course. Just note that the modulus determines the size of the key and can be configured from 360 bits to 2048 bits. The larger the modulus, the more secure the key, but the longer it takes to encrypt and decrypt information. The minimum recommended modulus length is 1024 bits.

Step 3.   Create a local database username entry using the **username** global configuration command.

Step 4.   Enable inbound SSH sessions using the line vty commands **login local** and **transport input ssh**.

The router can now be remotely accessed only by using SSH.

Refer to **Packet Tracer Activity** for this chapter

11.2.4.5   Packet Tracer - Configuring Secure Passwords and SSH

The network administrator has asked you to prepare a router for deployment. Before it can be connected to the network, security measures must be enabled.

Refer to **Lab Activity** for this chapter

11.2.4.6   Lab - Accessing Network Devices with SSH

In this lab, you will complete the following objectives:

- Part 1: Configure Basic Device Settings
- Part 2: Configure the Router for SSH Access

Refer to
Lab Activity
for this chapter

11.2.4.7   Lab - Examining Telnet and SSH in Wireshark

In this lab, you will complete the following objectives:

- Part 1: Examine a Telnet Session with Wireshark

- Part 2: Examine an SSH Session with Wireshark

Refer to
Lab Activity
for this chapter

11.2.4.8   Lab - Securing Network Devices

In this lab, you will complete the following objectives:

- Part 1: Configure Basic Device Settings

- Part 2: Configure Basic Security Measures on the Router

- Part 3: Configure Basic Security Measures on the Switch

Refer to
Online Course
for Illustration

11.3   Basic Network Performance

11.3.1   The ping Command

11.3.1.1   Interpreting Ping Results

Using the **ping** command is an effective way to test connectivity. The **ping** command uses the Internet Control Message Protocol (ICMP) and verifies Layer 3 connectivity. The **ping** command will not always pinpoint the nature of a problem, but it can help to identify the source of the problem, an important first step in troubleshooting a network failure.

IOS Ping Indicators

A ping issued from the IOS will yield one of several indications for each ICMP echo request that was sent. The most common indicators are:

- ! - indicates receipt of an ICMP echo reply message, as shown in Figure 1

- . - indicates a time expired while waiting for an ICMP echo reply message

- U - an ICMP unreachable message was received

The "." (period) may indicate that a connectivity problem occurred somewhere along the path. It may also indicate that a router along the path did not have a route to the destination and did not send an ICMP destination unreachable message. It also may indicate that the ping was blocked by device security. When sending a ping on an Ethernet LAN, it is common for the first echo request to timeout if the ARP process is required.

The "U" indicates that a router along the path responded with an ICMP unreachable message. The router either did not have a route to the destination address, or that the ping request was blocked.

Testing the Loopback

The ping command can also be used to verify the internal IP configuration on the local host by pinging the loopback address, 127.0.0.1, as shown in Figure 2. This verifies the proper operation of the protocol stack from the network layer to the physical layer, and back, without actually putting a signal on the media.

Refer to
Online Course
for Illustration

11.3.1.2   Extended Ping

The Cisco IOS offers an "extended" mode of the **ping** command. This mode is entered by typing **ping** in privileged EXEC mode, without a destination IP address. As shown in the figure, a series of prompts are then presented. Pressing **Enter** accepts the indicated default values. The example illustrates how to force the source address for a ping to be 10.1.1.1 (see R2 in the figure); the source address for a standard ping would be 209.165.200.226. By doing this, the network administrator can verify from R2 that R1 has a route to 10.1.1.0/24.

Note   The **ping ipv6** command is used for IPv6 extended pings.

Refer to
Online Course
for Illustration

11.3.1.3   Network Baseline

One of the most effective tools for monitoring and troubleshooting network performance is to establish a network baseline. Creating an effective network performance baseline is accomplished over a period of time. Measuring performance at varying times (Figures 1 and 2) and loads will assist in creating a better picture of overall network performance.

The output derived from network commands contributes data to the network baseline.

One method for starting a baseline is to copy and paste the results from an executed **ping**, **trace**, or other relevant commands into a text file. These text files can be time stamped with the date and saved into an archive for later retrieval and comparison (Figure 3). Among items to consider are error messages and the response times from host to host. If there is a considerable increase in response times, there may be a latency issue to address.

Corporate networks should have extensive baselines; more extensive than we can describe in this course. Professional-grade software tools are available for storing and maintaining baseline information. In this course, we cover a few basic techniques and discuss the purpose of baselines.

Best practices for baseline processes can be found here.

Refer to
Online Course
for Illustration

11.3.2   The traceroute and tracert Command

11.3.2.1   Interpreting Trace Messages

A trace returns a list of hops as a packet is routed through a network. The form of the command depends on where the command is issued. When performing the trace from a Windows computer, use **tracert**. When performing the trace from a router CLI, use **traceroute**, as shown in Figure 1.

Figure 2 shows example output of the **tracert** command entered on Host 1 to trace the route to Host 2. The only successful response was from the gateway on Router A. Trace requests to the next hop timed out, meaning that the next hop router did not respond. The trace results indicate that there is either a failure in the internetwork beyond the LAN, or that these routers have been configured to not respond to echo requests used in the trace.

Refer to
Online Course
for Illustration

11.3.2.2   Extended Traceroute

Designed as a variation of the **traceroute** command, the extended **traceroute** command allows the administrator to adjust parameters related to the command operation. This is helpful when troubleshooting routing loops, determining the exact next-hop router, or to help determine where packets are getting dropped by a router, or denied by a firewall. While the extended **ping** command can be used to determine the type of connectivity problem, the extended **traceroute** command is useful in locating the problem.

An ICMP "time exceeded" error message indicates that a router in the path has seen and discarded the packet. An ICMP "destination unreachable" error message indicates that a router has received the packet, but discarded it because it could not be delivered. Like ping, traceroute uses ICMP echo requests and echo replies. If the ICMP timer expires before an ICMP echo reply is received, **traceroute** command output displays an asterisk (*).

In IOS, the extended traceroute command terminates when any of the following occur:

- The destination responds with an ICMP echo reply

- The user interrupts the trace with the escape sequence

Note   In IOS, you can invoke this escape sequence by pressing **Ctrl+Shift+6**. In Windows, the escape sequence is invoked by pressing **Ctrl+C**.

To use **extended** traceroute, simply type **traceroute**, without providing any parameters, and press **ENTER**. IOS will guide you through the command options by presenting a number of prompts related to the setting of all the different parameters. Figure 1 shows the IOS extended **traceroute** options and their respective descriptions.

While the Windows **tracert** command allows the input of several parameters, it is not guided and must be performed through options in the command line. Figure 2 shows the available options for **tracert** in Windows.

Refer to **Packet Tracer Activity** for this chapter

11.3.2.3   Packet Tracer – Test Connectivity with Traceroute

This activity is designed to help you troubleshoot network connectivity issues using commands to trace the route from source to destination. You are required to examine the output of **tracert** (the Windows command) and **traceroute** (the IOS command) as packets traverse the network and determine the cause of a network issue. After the issue is corrected, use the **tracert** and **traceroute** commands to verify the completion.

Refer to **Lab Activity** for this chapter

11.3.2.4   Lab -Testing Network Latency with Ping and Traceroute

In this lab, you will complete the following objectives:

- Part 1: Use Ping to Document Network Latency

- Part 2: Use Traceroute to Document Network Latency

Refer to
Online Course
for Illustration

11.3.3   Show Commands

11.3.3.1   Common show Commands Revisited

The Cisco IOS CLI **show** commands display relevant information about the configuration and operation of the device.

Network technicians use **show** commands extensively for viewing configuration files, checking the status of device interfaces and processes, and verifying the device operational status. The **show** commands are available whether the device was configured using the CLI or Cisco Configuration Professional.

The status of nearly every process or function of the router can be displayed using a **show** command. Some of the more popular **show** commands are:

- **show running-config** (Figure 1)
- **show interfaces** (Figure 2)
- **show arp** (Figure 3)
- **show ip route** (Figure 4)
- **show protocols** (Figure 5)
- **show version** (Figure 6)

Click the buttons in the figure to see example output from each of these show commands.

Refer to **Video**
in online course

11.3.3.2   Video Demonstration - The show version Command

The show version command can be used to verify and troubleshoot some of the basic hardware and software components used during the boot process. Click Play to view a video from earlier in the course, to review an explanation of the **show version** command.

Click here to read the transcript of this video.

Refer to **Packet
Tracer Activity**
for this chapter

11.3.3.3   Packet Tracer - Using show Commands

This activity is designed to reinforce the use of router **show** commands. You are not required to configure, but rather examine, the output of several show commands.

Refer to
Online Course
for Illustration

11.3.4   Host and IOS Commands

11.3.4.1   The ipconfig Command

As shown in Figure 1, the IP address of the default gateway of a host can be viewed by issuing the **ipconfig** command at the command line of a Windows computer.

As shown in Figure 2, use the **ipconfig /all** command to view the MAC address, as well as a number of details regarding the Layer 3 addressing of the device.

The DNS Client service on Windows PCs also optimizes the performance of DNS name resolution by storing previously resolved names in memory. As shown in Figure 3, the **ipconfig /displaydns** command displays all of the cached DNS entries on a Windows computer system.

Refer to
Online Course
for Illustration

11.3.4.2   The arp Command

The **arp** command is executed from the Windows command prompt, as shown in the figure. The **arp –a** command lists all devices currently in the ARP cache of the host, which includes the IPv4 address, physical address, and the type of addressing (static/dynamic), for each device.

The cache can be cleared by using the **arp -d*** command in the event the network administrator wants to repopulate the cache with updated information.

Note   The ARP cache contains information only from devices that have been recently accessed. To ensure that the ARP cache is populated, ping a device so that it will have an entry in the ARP table.

Refer to
Online Course
for Illustration

11.3.4.3   The show cdp neighbors Command

There are several other IOS commands that are useful. For example, the Cisco Discovery Protocol (CDP) is a Cisco-proprietary protocol that runs at the data link layer. Because CDP operates at the data link layer, two or more Cisco network devices, such as routers that support different network layer protocols, can learn about each other even if Layer 3 connectivity does not exist.

Compare the output from the **show cdp neighbors** commands in Figure 1 with the topology in Figure 2. Notice that R3 has gathered some detailed information about R2 and the switch connected to the Fast Ethernet interface on R3.

When a Cisco device boots, CDP starts by default. CDP automatically discovers neighboring Cisco devices running CDP, regardless of which Layer 3 protocol or suites are running. CDP exchanges hardware and software device information with its directly connected CDP neighbors.

CDP provides the following information about each CDP neighbor device:

- **Device identifiers** – For example, the configured host name of a switch
- **Address list** – Up to one network layer address for each protocol supported
- **Port identifier** – The name of the local and remote port in the form of an ASCII character string, such as FastEthernet 0/0
- **Capabilities list** – For example, whether this device is a router or a switch
- **Platform** – The hardware platform of the device; for example, a Cisco 1841 series router

The **show cdp neighbors detail** command reveals the IP address of a neighboring device. CDP will reveal the neighbor's IP address regardless of whether or not you can ping that neighbor. This command is very helpful when two Cisco routers cannot route across their shared data link. The **show cdp neighbors detail** command will help determine if one of the CDP neighbors has an IP configuration error.

As helpful as CDP is, it can also be a security risk because it can provide useful network infrastructure information to attackers. For example, by default many IOS versions send CDP advertisements out all enabled ports. However, best practices suggest that CDP should be enabled only on interfaces that are connecting to other infrastructure Cisco devices. CDP advertisements should be disabled on user-facing ports.

Because some IOS versions send out CDP advertisements by default, it is important to know how to disable CDP. To disable CDP globally, use the global configuration command **no cdp run**. To disable CDP on an interface, use the interface command **no cdp enable**.

Refer to
Online Course
for Illustration

11.3.4.4   The show ip interface brief Command

In the same way that commands and utilities are used to verify a host configuration, commands can be used to verify the interfaces of intermediate devices. The Cisco IOS provides commands to verify the operation of router and switch interfaces.

Verifying Router Interfaces

One of the most frequently used commands is the **show ip interface brief** command. This command provides a more abbreviated output than the **show ip interface** command. It provides a summary of the key information for all the network interfaces on a router.

Figure 1 shows the topology that is being used in this example.

On Figure 2, click the R1 button. The **show ip interface brief** output displays all interfaces on the router, the IP address assigned to each interface, if any, and the operational status of the interface.

Verifying the Switch Interfaces

On Figure 2, click the S1 button. The **show ip interface brief** command can also be used to verify the status of the switch interfaces. The VLAN1 interface is assigned an IPv4 address of 192.168.254.250 and has been enabled, and is operational.

The output also shows that the FastEthernet0/1 interface is down. This indicates that either no device is connected to the interface or the device that is connected has a network interface that is not operational.

In contrast, the output shows that the FastEthernet0/2 and FastEthernet0/3 interfaces are operational. This is indicated by both the Status and Protocol being shown as up.

Refer to
Interactive Graphic
in online course

11.3.4.5   Activity - Show Commands

11.3.4.6   Lab - Using the CLI to Gather Network Device Information

In this lab, you will complete the following objectives:

Refer to
Lab Activity
for this chapter

- Part 1: Set Up Topology and Initialize Devices
- Part 2: Configure Devices and Verify Connectivity
- Part 3: Gather Network Device Information

Refer to
Online Course
for Illustration

11.3.5   Debugging

11.3.5.1   The debug Command

IOS processes, protocols, mechanisms and events generate messages to communicate their status. These messages can provide valuable information when troubleshooting or verifying system operations. The IOS **debug** command allows the administrator to display these messages in real-time for analysis. It is a very important tool for monitoring events on a Cisco IOS device.

All **debug** commands are entered in privileged EXEC mode. The Cisco IOS allows for narrowing the output of **debug** to include only the relevant feature or sub-feature. This is important because debugging output is assigned high priority in the CPU process and it can render the system unusable. For this reason, use **debug** commands only to troubleshoot specific problems. To monitor the status of ICMP messages in a Cisco router, use **debug ip icmp**, as shown in the figure.

To list a brief description of all the debugging command options, use the **debug ?** command in privileged EXEC mode at the command line.

To turn off a specific debugging feature, add the **no** keyword in front of the **debug** command:

```
Router# no debug ip icmp
```

Alternatively, you can enter the **undebug** form of the command in privileged EXEC mode:

```
Router# undebug ip icmp
```

To turn off all active debug commands at once, use the **undebug all** command:

```
Router# undebug all
```

Some debug commands such as **debug all** and **debug ip packet** generate a substantial amount of output and use a large portion of system resources. The router would get so busy displaying debug messages that it would not have enough processing power to perform its network functions, or even listen to commands to turn off debugging. For this reason, using these command options is not recommended and should be avoided.

11.3.5.2   The terminal monitor Command

Refer to **Online Course** for Illustration

Connections to grant access to the IOS command line interface can be established locally or remotely.

Local connections require physical access to the router or switch; therefore, a cable connection is required. This connection is usually established by connecting a PC to the router or switch console port using a rollover cable. In this course, we refer to a local connection as a console connection.

Remote connections are established over the network; therefore, they require a network protocol such as IP. No direct physical access is required for remote sessions. SSH and Telnet are two common connection protocols used for remote sessions. In this course, we use the protocol when discussing a specific remote connection, such as a Telnet connection or an SSH connection.

While IOS log messages are sent to the console by default, these same log messages are not sent to the virtual lines by default. Because debug messages are log messages, this behavior prevents any debug-related messages from being displayed on VTY lines.

To display log messages on a terminal (virtual console), use the **terminal monitor** privileged EXEC command.

To stop logging messages on a terminal, use the **terminal no monitor** privileged EXEC command.

User the Syntax Checker to practice using **terminal monito**r and **debug** for troubleshooting.

Refer to
Online Course
for Illustration

11.4   Network Troubleshooting

11.4.1   Troubleshooting Methodologies

11.4.1.1   Basic Troubleshooting Approaches

Network problems can be simple or complex, and can result from a combination of hardware, software, and connectivity issues. Technicians must be able to analyze the problem and determine the cause of the error before they can resolve the network issue. This process is called troubleshooting.

A common and efficient troubleshooting methodology is based on the scientific method and can be broken into the six main steps shown in the figure.

To assess the problem, determine how many devices on the network are experiencing the problem. If there is a problem with one device on the network, start the troubleshooting process at that device. If there is a problem with all devices on the network, start the troubleshooting process at the device where all other devices are connected. You should develop a logical and consistent method for diagnosing network problems by eliminating one problem at a time.

Refer to
Online Course
for Illustration

11.4.1.2   Resolve or Escalate?

In some situations, it may not be possible to resolve the problem immediately. A problem should be escalated when it requires a manager's decision, some specific expertise, or network access level unavailable to the troubleshooting technician.

For example, after troubleshooting, the technician concludes a router module should be replaced. This problem should be escalated for manager approval. The manager may have to escalate the problem again as it may require the financial department's approval before a new module can be purchased.

A company's policy should clearly state when and how a technician should escalate a problem.

Refer to
Online Course
for Illustration

11.4.1.3   Verify and Monitor Solution

Cisco IOS includes powerful tools to with help troubleshooting and verification. When a problem has been solved and a solution implemented, it is important to verify the system operation. Verification tools include the **ping**, **traceroute** and **show** commands. The **ping** command can be used to verify successful network connectivity.

If a **ping** is successful, as shown in Figure 1, it is safe to conclude packets are being routed from source to destination.

Note   A failed **ping** usually does not provide enough information to draw any conclusions. It could be the result of an ACL or firewall blocking ICMP packets, or the destination device may be configured to not respond to pings. A failed ping is usually indication that further investigation is required.

The **traceroute** command, as shown in Figure 2, is useful for displaying the path that packets are using to reach a destination. While output from the **ping** command shows whether a packet has arrived at the destination, output from the **traceroute** command shows what path it took to get there, or where the packet was stopped along the path.

The Cisco IOS **show** commands are some of the most useful troubleshooting and verification tools included the Cisco IOS. Taking advantage of a large variety of options and sub-options, the **show** command can be used to narrow down and display information about practically any specific aspect of IOS.

Figure 3 displays the output of a **show ip interface brief** command. Notice that the two interfaces configured with IPv4 addresses are both "up" and "up". These interfaces can send and receive traffic. The other three interfaces have no IPv4 addressing and are administratively down.

> Refer to
> **Interactive Graphic**
> in online course

11.4.1.4   Activity – Order the Troubleshooting Steps

Enter storyboard text here

> Refer to
> **Online Course**
> for Illustration

11.4.2   Troubleshoot Cables and Interfaces

11.4.2.1   Duplex Operation

In data communications, duplex refers to the direction of data transmission between two devices. If the communications are restricted to the exchange of data in one direction at a time, this connection is called half-duplex. Full-duplex allows the sending and receiving of data to happen simultaneously.

For best communication performance, two connected Ethernet network interfaces must operate in the same duplex mode to avoid inefficiency and latency on the link.

Ethernet autonegotiation was designed to facilitate configuration, minimize problems and maximize link performance. The connected devices first announce their supported capabilities and then choose the highest performance mode supported by both ends. For example, the switch and router in in the figure successfully autonegotiated full-duplex mode.

If one of the two connected devices is operating in full-duplex and the other is operating in half-duplex, a duplex mismatch occurs. While data communication will occur through a link with a duplex mismatch, link performance will be very poor. Duplex mismatch may be caused by incorrect manual configuration, which is manually setting the two connected devices to different duplex modes. Duplex mismatch can also occur by connecting a device performing auto-negotiation to another that is manually set to full-duplex. Although rare, duplex mismatch can also occur due to failed autonegotiation.

> Refer to
> **Online Course**
> for Illustration

11.4.2.2   Duplex Mismatch

Duplex mismatches may be difficult to troubleshoot as the communication between devices still occurs. A duplex mismatch may not become apparent even when using tools such as ping. Single small packets may fail to reveal a duplex mismatch problem. A terminal session which sends data slowly (in very short bursts) could also communicate successfully through a duplex mismatch. Even when either end of the connection attempts to send any significant amount of data and the link performance drops considerably, the cause may not be readily apparent because the network is otherwise operational.

CDP, the Cisco proprietary protocol, can easily detect a duplex mismatch between two Cisco devices. Consider the topology and log messages in Figure 1 where the G0/0 interface on R1 has been erroneously configured to operate in half-duplex mode. CDP will display log messages about the link with the duplex mismatch. The messages also contain the device names and ports involved in the duplex mismatch, which makes it much easier to identify and fix the problem.

Note   Because these are log messages, they are only displayed on a console session by default. You would only see these messages on a remote connection if the terminal monitor command is enabled.

Figure 2 shows that the S1 interface is properly configured for full-duplex operation. Figure 3 shows that the half-duplex configuration on R1 caused the problem.

Refer to
Online Course
for Illustration

11.4.3   Troubleshooting Scenarios

11.4.3.1   IP Addressing Issues on IOS Devices

IP address-related problems will likely keep remote network devices from communicating. Because IP addresses are hierarchical, any IP address assigned to a network device must conform to that network's range of addresses. Wrongly assigned IP addresses create a variety of issues, including IP address conflicts and routing problems.

Two common causes of incorrect IPv4 assignment are manual assignment mistakes or DHCP-related issues.

Network administrators often have to manually assign IP addresses to devices such as servers and routers. If a mistake is made during the assignment, then communications issues with the device are very likely to occur.

On an IOS device, use the **show ip interface** or **show ip interface brief** commands to verify what IPv4 addresses are assigned to the network interfaces. The figure displays the output of the **show ip interface** command issued on a R1. Notice that the output displays IPv4 information (OSI Layer 3), while the previously mentioned **show interfaces** command displays the physical and data link details of an interface.

Refer to
Online Course
for Illustration

11.4.3.2   IP Addressing Issues on End Devices

In Windows-based machines, when the device cannot contact a DHCP server, Windows will automatically assign an address belonging to the 169.254.0.0/16 range. This process is designed to facilitate communication within the local network. Think of it as Windows saying "I will use this address from the 169.254.0.0/16 range because I could not get any other address". More often than not, a computer with a 169.254.0.0/16 will not be able to communicate with other devices in the network because those devices will most likely not belong to the 169.254.0.0/16 network. This situation indicates an automatic IPv4 address assignment problem that should be fixed.

Note   Other operating systems, such Linux and OS X, will not assign an IPv4 address to the network interface if communication with a DHCP server fails.

Most end devices are configured to rely on a DHCP server for automatic IPv4 address assignment. If the device is unable to communicate with the DHCP server, then the server cannot assign an IPv4 address for the specific network and the device will not be able to communicate.

To verify the IP addresses assigned to a Windows-based computer, use the **ipconfig** command, as shown in the figure.

Refer to
Online Course
for Illustration

11.4.3.3   Default Gateway Issues

The default gateway for an end device is the closest networking device that can forward traffic to other networks. If a device has an incorrect or nonexistent default gateway address, it will not be able to communicate with devices in remote networks. Because the default gateway is the path to remote networks, its address must belong to the same network as the end device.

The address of the default gateway can be manually set or obtained from a DHCP server. Similar to IPv4 addressing issues, default gateway problems can be related to misconfiguration (in the case of manual assignment) or DHCP problems (if automatic assignment is in use).

To solve misconfigured default gateway issues, ensure that the device has the correct default gateway configured. If the default address was manually set but is incorrect, simply replace it with the proper address. If the default gateway address was automatically set, ensure the device can properly communicate with the DHCP server. It is also important to verify that the proper IPv4 address and subnet mask were configured on the router's interface and that the interface is active.

To verify the default gateway on Windows-based computers, use the **ipconfig** command, as shown in Figure 1.

On a router, use the **show ip route** command to list the routing table and verify that the default gateway, known as a default route, has been set. This route is used when the destination address of the packet does not match any other routes in its routing table. Figure 2 shows that R2 is the default route for R1 and the output of the **show ip route** command shows that the default gateway has been set with a default route of 10.1.0.2.

Refer to
Online Course
for Illustration

11.4.3.4   Troubleshooting DNS Issues

Domain Name Service (DNS) defines an automated service that matches names, such as www.cisco.com, with the IP address. While DNS resolution is not crucial to device communication, it is very important to the end user.

It is common for users to mistakenly relate the operation of an Internet link to the availability of the DNS service. User complaints such as "the network is down" or "the Internet is down" are often caused by an unreachable DNS server. While packet routing and all other network services are still operational, DNS failures often lead the user to the wrong conclusion. If a user types in a domain name such as www.cisco.com in a web browser and the DNS server is unreachable, the name will not be translated into an IP address and the website will not display.

DNS server addresses can be manually or automatically assigned. Network administrators are often responsible for manually assigning DNS server addresses on servers and other devices, while DHCP is used to automatically assign DNS server addresses to clients.

Although it is common for companies and organizations to manage their own DNS servers, any reachable DNS server can be used to resolve names. Small office and home office (SOHO) users often rely on the DNS server maintained by their ISP for name resolution. ISP-maintained DNS servers are assigned to SOHO customers via DHCP. For example, Google maintains a public DNS server that can be used by anyone and it is very useful for testing. The IPv4 address of Google's public DNS server is 8.8.8.8 and 2001:4860:4860::8888 for its IPv6 DNS address.

Use the **ipconfig /all**, as shown in Figure 1, to verify which DNS server is in use by the Windows computer.

The **nslookup** command is another useful DNS troubleshooting tool for PCs. With **nslookup** a user can manually place DNS queries and analyze the DNS response. Figure 2 shows the output of **nslookup** when placing a query for www.cisco.com.

> Refer to
> **Lab Activity**
> for this chapter

11.4.3.5   Lab - Troubleshooting Connectivity Issues

In this lab, you will complete the following objectives:

- Identify the Problem
- Implement Network Changes
- Verify Full Functionality
- Document Findings and Configuration Changes

> Refer to **Packet**
> **Tracer Activity**
> for this chapter

11.4.3.6   Packet Tracer - Troubleshooting Connectivity Issues

The objective of this Packet Tracer activity is to troubleshoot and resolve connectivity issues, if possible. Otherwise, the issues should be clearly documented and so they can be escalated.

11.5   Summary

11.5.1   Conclusion

> Refer to
> **Lab Activity**
> for this chapter

11.5.1.1   Class Activity - Design and Build a Small Business Network

Use Packet Tracer and a word processing application to complete this activity – 2-3 students per group.

Design and build a network from scratch.

- Your design must include a minimum of one router, one switch, and one PC.
- Fully configure the network - use IPv4 or IPv6 (subnetting must be included as a part of your addressing scheme).
- Verify the network using at least five show commands.
- Secure the network using SSH, secure passwords, and console passwords (minimum).

Create a rubric to use for peer grading – or your instructor may choose to use the rubric provided with this activity.

Present your capstone project to the class – be able to answer questions from your peers and instructor!

Refer to **Packet Tracer Activity** for this chapter

11.5.1.2   Packet Tracer - Skill Integration Challenge

In this activity, you will design and implement an addressing scheme in a two router, three switch topology. You will configure basic device settings including line access, banners, passwords, and SSH. You will then verify that all devices can access network resources.

Refer to **Packet Tracer Activity** for this chapter

11.5.1.3   Packet Tracer - Troubleshooting Challenge

In this activity, you will troubleshoot the configurations in a two router, three switch topology. Once all issues are resolved, all devices should be able to access network resources.

Refer to **Online Course** for Illustration

11.5.1.4   Build a Small Network

In order to meet user requirements, even small networks require planning and design. Planning ensures that all requirements, cost factors, and deployment options are given due consideration. An important part of network design is reliability, scalability, and availability.

Supporting and growing a small network requires being familiar with the protocols and network applications running over the network. Protocol analyzers enable a network professional to quickly compile statistical information about traffic flows on a network. Information gathered by the protocol analyzer is evaluated based on the source and destination of the traffic as well as the type of traffic being sent. This analysis can be used by a network technician to make decisions on how to manage the traffic more efficiently. Common network protocols include DNS, Telnet, SMTP, POP, DHCP, HTTP, and FTP.

It is a necessity to consider security threats and vulnerabilities when planning a network implementation. All network devices must be secured. This includes routers, switches, end-user devices, and even security devices. Networks need to be protected from malicious software such as viruses, Trojan horses, and worms. Antivirus software can detect most viruses and many Trojan horse applications and prevent them from spreading in the network. The most effective way to mitigate a worm attack is to download security updates from the operating system vendor and patch all vulnerable systems.

Networks must also be protected from network attacks. Network attacks can be classified into three major categories: reconnaissance, access attacks, and denial of service. There are several ways to protect a network from attacks.

- Authentication, authorization, and accounting (AAA, or "triple A") network security services provide the primary framework to set up access control on a network device. AAA is a way to control who is permitted to access a network (authenticate), what they can do while they are there (authorize), and to watch the actions they perform while accessing the network (accounting).

- A firewall is one of the most effective security tools available for protecting internal network users from external threats. A firewall resides between two or more networks and controls the traffic between them and also helps prevent unauthorized access.

- To protect network devices, it is important to use strong passwords. Also, when accessing network devices remotely, it is highly recommended to enable SSH instead of the unsecured telnet.

After the network has been implemented, a network administrator must be able to monitor and maintain network connectivity. There are several commands available toward this end. For testing network connectivity to local and remote destinations, commands such as **ping**, **telnet**, and **traceroute** are commonly used.

On Cisco IOS devices, the **show version** command can be used to verify and troubleshoot some of the basic hardware and software components used during the boot process. To view information for all network interfaces on a router, the **show ip interface** command is used. The **show ip interface brief** can also be used to view a more abbreviated output than the **show ip interface** command. Cisco Discovery Protocol (CDP) is a Cisco-proprietary protocol that runs at the data link layer. Because CDP operates at the data link layer, two or more Cisco network devices, such as routers that support different network layer protocols, can learn about each other even if Layer 3 connectivity does not exist.

Cisco IOS configuration files such as startup-config or running-config should be archived. These files can be saved to a text file or stored on a TFTP server. Some models of routers also have a USB port, and a file can be backed up to a USB drive. If needed, these files can be copied to the router and or switch from the TFTP server or USB drive.

Go to the online course to take the quiz and exam.

Chapter 11 Quiz

This quiz is designed to provide an additional opportunity to practice the skills and knowledge presented in the chapter and to prepare for the chapter exam. You will be allowed multiple attempts and the grade does not appear in the gradebook.

Chapter 11 Exam

The chapter exam assesses your knowledge of the chapter content.

Your Chapter Notes

Z